D0161172

GREGG SHORTHAND FOR COLLEGES Volume Two

Diamond Jubilee Series

Second Edition

Louis A. Leslie
Coauthor Diamond Jubilee Series of Gregg Shorthand

Charles E. Zoubek
Coauthor Diamond Jubilee Series of Gregg Shorthand

A. James Lemaster
Assistant Professor of Education
Baruch College, City University of New York

Russell J. Hosler
Professor of Education
University of Wisconsin

Shorthand written by
Charles Rader

GREGG SHORTHAND FOR COLLEGES Volume Two

Diamond Jubilee Series

Second Edition

Gregg Division | McGraw-Hill Book Company

New York | St. Louis | Dallas | San Francisco
Düsseldorf | Johannesburg | Kuala Lumpur
London | Mexico | Montreal | New Delhi | Panama
Rio de Janeiro | Singapore | Sydney | Toronto

Art Director	Frank Medina
Designer	Barbara Bert
Chapter Illustrations	Neil Boyle
Shorthand Production Supervisor	Charles Rader
Editorial Staff	Jerome Edelman, Mary Buchanan, Kathy Flynn
Compositor	King Typographic Service
Printer	R. R. Donnelley & Sons Company

Library of Congress Cataloging in Publication Data

Main entry under title:
Gregg shorthand for colleges.

(Diamond jubilee series)
First ed. by L. A. Leslie, C. E. Zoubek, and R. J. Hosler.

1. Shorthand—Gregg. I. Leslie, Louis A., date. II. Leslie, Louis A., date Gregg shorthand for colleges.
Z56.G833G74 653'.427 72-10140
ISBN 0-07-037401-5 (v. 1)
ISBN 0-07-037406-6 (v. 2)

GREGG SHORTHAND FOR COLLEGES, Volume Two
Diamond Jubilee Series
Second Edition

567890 DODO 2109876

Preface

In *Gregg Shorthand for Colleges, Diamond Jubilee Series, Volume One, Second Edition,* the student studied all the word-building principles of Gregg Shorthand. In addition, he studied many nonshorthand elements designed to help him become an efficient transcriber.

Volume Two, as its title indicates, is designed to be used following Volume One.

Objectives

Volume Two has the following major objectives:

1 To review the principles of Gregg Shorthand.

2 To develop the student's ability to construct outlines for unfamiliar words under the stress of dictation.

3 To develop the student's dictation speed to the highest point possible.

4 To extend the student's knowledge of the basic elements of transcription, which include spelling, punctuation, word usage, and typing style.

5 To lay a firm foundation for rapid and accurate typewritten transcription—the student's ultimate goal.

6 To teach the student to handle simple problems of office-style dictation.

Organization

Volume Two is organized into 16 chapters, each containing 5 lessons, for a total of 80 lessons. Each lesson consists of 3 parts:

- Developing Word-Building or Phrasing Power
- Building Transcription Skills
- Reading and Writing Practice

Developing Word-Building or Phrasing Power

The 5 lessons comprising each of the 16 chapters contain a carefully planned cycle of word-building or phrasing drills that provide a quick, intensive recall in list form of the important elements of Gregg Shorthand.

The first lesson in each chapter concentrates on brief forms. It contains a chart of 36 brief forms and derivatives. All the brief forms of the system are reviewed at least once; many of them, several times. (The first letter in the Reading and Writing Practice of each first lesson contains many brief forms.)

The second lesson in each chapter concentrates on useful business phrases. The phrases in the drills have been selected from a study of the phrase content of more than 2,500 actual business letters containing more than 250,000 running words. (The first letter in the Reading and Writing Practice of each second lesson is a letter containing a high concentration of useful phrases.) In addition, each second lesson contains a drill on cities, states, and other geographical expressions.

The third lesson in each chapter is devoted to shorthand word families. These shorthand word families enable the student to take advantage of a very effective aid in word building—analogy. Shorthand word families are an important factor in helping the student construct outlines for unfamiliar words.

The fourth lesson in each chapter is devoted to an intensive drill on word beginnings and endings. Through these drills, the student reviews all the word beginning and endings of the system at least once; some of the more important ones, several times.

The fifth lesson in each chapter contains a shorthand vocabulary builder that provides drills on major principles of Gregg Shorthand—blends, vowel combinations, omissions of vowels, and so on.

Building Transcription Skills

Transcription teachers will agree that one of the basic problems in shorthand classes is the difficulty that students have in handling the mechanics of the English language. Businessmen frequently comment that stenographers cannot spell, cannot punctuate, and have no grasp of correct grammar.

To cope with this basic problem, a number of transcription skill-building features were introduced in Volume One. In Volume Two the emphasis on the mechanics of the English language has been intensified, beginning with the very first lesson. Volume Two contains the following transcription skill-building features:

SPELLING

Two types of spelling exercises are provided.

Marginal Reminders Words have been selected from the Reading and Writing Practice for special spelling attention. These words are printed in a second color in the shorthand and appear in type, correctly syllabicated, in the margins of the shorthand.

Spelling Families Each spelling family contains a list of words that present common spelling problems—for example, words ending in -ible, -able; -ance, -ence.

PUNCTUATION

In Volume One the student studied several of the most frequent uses of the comma. In Volume Two he continues to drill on those uses of the comma. In addition, he studies other important punctuation marks, including the semicolon, the hyphen, and the apostrophe.

To test the student's grasp of the punctuation rules studied, each lesson (except the fifth lesson in each chapter) contains a Transcription Quiz in which the student must supply all internal punctuation. The Transcription Quiz also teaches the student to supply from context words that have been omitted in the shorthand.

VOCABULARY DEVELOPMENT

Three types of drills are provided to help the student expand his vocabulary and develop his understanding of words.

Business Vocabulary Builder In each lesson the student studies several words or expressions, selected from the Reading and Writing Practice, with which he may not be familiar. Each word or expression is briefly defined.

Similar-Words Drill The Similar-Words Drills make the student aware of groups of words that sound alike, or almost alike—words that are responsible for many transcription errors. Examples of similar words are *their-there; here-hear; to-two-too.* In Volume Two there are 14 groups of similar words.

Common Prefixes An effective device to aid the student increase his understanding of words is the study of common prefixes. In Volume Two the student studies 7 common prefixes.

GRAMMAR CHECKUP

A number of the lessons contain drills dealing with common errors in grammar that the unwary stenographer often makes.

TYPING STYLE STUDIES

In the Typing Style Studies the student is taught how to handle quantities, dates, addresses, and other situations in which numbers occur.

OFFICE-STYLE DICTATION

In Chapters 13 through 16 the student learns how to handle some of the office-style dictation problems he will meet when he takes dictation on the job—insertions, deletions, and changes during dictation. Each problem is explained and illustrated.

LETTER PLACEMENT BY JUDGMENT

In Chapter 13 the student is taught how to place short letters, the most common type in business, attractively on a letterhead the way an experienced stenographer or secretary would place them—by judgment.

Reading and Writing Practice

An extremely important part of a student's practice program is the reading and copying of large quantities of well-written shorthand. This reading and copying provides a constant, automatic review of the principles of the system. In addition, it stocks the student's mind with correct joinings of shorthand characters and with the shapes of individual characters so that he can effectively construct a shorthand outline for any word that is dictated to him.

Volume Two contains 65,473 words of practice material on business letters and interesting, informative articles. Much of the practice material in this Second Edition is new. That which has been retained from the First Edition has been revised and brought up to date.

The publishers are confident that the Second Edition of *Gregg Shorthand for Colleges, Diamond Jubilee Series, Volume Two,* will enable the teacher to do an even more effective job of training accurate and rapid transcribers.

The Publishers

Contents

DEVELOPMENT OF SHORTHAND SPEED

You are about to begin the second, and extremely important, phase of your shorthand training—the development of shorthand speed. Before doing so, take a few moments to review what you have already accomplished. Upon completion of *Gregg Shorthand for Colleges, Volume One,* you have:

Learned the alphabet of Gregg Shorthand; consequently, you have the means with which to construct a legible outline for any word in the English language.

Learned many useful abbreviating devices such as brief forms, word beginnings and endings, and phrases that will help you write shorthand more rapidly and easily.

Improved your command of the nonshorthand elements of transcription—spelling, punctuation, word usage, and grammar.

You now have a firm foundation for the task ahead—developing your ability to take dictation and transcribing accurately on the typewriter. With this foundation, and an efficient practice program, you will experience the thrill of watching your shorthand speed grow and your ability to handle the mechanics of the English language improve almost from day to day.

YOUR PRACTICE PROGRAM—OUTSIDE OF CLASS

Your assignments outside of class will consist largely of reading and copying well-written shorthand. Reading and copying shorthand will help your shorthand speed develop rapidly. This part of your practice program should be easy and pleasant, for your have no new shorthand principles or abbreviating devices to learn.

To get the most of your out-of-class practice, follow these suggestions:

Read the word and phrase drills at the beginning of each lesson. Cover up the key as you read. The moment you cannot read an outline, refer to the key.

Read and study the material in "Building Transcription Skills" which follows the word and phrase drills.

Read and copy the Reading and Writing Practice in each lesson in this way:

1 Read a letter or article from the shorthand. When you cannot read an outline, spell the shorthand characters in it; this spelling will often give you the meaning. If it does not, refer to your transcript if you have been provided with one. If you do not have a transcript, encircle the outline in your book if it is your personal property. If not, write the outline on a slip of paper. Do not spend more than a few seconds trying to decipher an outline. The next day in class find out the meaning of the outlines that you have written on your slip of paper.

2 After you have read the material from the shorthand, make a shorthand copy of it in your notebook. Read a convenient group of words—aloud if possible—and then write that group in your notebook. Write as rapidly as you can, but be sure that what you write is legible.

3 If time permits, read what you have written. You will be glad you did if you are called upon to read from your notes in class the next day.

4 Complete the corresponding lesson in the *Workbook for Gregg Shorthand for Colleges, Volume Two,* if you have been provided with one.

YOUR PRACTICE PROGRAM—IN CLASS

Most of your time in class will be devoted to taking dictation at constantly increasing speeds. Your instructor will see to it that you get the proper kind of dictation at the proper speeds so that your skill will increase easily and rapidly.

1 General

Comma Brushup

The competent secretary must, of course, be able to take her employer's dictation and read it back. In addition, however, she must be able to punctuate correctly if she is to produce letters that her employer will sign.

In *Gregg Shorthand for Colleges, Volume One,* you studied nine of the most frequent uses of the comma. In Chapter 1 of Volume Two, you will "brush up" on five of these uses of the comma; in Chapter 2, the remaining four uses.

Beginning with Chapter 3 you will take up additional, more advanced points of punctuation.

PRACTICE PROCEDURES

To be sure that you derive the greatest benefit from your study of punctuation and spelling in each Reading and Writing Practice, follow these suggestions:

1 Read carefully each punctuation rule and the illustrative examples.

2 Read the Reading and Writing Practice. Each time you see an encircled punctuation mark, note the reason for its use, which is indicated directly above the encircled mark.

3 Make a shorthand copy of the Reading and Writing Practice. As you copy, insert the punctuation marks in your shorthand notes, encircling them as in the textbook.

4 When you encounter a shorthand outline printed in a second color, that indicates the word has been singled out for spelling attention. Finish reading the sentence in which it occurs. Then glance at the margin of the shorthand, where the word appears in type. Spell the word, aloud if possible, pausing slightly after each word division. (The word divisions indicated are those given in Webster's Seventh New Collegiate Dictionary.)

In Chapter 1 you will review:

, parenthetical

In order to make his meaning absolutely clear, a writer sometimes inserts a comment or an explanation that could be omitted without changing the meaning of the sentence. These added comments and explanations are called *parenthetical* and are separated from the rest of the sentence by commas.

If the parenthetical word or expression occurs at the beginning or end of a sentence, only one comma is needed.

I want to urge you, however, not to worry.

Thank you, Mr. Smith, for your help.

We shall miss you, of course.

par

Each time a parenthetical expression occurs in the Reading and Writing Practice, it will be indicated as shown in the margin.

, apposition

Sometimes a writer mentions a person or thing and then, in order to make his meaning perfectly clear to the reader, says the same thing again in different words. This added explanation is known as an expression in *apposition.*

An expression in apposition is set off by two commas, except at the end of a sentence, when only one comma is necessary.

Your secretary, Miss Smith, tells me you are improving.

I met Mr. Smith, president of Smith and Company.

I will see you on Friday, June 1.

ap

Each time an expression in apposition occurs in the Reading and Writing Practice, it will be indicated as shown in the margin.

, series

When the last member of a series of three or more items is preceded by *and, or* or *nor,* place a comma before the conjunction as well as between the other items.

Please accept my best wishes for your success, prosperity, and happiness.

I can see him on March 1, on March 18, or on April 10.

Each time a series occurs in the Reading and Writing Practice, it will be indicated as shown in the margin.

ser 

, conjunction

A comma is used to separate two independent clauses that are joined by a conjunction.

I am proud that you are one of us, and I want you to know that I appreciate your work.

Each time this use of the comma occurs in the Reading and Writing Practice, it will be indicated as shown in the margin.

conj 

, and omitted

When two or more adjectives modify the same noun, they are separated by commas.

He was a quiet, efficient worker.

However, the comma is not used if the first adjective modifies the combined idea of the second adjective plus the noun.

She wore a beautiful green dress.

Each time this use of the comma occurs in the Reading and Writing Practice, it will be indicated as shown in the margin.

and o 

LESSON 1

Developing Word-Building Power

1 BRIEF FORMS

There are 36 brief forms in the following chart. You have already practiced these brief forms many times, and you should be able to read them rapidly. First read each line from left to right; then read each line from right to left. Finally, read down each column.

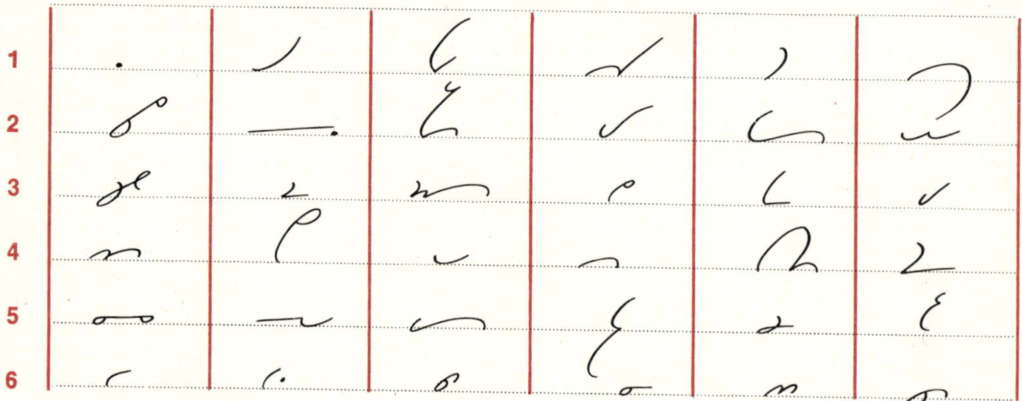

1 A-an, and, but, could, for, govern.
2 Idea, morning, object, ordinary, progress, railroad.
3 Satisfy-satisfactory, soon, suggest, they, upon, what.
4 Work, about, are-our-hour, can, difficult, from.
5 Immediate, Mr., organize, public, send, speak.
6 Than, thing-think, use, when, world, acknowledge.

Building Transcription Skills

2 BUSINESS VOCABULARY BUILDER

The greater command you have of the English language, the more efficient stenographer or secretary you will be. In each lesson a Business Vocabulary Builder will help you to continue to build your vocabulary.

Be sure to study each Business Vocabulary Builder before you begin your work on the Reading and Writing Practice of each lesson.

Business Vocabulary Builder

clients Customers; patrons.

itinerary Outline of travel; a guide.

consultant Expert; adviser.

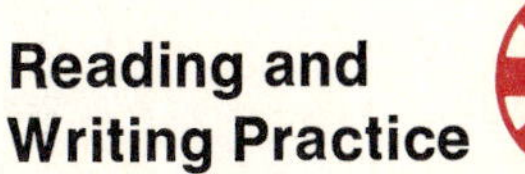

Reading and Writing Practice

3 Brief-Form Letter The following letter contains many brief forms and derivatives. You will profit by reading and copying it several times.

ser

of·fer·ing

ap

par

par

par

chal·leng·ing

[127]

4

par

ac·cept

par

ad·vance·ment

de·pend·able

and o

conj

ea·ger

[102]

5

ac·quaint·ed

ini·tial

ser

priv·i·leges

[173]

6

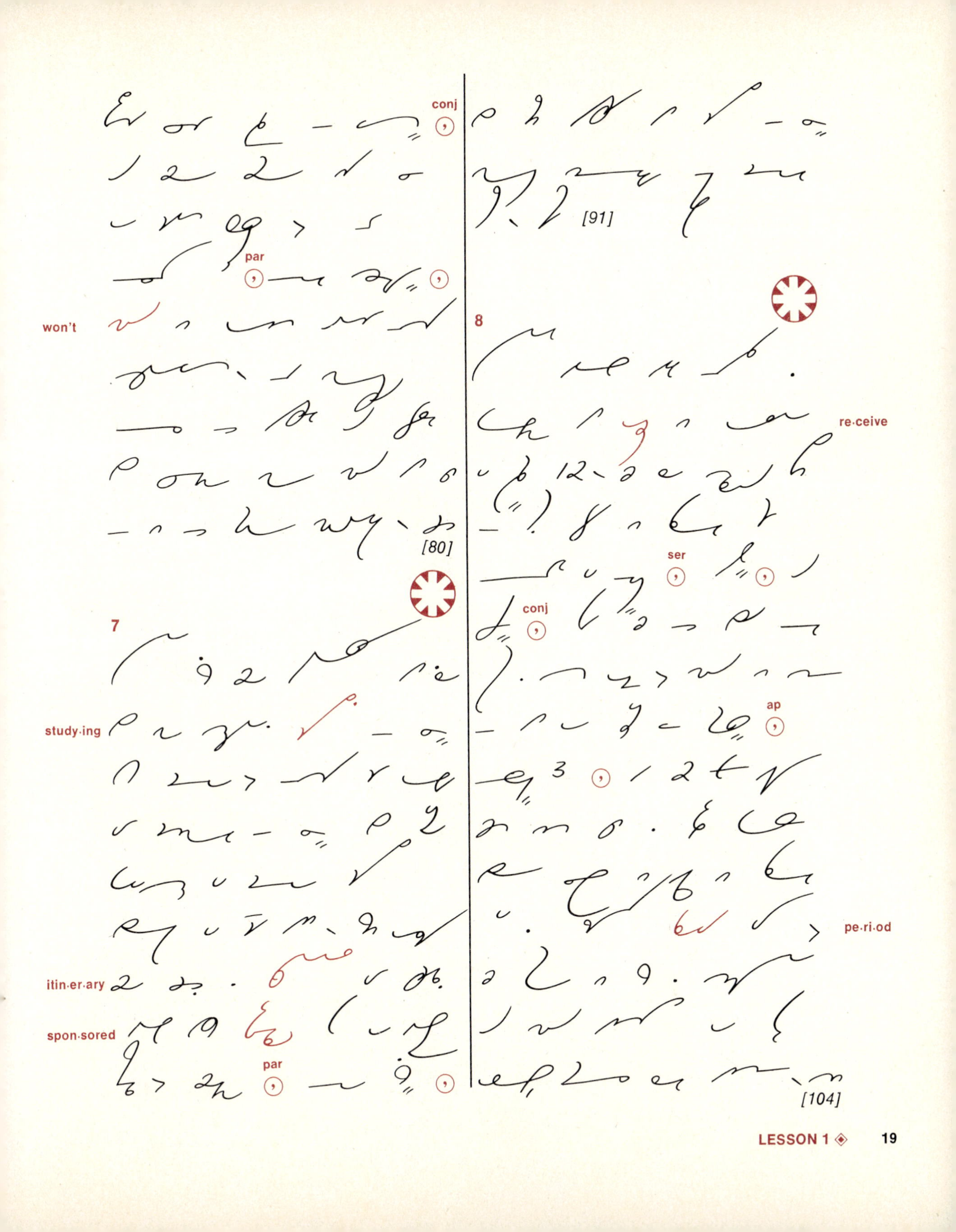

conj

par

won't

[80]

7

study·ing

itin·er·ary

spon·sored

par

[91]

8

re·ceive

ser

conj

ap

pe·ri·od

[104]

9 Transcription Quiz You are already familiar with the Transcription Quiz from your work in Volume One. This quiz gives you an opportunity to see how well you can apply the comma rules you have studied thus far.

In Chapters 1 and 2 of Volume Two, the Transcription Quiz will contain the same type of problems as those in Volume One. In later chapters, as new points of punctuation are introduced, the quizzes will become more advanced.

As you read the letter, decide what punctuation should be used. Then as you make a shorthand copy of it, insert the correct punctuation marks in the proper places in your notes.

For you to supply: 4 commas series.

[142]

Building Phrasing Skill

10 USEFUL BUSINESS-LETTER PHRASES

Below are a number of phrases that are used frequently in business letters. Can you read the entire list in 40 seconds?

We

1

Ago

2

Every

3

You will

4

I

5

1. We are, we are not, we will, we will not, we have, we have not, we may, we may not.
2. Years ago, months ago, days ago, weeks ago, several months ago.
3. Every one, every minute, every month, every other, every day.
4. You will, you will not, you will have, you will not have, you will be, you will not be, you will see.
5. I could, I cannot, I met, I should, I will, I have, I did not, I do not.

11 GEOGRAPHICAL EXPRESSIONS

1 Seattle, Los Angeles, San Francisco, New York, Hartford, Chicago.
2 Washington, Connecticut, California, Oregon, New Jersey, Illinois.

Building Transcription Skills

12 SIMILAR-WORDS DRILL

In Volume Two you will continue your study of similar words—words that sound alike and words that sound or look *almost* alike. Such words are often confused by stenographers when they transcribe.

Study each definition carefully. As you read and copy the Reading and Writing Practice of the lesson, watch for these similar words; you will find them in the lesson.

SIMILAR-WORDS DRILL ■ except, accept

except Left out; omitted.

I am free every day *except* Thursday.

accept To take.

Everybody must *accept* the responsibility of keeping our country beautiful.

13 Business Vocabulary Builder

stipulation Condition; requirement.

severe Critical; harsh.

ecology Science of the relations of man to his environment.

open-shelf files Business files on book-type shelves rather than in enclosed cases.

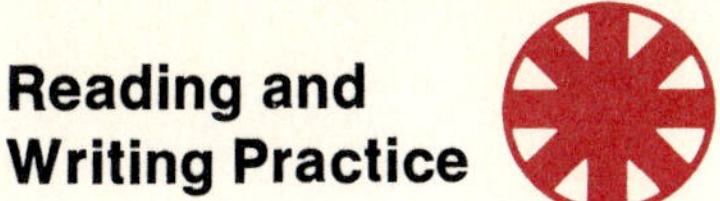

Reading and Writing Practice

14 Phrase Letter The following letter contains many useful phrases. You should read and copy it several times.

ap

par

ar·ea

ex·cept

con·ve·nient

[84]

too

droughts

conj

par

15

se·vere

dam·ag·ing

Cri·sis

ap

and o

[160]

16

ecol·o·gy

ac·cept

en·vi·ron·ment

ap

par

[113]

17

fur·ther

conj

sal·a·ry

par

el·i·gi·ble

[94]

18

rec·om·mend·ing

conj

ser

ap

chal·leng·ing

[127]

19 Transcription Quiz For you to supply: 7 commas—2 commas apposition, 2 commas series, 1 comma conjunction, 2 commas parenthetical.

5

12

[150]

SABIN SALES SPECIALTY CORP.

216 Williams Avenue • Jackson, Mississippi 39219

June 20, 197-

Mrs. Carole Thomas
730 Clark Street
Philadelphia, Pennsylvania 19150

Dear Mrs. Thomas:

It was indeed a pleasure to receive your letter of February 12. We were concerned about your not having paid your bills for the months of November, December, and January, but we knew that there must have been a good reason.

Won't you come in to our office on Friday, March 3, at 2 p.m., at which time we can work out a special plan that will enable you to pay your bills over an extended period of time.

We value you as a customer and want to continue our business relationship for many years to come.

Cordially yours,

Donald H. Wright
Customer Relations Manager

DHW:KD

Short Letter
Blocked Style
Standard Punctuation

Developing Word-Building Power

20 WORD FAMILIES

The principle of analogy will be of great help to you as you construct new shorthand outlines. The word families that you will find in the third lesson of each chapter will enable you to take advantage of that principle.

Read the following Word Families, referring to the key whenever you cannot read an outline in a few seconds.

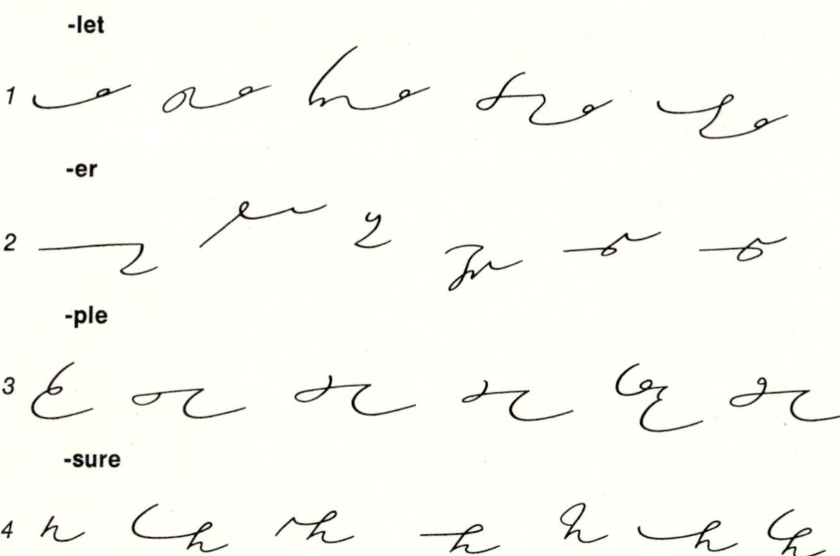

1 Let, outlet, booklet, pamphlet, leaflet.

2 Manufacturer, dealer, offer, computer, meter, matter.

3 People, ample, sample, simple, principle, example.

4 Sure, pleasure, treasure, measure, assure, leisure, pressure.

Building Transcription Skills

21 SPELLING FAMILIES ■ -ize, -ise, -yze

Words Ending in -ize

re·al·ize	equal·ize	crit·i·cize
mod·ern·ize	sum·ma·rize	sym·pa·thize
apol·o·gize	econ·o·mize	or·ga·nize

Words Ending in -ise

ad·vise	com·pro·mise	mer·chan·dise
ad·ver·tise	en·ter·prise	com·prise

Words Ending in -yze

par·a·lyze	an·a·lyze

22 Business Vocabulary Builder

computer Business machine that can, when programmed properly, perform numerous routine calculations electronically.

pertinent Applicable; pertaining to.

computer terminal A keyboard or other keying device connected to a computer.

Reading and Writing Practice

23

par

ad·vise

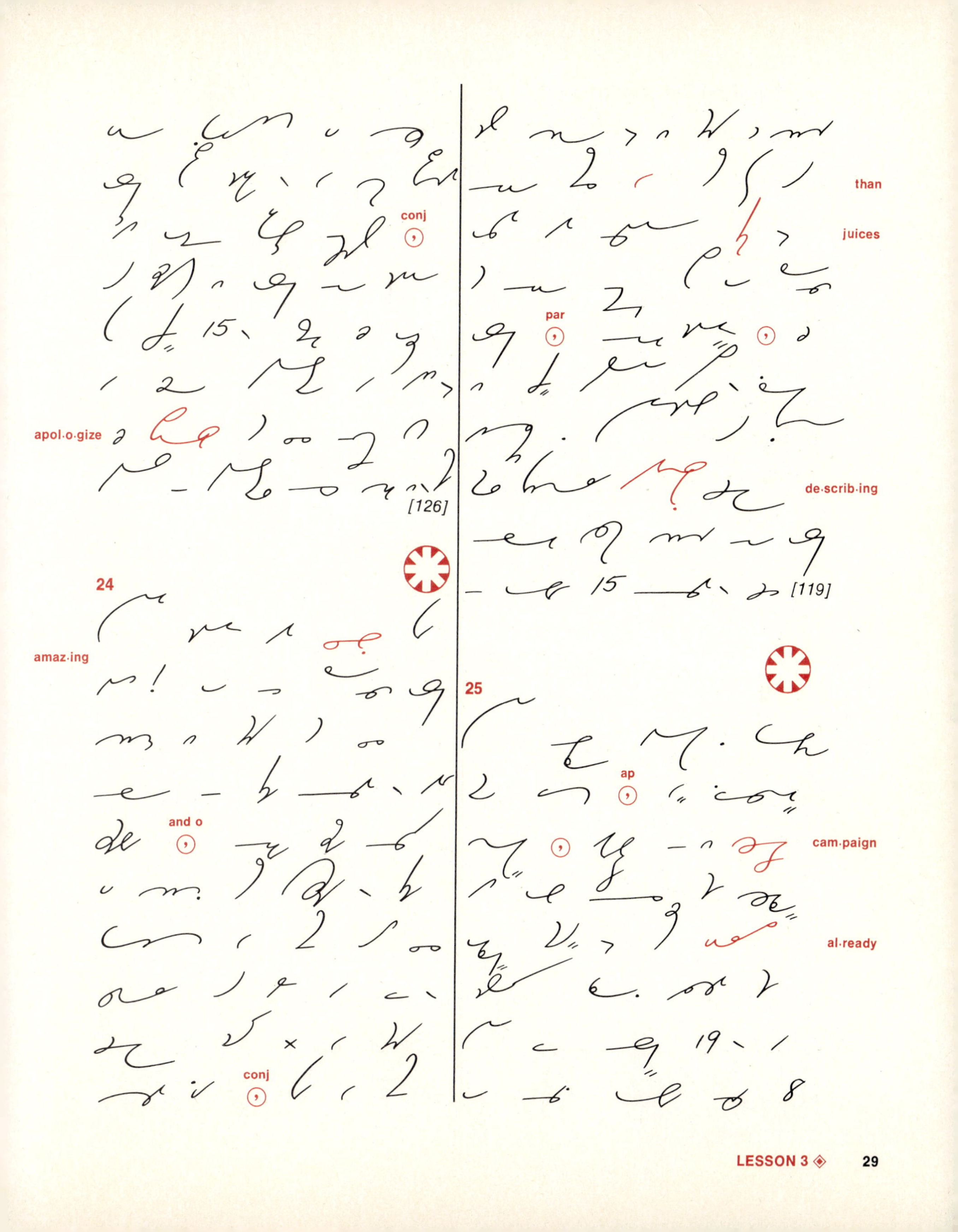

conj

apol·o·gize

[126]

24

amaz·ing

and o

conj

than

juices

par

de·scrib·ing

[119]

25

ap

cam·paign

al·ready

conj

ap

12

[108]

26

ser

than

an·a·lyze

ac·com·pa·ny·ing

par

per·ti·nent

par

wor·ries

bur·ied

[239]

27 Transcription Quiz For you to supply: 4 commas—2 commas parenthetical, 2 commas conjunction.

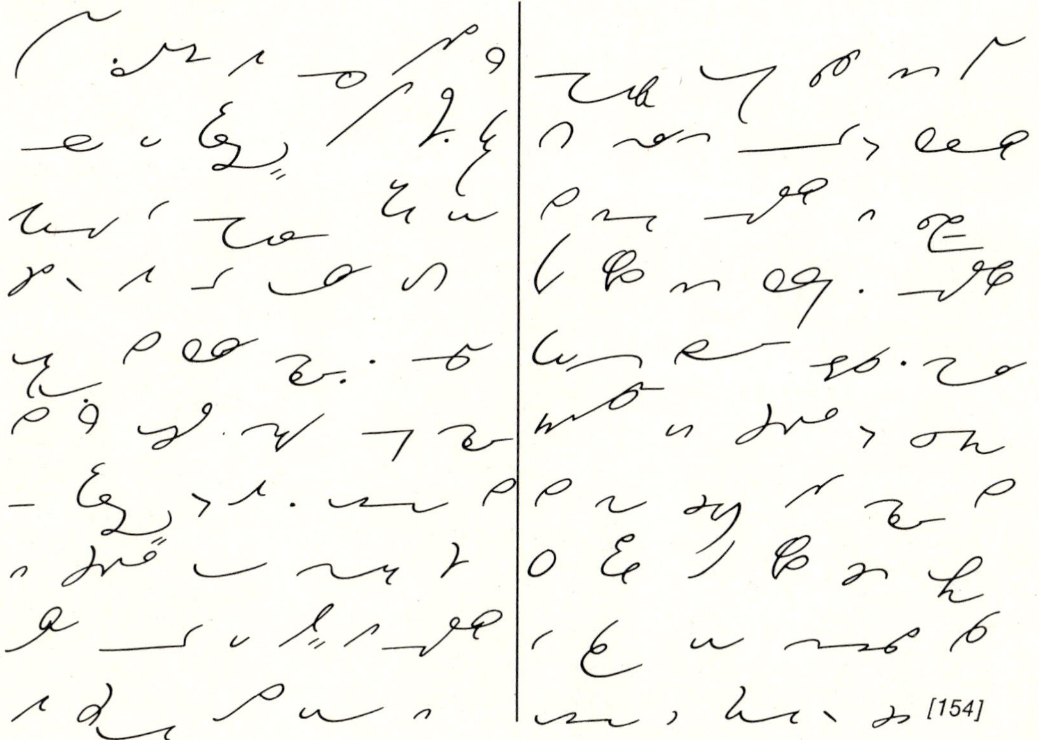

■ *Don't be discouraged if your first invasion of the business world produces only a position that you feel is of a menial nature. No one starts at the top of a ladder. Hard work and an honest interest in your job are still the best aids to success.*

LESSON 4

Developing Word-Building Power

28 WORD BEGINNINGS AND ENDINGS

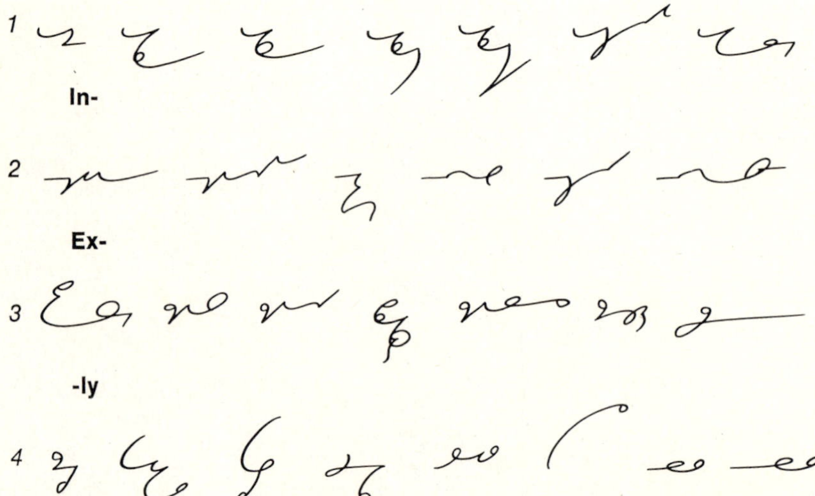

1 Reason, repel, resale, reserve, reserved, residents, replenish.
2 Install, instructor, inspection, increase, incident, incline.
3 Explanation, extra, extract, exercises, extremely, excuse, examine.
4 Essentially, properly, briefly, simply, thoroughly, timely, nearly, merely.

Building Transcription Skills

29 GRAMMAR CHECKUP ■ pronouns

A pronoun must agree with its antecedent in person, number, and gender.

Each person must complete his (*not* their) *work.*
The description you gave of this property indicates that it *is just the type we want.*
The children must do their *assignments.*

30 Business Vocabulary Builder

extractor A device to remove objects.

enhance To make better.

precisely Exactly.

Reading and Writing Practice

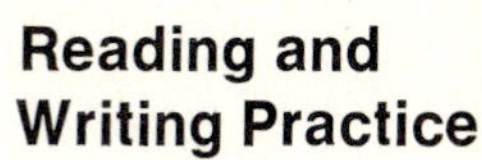

31

es·sen·tial·ly

conj

pro·hib·i·tive

copies

conj

par

[162]

32

par

car·pets

ser

sur·faces

ad·ja·cent

ex·trac·tor

ser

[122]

33

fur·ther

les·sons

ser

ex·er·cises

[77]

34

par

col·ors

en·hance

pre·cise·ly

[121]

35

and o

than

whisk·er

ap

unique

[134]

36

conj

hus·tle
bus·tle

[121]

37 **Transcription Quiz** For you to supply: 7 commas—5 commas apposition, 2 commas parenthetical.

[122]

Developing Word-Building Power

38 SHORTHAND VOCABULARY BUILDER

Ngk

Ted

Ow

Ind-, Int-

U

1 Ink, blank, frank, punctuation, rink, sink, sank.

2 Permitted, decorated, adopted, consisted, resisted, estimated.

3 Now, round, pound, bound, found, down, discount, mount.

4 Industry, India, index, induce, independent, into, integrity.

5 Few, beautiful, document, refuse, review, reviewed, futile, tube.

Building Transcription Skills

39 **Business Vocabulary Builder**

crudely Roughly.

posterity Future generations.

innovation New idea, method, or device.

subsidiaries Something which supports; a branch.

Reading and Writing Practice

40 **The History of Pens**

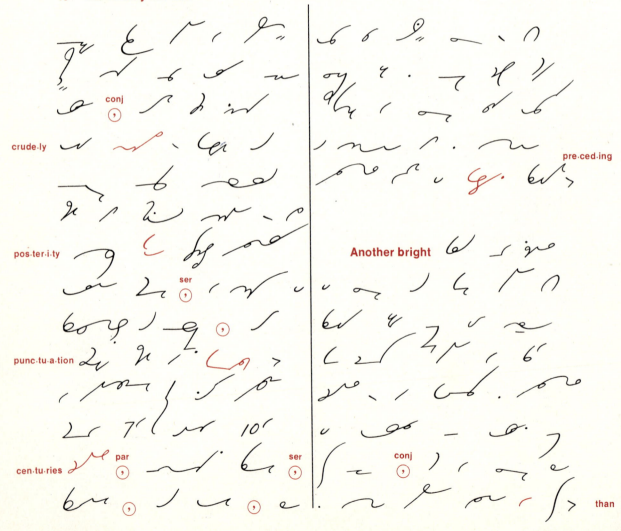

conj

crude·ly

pos·ter·i·ty

ser

punc·tu·a·tion

cen·tu·ries par ser

pre·ced·ing

Another bright

conj

than

par

roles

conj

par

Quill pens

man's

wear

conj

dis·ad·van·tages

par

par

sim·i·lar

amaz·ing

Capitals took

1780 conj

ac·cep·tance

rough

ser

bar·rel

chis·el

In 1803

conj

Although it

de·vel·op·ment

1800

1835

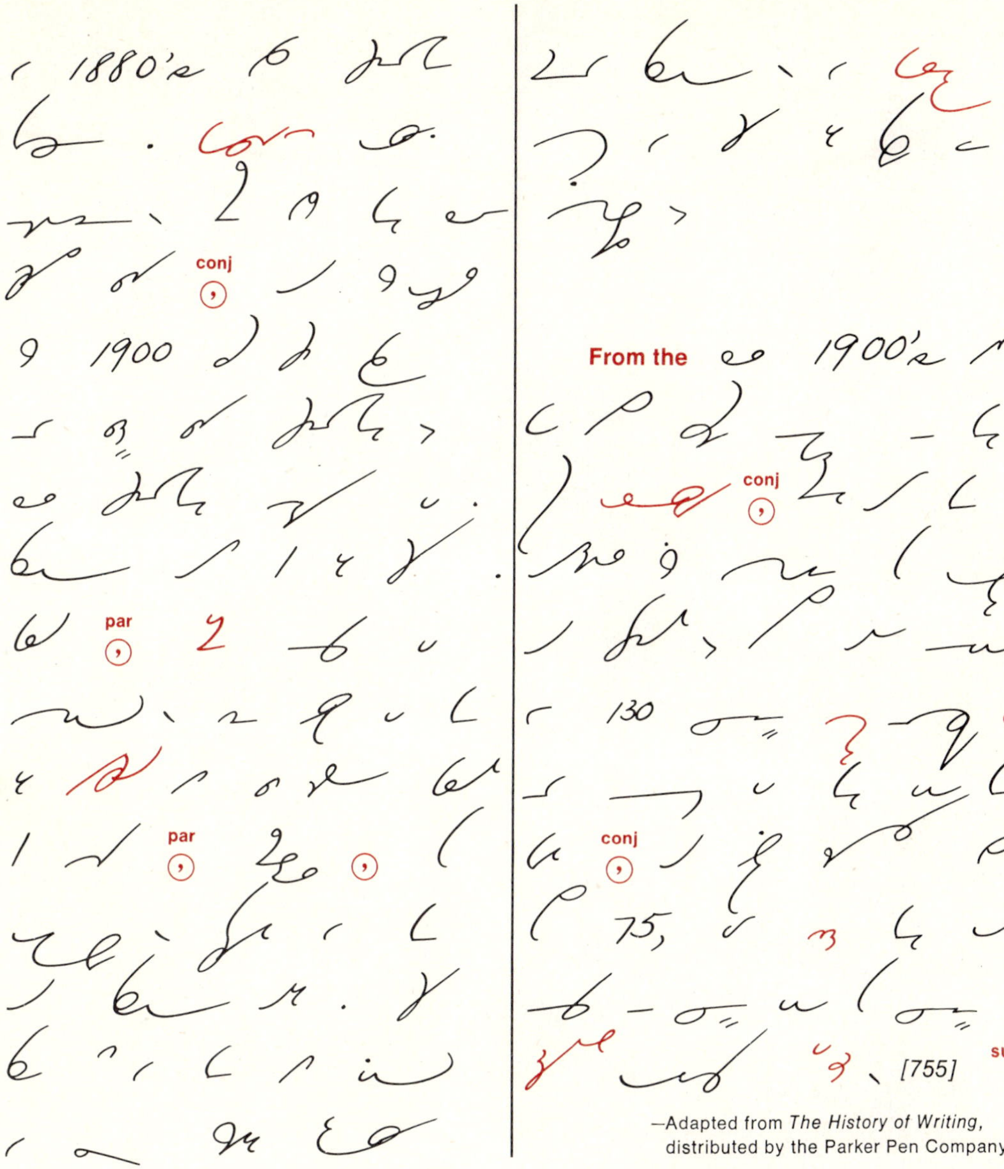

prin·ci·ple

prac·ti·cal

conj

From the

re·al·ized

conj

of·ten

par

com·pa·nies

de·signed

par

conj

world's

sub·sid·iaries

over·seas

[755]

—Adapted from *The History of Writing*, distributed by the Parker Pen Company.

■ *Cheerfulness is contagious! Even over the telephone a pleasant disposition and a friendly tone of voice are easily communicated to the invisible person at the other end of the wire.*

2 General

Comma Brushup (Concluded)

Introductory Commas

In Chapter 2 you will review the remaining four uses of the comma that you studied in Volume One—commas with introductory expressions. As in Volume One, introductory commas will be treated under the four headings given below. Next to each heading is the indication that will appear in the shorthand of the Reading and Writing Practice for that use of the comma.

, when clause	**when** (,)	**, if clause**	**if** (,)
, as clause	**as** (,)	**, introductory**	**intro** (,)

All introductory dependent clauses beginning with words other than *when, as,* and *if* will be classified as ", introductory."

When the original shipment is located, we will make the necessary adjustments.

As you know, we guarantee our cameras for a year.

If you are in urgent need of the notebooks, wire us.

Unless we receive our supplies soon, we will be in difficulty.

When the main clause comes first, however, no comma is usually necessary between the main clause and the dependent clause.

We will be in difficulty unless we receive our supplies soon.

Wire us if you are in urgent need of the notebooks.

A comma is also required after introductory words and explanatory expressions such as *frankly, consequently, on the contrary, for instance.*

Frankly, I cannot wait any longer.

On the contrary, you are the one who made the error.

Developing Word-Building Power

41 BRIEF FORMS

Can you read these brief forms in 35 seconds or less?

1 It-at, character, during, general, great, important-importance.

2 Mrs., of, over, publish-publication, recognize, several.

3 State, thank, this, value, where, worth.

4 Advantage, be-by, railroad, enclose, gentlemen, have.

5 In-not, must, one (won), part, purpose, regard.

6 Shall, street, that, those, very, which.

Building Transcription Skills

42 Business Vocabulary Builder

flat rate A set fee; no additional charge.

extension An addition.

equivalent An amount equal to.

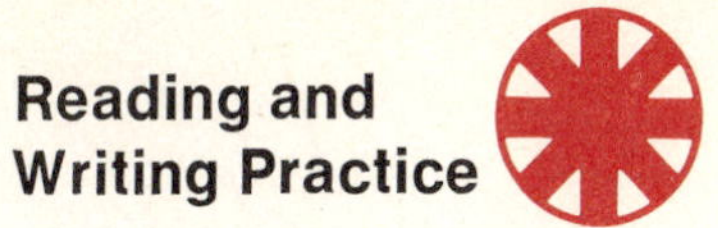

Reading and Writing Practice

43 Brief-Form Letter

if

conj

prac·tices

conj

cloth·ing

ser

intro

mon·ey's

[110]

44

as

swim·ming

when

for·eign

fac·tor

trav·el·ers

intro

any·where

mile·age

[146]

45

par

in·stalled

if

pi·ano

ser

pan·el·ing

if

par

ef·fects

and o

oily

stain

intro

[137]

46

10

Ha·waii

15

15

intro

per·son·nel

conj

as·sis·tance

intro

[120]

47

conj

intro

fair·ly

ex·pands

shank

conj

[94]

48

ware·house

if

leas·ing

cap·i·tal

[125]

49 Transcription Quiz For you to supply: 5 commas—1 comma conjunction, 2 commas parenthetical, 2 commas introductory.

[127]

Building Phrasing Skill

50 USEFUL BUSINESS-LETTER PHRASES

The following groups contain a number of phrases. Can you read them in 55 seconds?

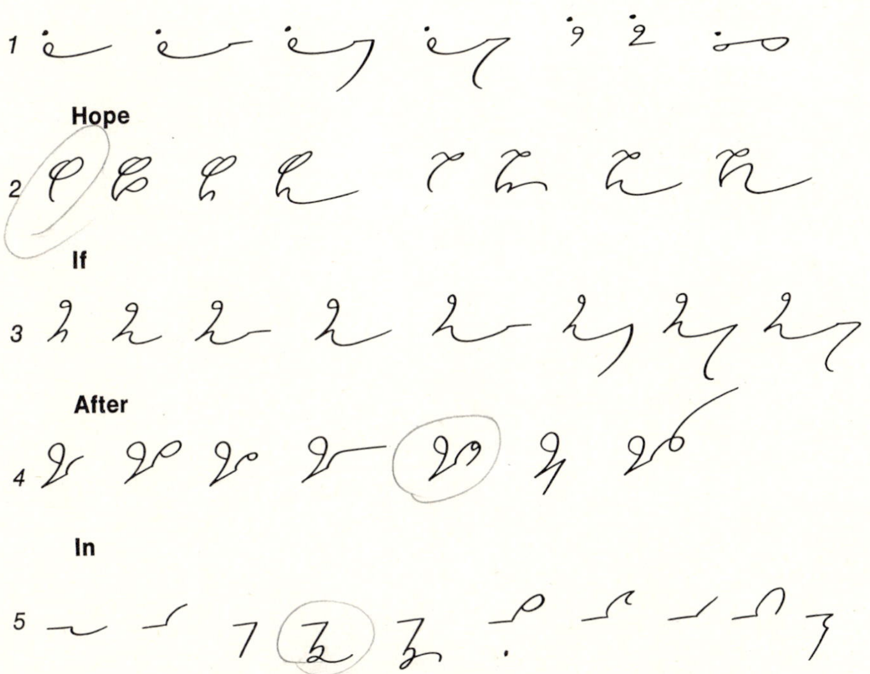

1 He will, he will not, he will not have, he will not be, he is, he is not, he may.

2 I hope, I hope that, I hope you, I hope you will, we hope, we hope you can, we hope you will, we hope this will.

3 If you, if you are, if you are not, if you will, if you will not, if you will have, if you will be, if you will not be.

4 After the, after that, after they, after them, after these, after which, after that time.

5 In our, in the, in which, in which we are, in which we can, in that, in those, in it, in this, in such.

51 GEOGRAPHICAL EXPRESSIONS

1 Miami, Boston, New York, Des Moines, Minneapolis, St. Paul, Indianapolis.

2 Iowa, Minnesota, Florida, Massachusetts, Indiana, Pennsylvania, Ohio, Kansas.

Building Transcription Skills

52 SIMILAR-WORDS DRILL ■ billed, build

billed (past tense of *bill*) Charged.

We should have *billed* you for $50.

build To create or produce; to construct.

The title of the talk was "How to *Build* Goodwill."

53 Business Vocabulary Builder

competent Capable.

flatware Knives, forks, spoons, etc.

proficiency Progress, as in attaining skill.

Reading and Writing Practice

54 Phrase Letter

intro

billed

par

ea·ger

and o

[98]

55

gram·mar
us·age

ap

writ·ing

intro
ex·cel·lent

re·ceive

if

intro

con·fi·dent

[156]

56

flat·ware

Feb·ru·ary

conj

ser

bot·tom

intro

[93]

57

ac·cept·ing

Busi·ness·men's

Build

ap

pre·vi·ous

as

ap

conj

if

ea·ger

[109]

58

won't

its

when

scarce

if

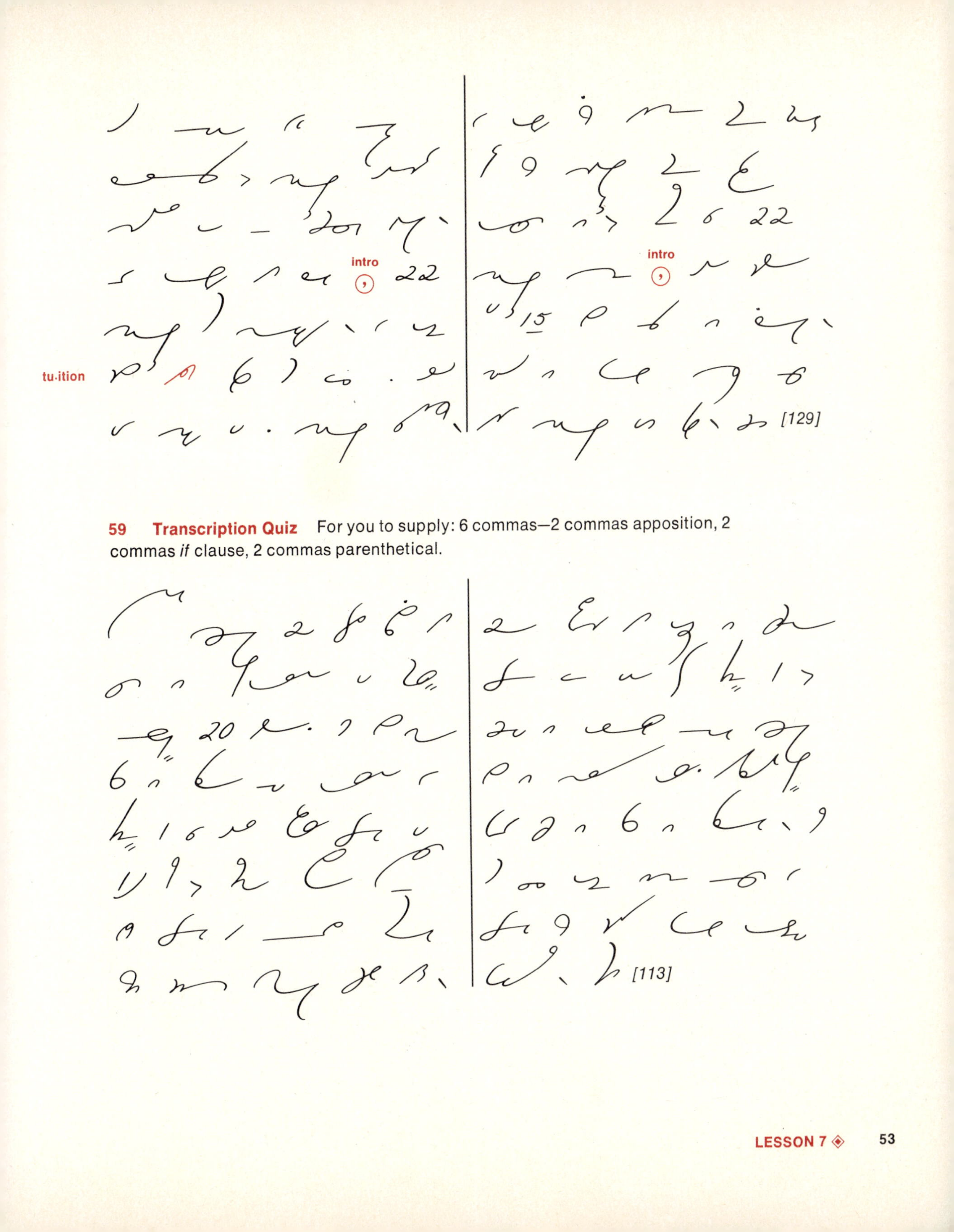

intro

intro

tu·ition

[129]

59 Transcription Quiz For you to supply: 6 commas—2 commas apposition, 2 commas *if* clause, 2 commas parenthetical.

[113]

LESSON 8

Developing Word-Building Power

60 WORD FAMILIES

Pro-

1

-st

2

-port

3

-time

4

1 Promotion, provide, problems, products, protect, protection.
2 Best, test, thirst, list, protest, honest, earnest.
3 Sport, import, export, report, deport, importation, exportation.
4 Time, daytime, nighttime, sometime, overtime, meantime.

Building Transcription Skills

61 SPELLING FAMILIES ■ -ar, -er, -or

Always be careful when you transcribe a word ending in the sound of *-er*—sometimes it is spelled *ar,* sometimes *er,* and sometimes *or.*

Words Ending in -ar

sug·ar	**col·lar**	**reg·u·lar**
gram·mar	**par·tic·u·lar**	**cel·lar**

Words Ending in -er

pa·per	fold·er	em·ploy·er
nev·er	let·ter	larg·er
lon·ger	deal·er	man·ag·er

Words Ending in -or

ma·jor	gov·er·nor	hu·mor
su·per·vi·sor	pro·fes·sor	el·e·va·tor

62 **Business Vocabulary Builder**

direct-mail piece Advertising mailed directly to potential buyer.

lease Rent agreement over a fixed period for a predetermined fee.

inventory Stock of merchandise on hand.

monopoly Exclusive control over an area.

Reading and Writing Practice

63

as

major

par

car·toons

[101]

64

piece

be·lieve

sup·pli·ers

ser

won't

par

[122]

65

when

ser

ad·vice

flex·i·ble

and o

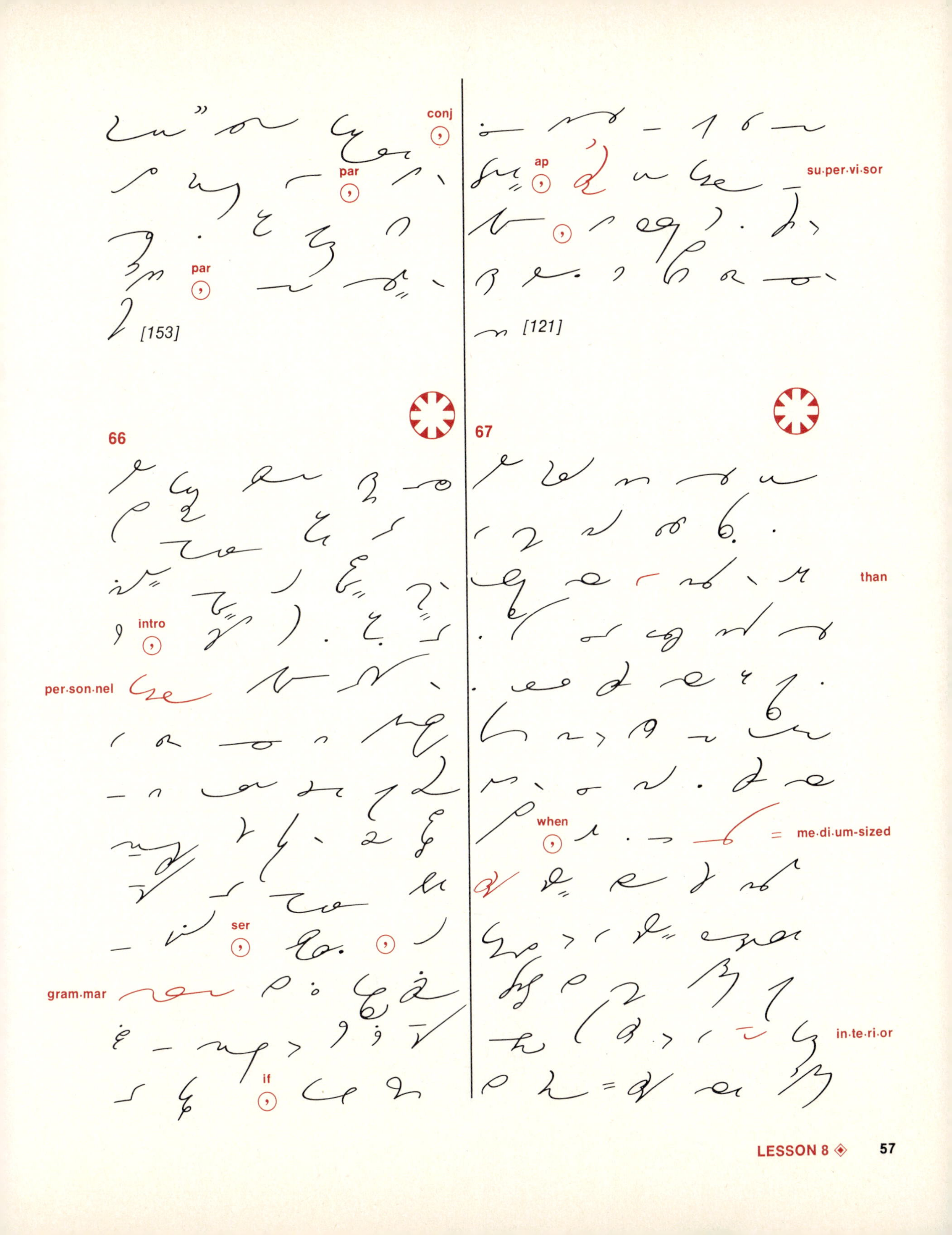

conj

par

par

[153]

ap

su·per·vi·sor

[121]

66

intro

per·son·nel

ser

gram·mar

if

67

than

when

me·di·um-sized

in·te·ri·or

mo·nop·o·ly

el·e·gance

[130]

68

ap

15

fare·well

as

as

18

quite

if

[78]

69 Transcription Quiz For you to supply: 2 commas—1 comma *and* omitted, 1 comma *if* clause.

[114]

LESSON 9

Developing Word-Building Power

70 WORD BEGINNINGS AND ENDINGS

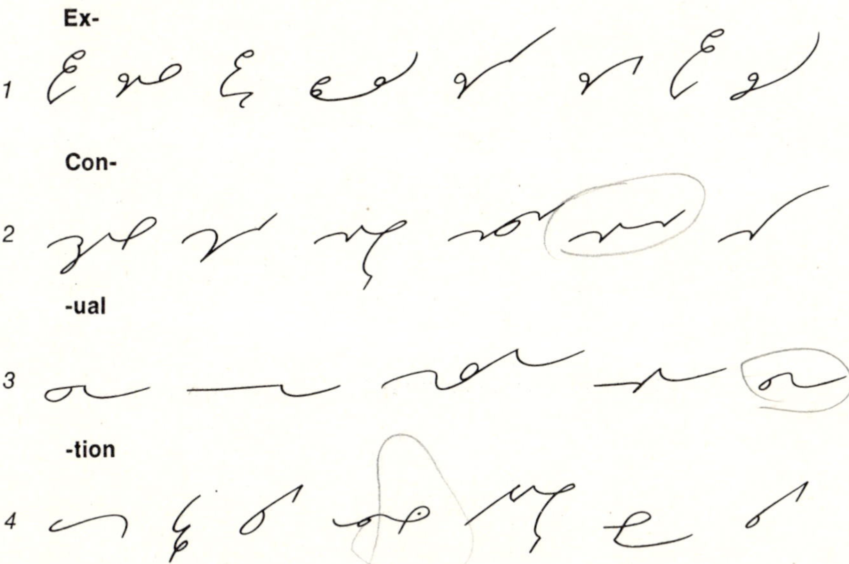

1 Except, extra, expense, excellent, extend, extension, exhibit, exempt.
2 Consideration, confident, contribution, contact, contract, condemn.
3 Annual, manual, gradual, mutual, equal.
4 Organization, position, addition, recreation, distribution, national, edition.

Building Transcription Skills

71 GRAMMAR CHECKUP ■ between, among

Between is used when referring to two things or persons; *among,* to more than two.

Between *you and me, I do not think he will complete the job.*
She divided the work among *the three secretaries.*

◈ Remember that when the word *between* is used as a preposition, any pronoun that follows it must be in the objective case.

Correct: *"Between you and me . . . ."*

Incorrect: *"Between you and I . . . ."*

72 **Business Vocabulary Builder**

conscientious Thoughtful; hard-working; self-checking.

mutual Given or received equally.

electronic calculator Machine which does mathematical computations electronically rather than mechanically.

Reading and Writing Practice

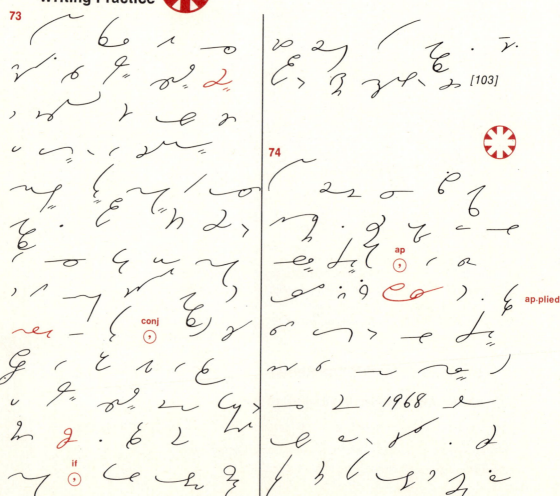

73

Fair

ca·reers

conj

as·sign

if

[103]

74

ap

ap·plied

1968

con·sci·en·tious

and o

conj

en·trust

[120]

75

ac·cept·ing

ser

conj

man·u·al

intro

par

[104]

76

intro

ap

conj

oc·ca·sion

intro

be·lieve

intro

res·i·dents

rec·re·ation·al

conj

[157]

77

its

ap

par

priv·i·leges

conj

dues

intro

ser

12 13 [133]

78

be·lieve

intro

[143]

79

ac·com·mo·date

as

141-2589

intro

for·eign

[55]

80 Transcription Quiz For you to supply: 6 commas—1 comma *as* clause, 4 commas series, 1 comma *if* clause.

18 19

20

[88]

NEW ENGLAND PRODUCTS

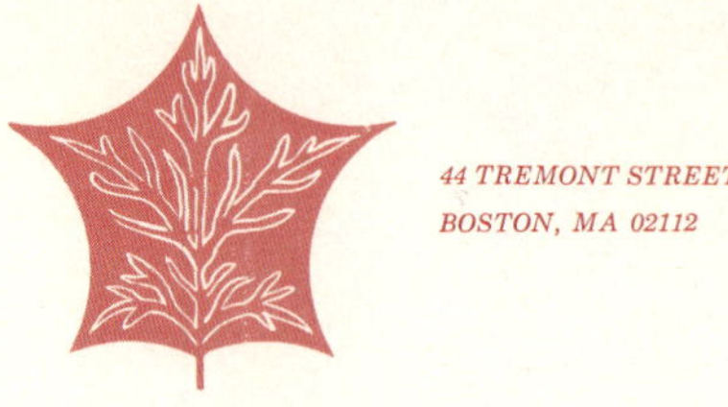

44 TREMONT STREET
BOSTON, MA 02112

August 17, 197-

Union Manufacturing Company
130 Randolph Street
Springfield, MA 01126

ATTENTION: Mr. Martin

Gentlemen:

In many business organizations, sending out a big mailing creates difficult problems. High-paid workers are diverted from their regular jobs to fold and stuff circulars and other advertising material into envelopes in order to meet a mailing deadline. The operation of the office is disrupted, and important work must be neglected.

This will not happen, however, in an organization that has installed a Harper Mailer 161. This unit folds mailing pieces, inserts them in envelopes, and seals the envelopes at the rate of 5,000 an hour. Thus in one ordinary working day you can process as many as 40,000 pieces while your regular staff goes about its regular duties.

Wouldn't you like to have us install a Harper 161 in your office on a ten-day trial basis? To arrange this, simply return the enclosed card.

Very truly yours,

Howard C. West

Howard C. West
Product Manager

HCW:DS

Average-Length Letter
Semiblocked Style,
with Attention Line
Standard Punctuation

LESSON 10

Developing Word-Building Power

81 SHORTHAND VOCABULARY BUILDER

Rd

1

Omission of Short U

2

Dif-, Div-, Etc.

3

Men, Etc.

4

1 According, compared, standards, yardstick, guard, card, feared.
2 Much, income, judge, budget, sums, someone, welcome.
3 Different, difference, definition, divide, devote, individual.
4 Businessmen, many, month, manner, harmony, women.

Building Transcription Skills

82 Business Vocabulary Builder

formulate To put together; to plan.

retained profits Receipts above expenses kept by a company.

per capita Per head; per person.

vague Not clear.

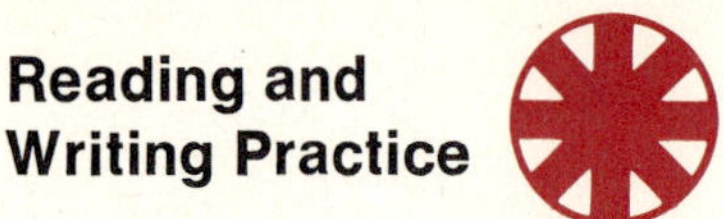

Reading and Writing Practice

83 GNP—Scorecard of Progress

yard·stick

intro

than

fa·mil·iar·ly

A concise

intro

ser

clothes

ser

sal·a·ries

intro

coun·try's

A word

par

ap·pro·pri·ate

intro

intro

to·day's

1950

stand·still

par

GNP's

growth

By subtracting GNP

year's

intro

intro

re·act·ed

les·sons

intro

intro

intro

bud·get

intro

wheth·er

All this

par

GNP

GNP

na·tion's

when

cit·i·zens

ser

sums

to·tal

if

per cap·i·ta

Of course,

in·di·vid·u·al's

cited

ser

wheth·er

Such

ser

vague

[637]

—Adapted from "GNP—Scorecard of Progress," *Senior Scholastic,* (Oct. 21, 1964).

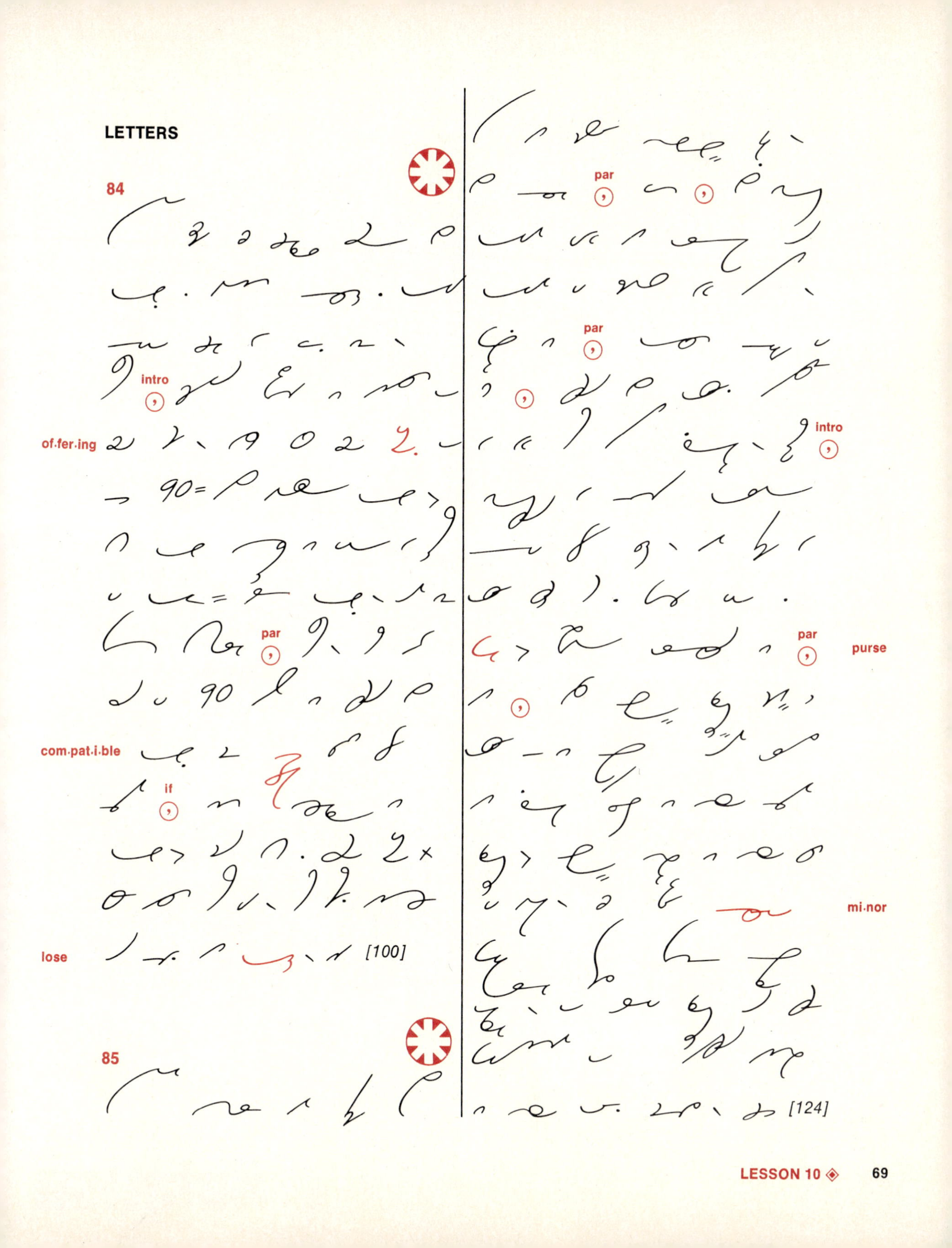

LETTERS

84

intro

of·fer·ing

par

compat·i·ble

if

lose

[100]

85

par

par

intro

par

purse

mi·nor

[124]

3 Aviation

LESSON 

Developing Word-Building Power

86 BRIEF FORMS

Can you read these brief forms in 35 seconds or less?

1 Would, advertise, between, circular, envelope, glad.

2 Is-his, manufacture, never, opinion, particular, put.

3 Regular, short, subject, the, throughout, was.

4 Why, yesterday, after, big, business, company.

5 Ever-every, gone, how-out, merchandise, newspaper, opportunity.

6 Present, quantity, request, should, success, there (their).

Building Transcription Skills

87 PUNCTUATION PRACTICE

You have now reviewed all the uses of the comma that you studied in Volume One. Beginning with this lesson, which introduces another important use of the comma, you will take up new punctuation pointers.

PUNCTUATION PRACTICE ■ , nonrestrictive

A nonrestrictive clause or phrase is one that may be omitted without changing the meaning of the sentence. Nonrestrictive clauses are set off by commas and might be classified as parenthetical. It is important that you follow the meaning of the dictation in order to be able to identify nonrestrictive clauses and phrases and punctuate them correctly.

Nonrestrictive—commas *Betty Jones, who is enrolling in college, should have a physical checkup.*

Restrictive—no commas *All students who are enrolling in college should have a physical checkup.*

In the first sentence, *who is enrolling in college* is a nonrestrictive descriptive or parenthetical clause that must be set off with commas. It is not needed to identify the particular person who should have a checkup and could be omitted without changing the meaning of the sentence.

In the second sentence, *who are enrolling in college* is a restrictive clause and must not be set off by commas. The expression identifies persons who should have a checkup.

Each time a nonrestrictive use of the comma occurs in the Reading and Writing Practice, it will be indicated thus in the shorthand: nonr (,)

88 Business Vocabulary Builder

substantially In a major way; having a big effect.

comptroller An accountant in charge of financial control.

comprehensive Complete; inclusive.

terminate Stop, cease.

Reading and Writing Practice

89 Brief-Form Letter

ex·pe·ri·ence

los·ing

ser

intro

intro

mer·chan·dise

if

[138]

90

de·ci·sion

conj

al·though

intro

intro

cat·e·go·ries

if

han·gar

[152]

91

nonr

ex·ten·sive

ac·cu·rate

and o

par

ad·di·tion·al

if

[96]

92

nonr

ac·com·mo·date

when

[75]

than

93

conj

nonr

com·pre·hen·sive

raise

ap

com·mis·sion·er

rec·om·men·da·tion

wit·nesses

ap

[114]

94

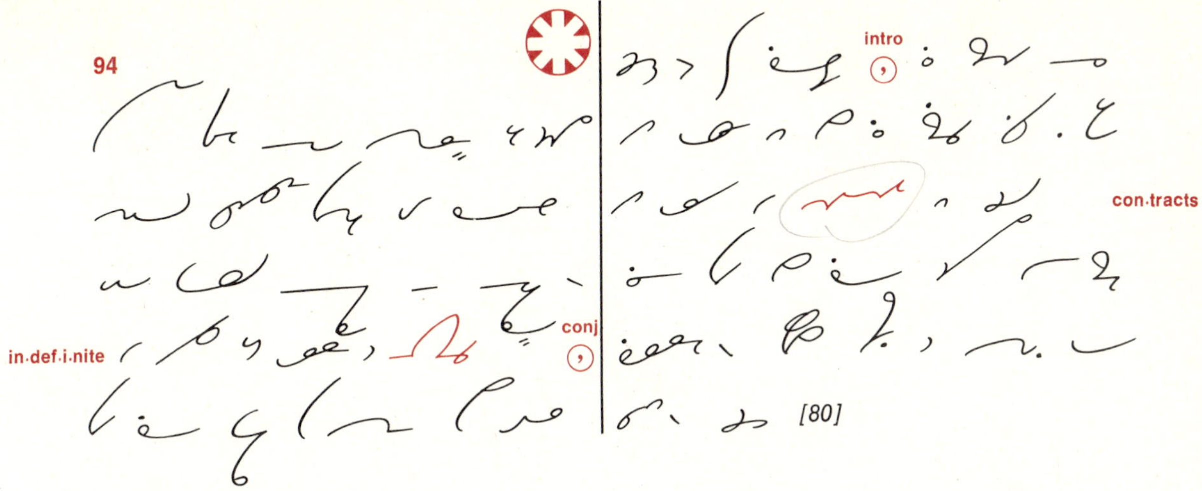

95 Transcription Quiz In this and succeeding Transcription Quizzes, a challenging new factor will be added. In addition to supplying the necessary punctuation, you will have to supply a number of words that have been omitted from the printed shorthand.

Occasionally a stenographer will omit a word when she is taking dictation, either through lack of attention or because she did not hear it. Then as the meaning of the sentence becomes clear, she will supply the missing word when transcribing.

You should have no difficulty supplying the missing words in these Transcription Quizzes since in each case only one possible word makes sense.

For you to supply: 4 commas—2 commas apposition, 1 comma introductory, 1 comma conjunction; 2 missing words.

[101]

Building Phrasing Skill

96 USEFUL BUSINESS-LETTER PHRASES

Below are a number of phrases. Can you read them in 50 seconds?

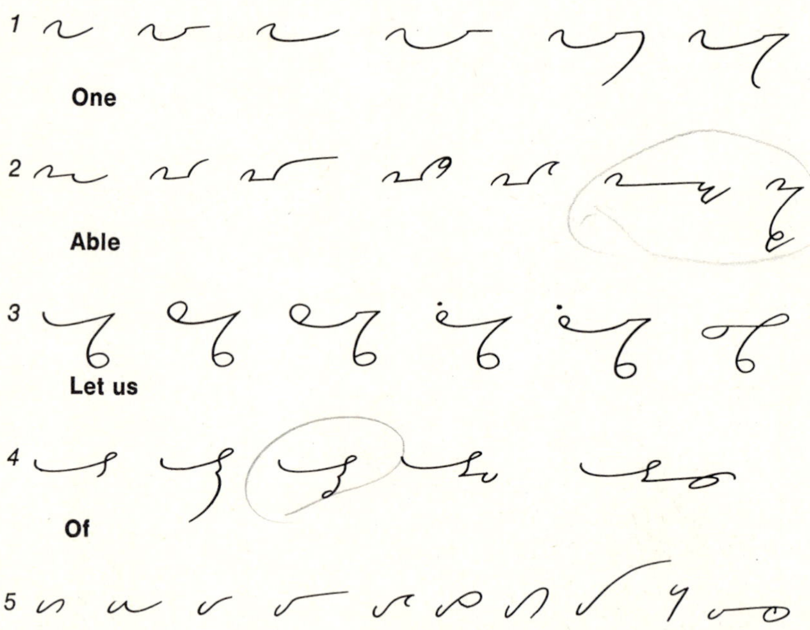

1 You are, you are not, you will, you will not, you will not have, you will not be.

2 One of our, one of the, one of them, one of these, one of those, one of the most, one of the best.

3 Will be able, I will be able, I will not be able, he will be able, he will not be able, I may be able.

4 Let us, let us have, let us see, let us know, let us make.

5 Of your, of our, of the, of them, of those, of that, of this, of time, of which, of my.

97 GEOGRAPHICAL EXPRESSIONS

1 Portland, Fort Worth, New Orleans, Salt Lake City, St. Louis, Denver.

2 Missouri, Colorado, Utah, Idaho, Montana, New Mexico, Texas.

Building Transcription Skills

98 PUNCTUATION PRACTICE ■ commas in numbers

1 When a number contains four or more digits, a comma is used to separate thousands, millions, billions.

$1,000 (*not* $1000) 798,196 6,123,000 9,100,000,000

2 Commas, however, are not used in serial numbers, house or street numbers, telephone numbers, page numbers, and between the digits of a year.

No. 15608 6201 Third Avenue 991-6872
page 1301 the year 1974

These uses of the comma in numbers will be called to your attention in the margin of the Reading and Writing Practice thus: ***Transcribe:*** **$1,115** **No. 11561**

99 Business Vocabulary Builder

contemplate Consider carefully.

invalid Being without foundation, fact, or truth.

frustrating Causing anxiety.

Reading and Writing Practice

100 Phrase Letter

vol·ume

Transcribe: 1970

intro

Transcribe: 6134

intro

Transcribe: No. 1156

Transcribe: $1,450

1,450

par

intro

ef·fect

and o

par

[152]

101

air·freight

par

par

30

ship·ping

conj

[113]

102

sep·a·rate·ly

1986

nonr

Transcribe: No. 1986

li·censes

conj

intro

an·swer

Transcribe:
788-8999

788-8999 [111]

103

le·gal

re·ferred

com·plet·ing

when

intro

reg·u·la·tions

filed

re·ceive

if

rec·og·nize

ser

time-con·sum·ing

par

if

fur·ther

[165]

104

conj

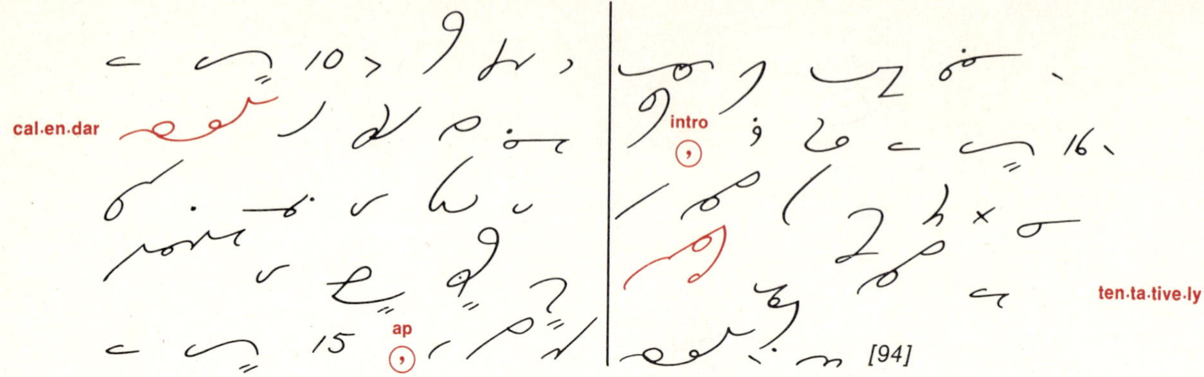

105 Transcription Quiz For you to supply: 4 commas—2 commas conjunction, 1 comma *when* clause, 1 comma nonrestrictive; 2 missing words.

[136]

LESSON 13

Developing Word-Building Power

106 WORD FAMILIES

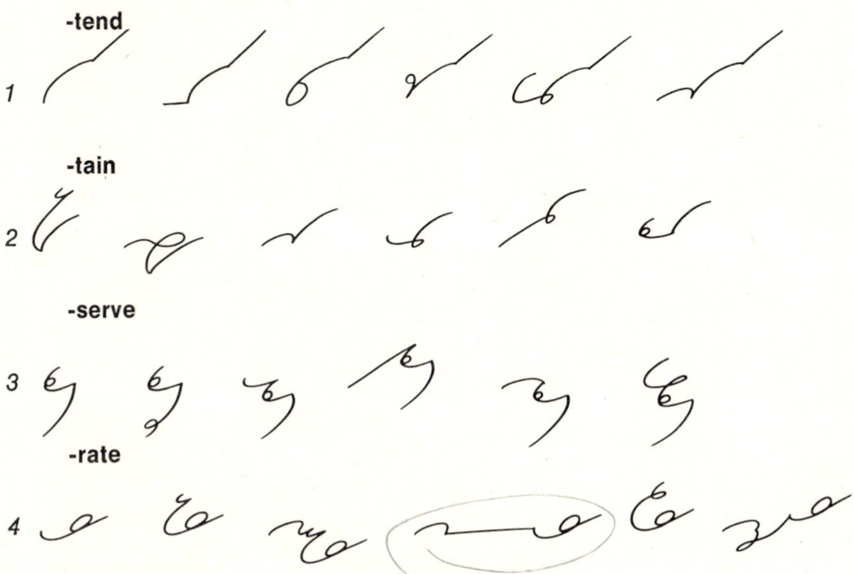

1 Tend, intend, attend, extend, pretend, contend.
2 Obtain, captain, contain, retain, detain, certain.
3 Serve, service, reserve, deserve, conserve, preserve.
4 Rate, operate, cooperate, commemorate, separate, concentrate.

Building Transcription Skills

107 TYPING STYLE STUDY ■ numbers at the beginning of a sentence

1 Always spell out a number that begins a sentence.

Twenty-seven *crates of fruit have been shipped.*
Five hundred *people attended the convention.*

2 For consistency, also spell out related numbers.

Twenty *or* twenty-five (*not* 25) *boxes were missing.*

108 Business Vocabulary Builder

Chartered trip A specially planned trip for which reservations are necessary.

memorandum Short note.

hearings Meetings held to discuss stated subjects.

Reading and Writing Practice

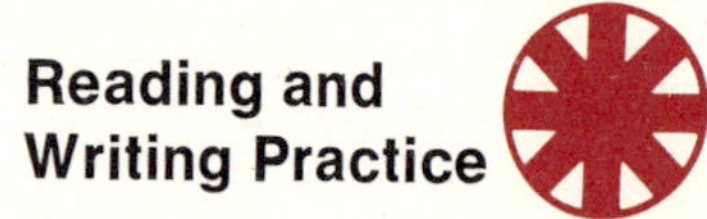

109

year's

intro

nonr

fare

ser

ap

com·mit·tee

if

de·pos·it

[131]

110

char·tered

nonr

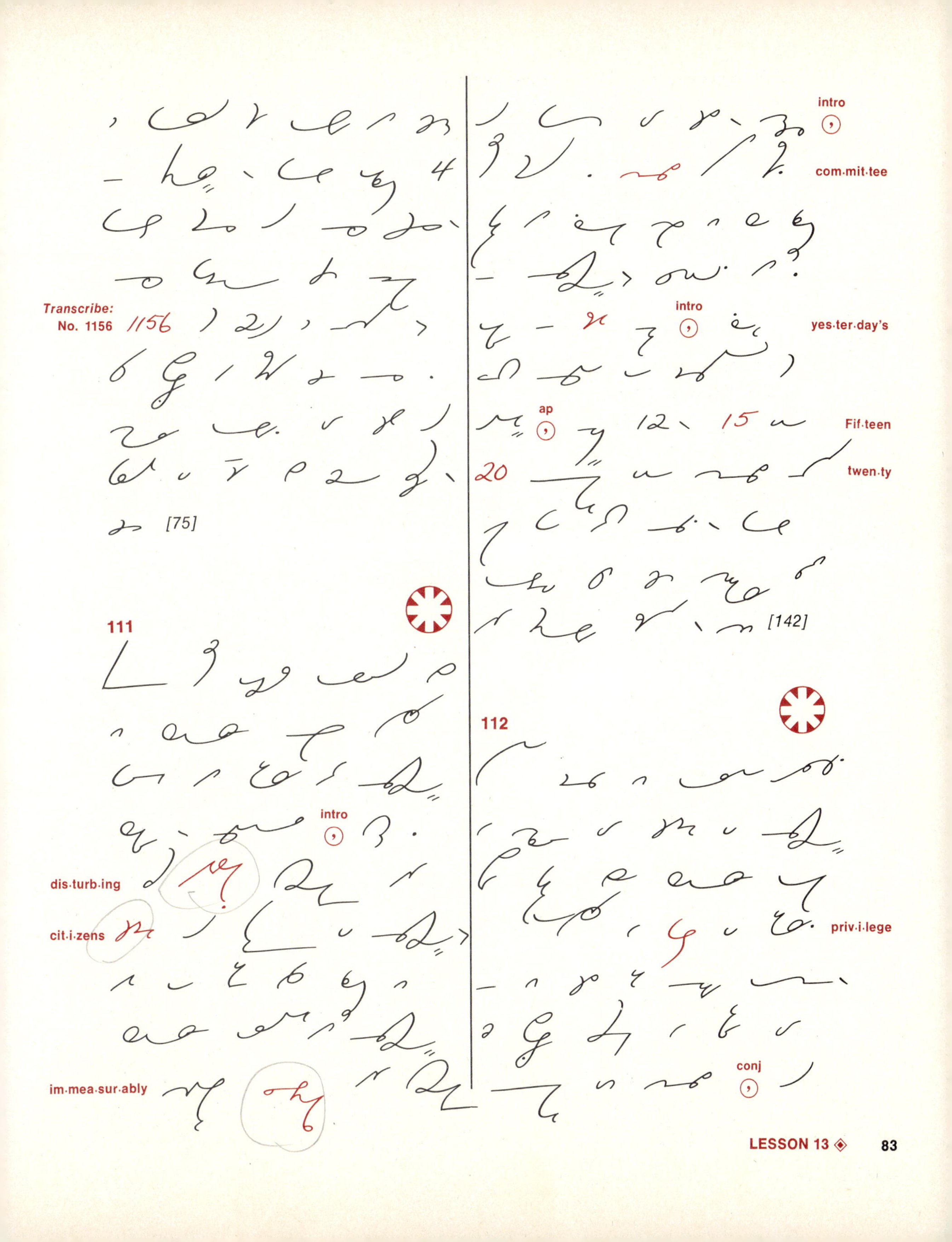

intro

com·mit·tee

Transcribe:
No. 1156

intro

yes·ter·day's

ap

Fif·teen

twen·ty

[75]

[142]

111

112

intro

dis·turb·ing

cit·i·zens

priv·i·lege

conj

im·mea·sur·ably

cor·dial

ap

[103]

113

re·fu·el·ing

as

when

nat·u·ral·ly

and o

con·ve·nient

par

in·stal·la·tion

[155]

114

when

flights

when

ser

intro

lis·ten

if

com·pli·ments

if

intro

116-1189 [144]

115 Transcription Quiz For you to supply: 6 commas—1 comma conjunction, 2 commas parenthetical, 2 commas apposition, 1 comma *if* clause.

12

16 9

[106]

Developing Word-Building Power

116 WORD BEGINNINGS AND ENDINGS

For-, Fore-

-ment

Per-, Pur-

De-, Di-

-ly

1 Effort, form, ford, afford, forward, foreman, forecasting, forget.
2 Development, adjustment, replacement, department, compartment, moment.
3 Person, perfect, personnel, purchase, purchasing, purple, pursue.
4 Deliver, delay, delightful, direct, direction, directly.
5 Badly, only, early, surely, thoroughly, closely, daily, freely.

Building Transcription Skills

117 PUNCTUATION PRACTICE ■ ; no conjunction

A semicolon is used to separate two independent but closely related clauses when no conjunction is used between them.

Bill came to work early; Harry was late.

The above sentence could be written as two sentences.

Bill came to work early. Harry was late.

Because the two thoughts are closely related, the use of the semicolon is more appropriate than the use of the period.

Each time this use of the semicolon occurs in the Reading and Writing Practice, it will be indicated thus in the shorthand: nc (;)

118 Business Vocabulary Builder

numerous Many.

direct air service One plane service between cities—not necessarily nonstop.

compensated Paid for.

Reading and Writing Practice

119

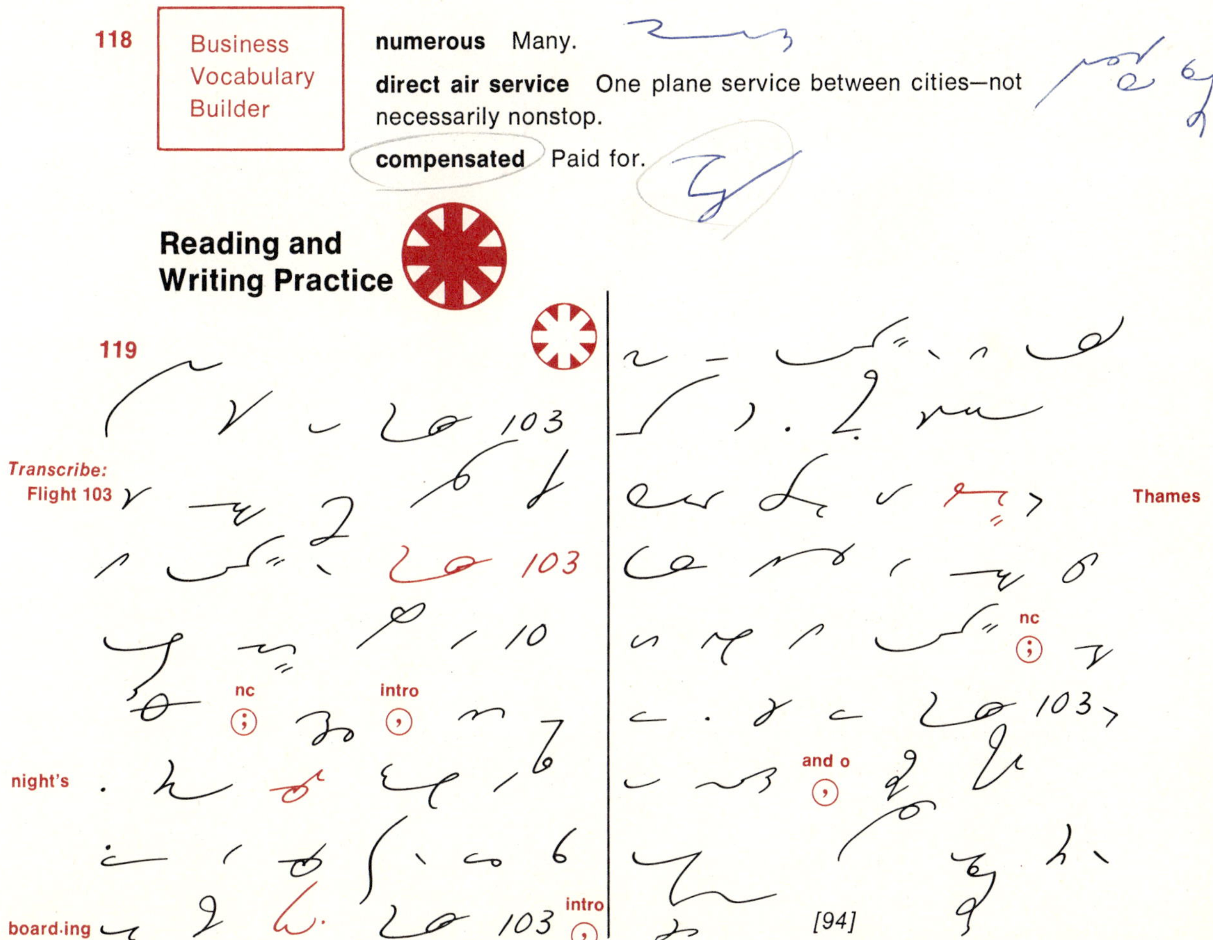

120

Transcribe:
Flight 161

161

15

conj

weath·er

can·cel·la·tions

nc

intro

safe·ty

par

routes

and o

[121]

121

ap

Ad·ver·tis·ers

26

ser

27

28

con·ve·nient·ly

intro

rec·re·ation

cur·rent

if

[144]

122

ap

trav·eled

Pitts·burgh

when

nc

leath·er

as

oc·curred

nonr

pur·chased

[124]

123

intro

intro

Transcribe: 86,000

par

conj

re·li·abil·i·ty

ser

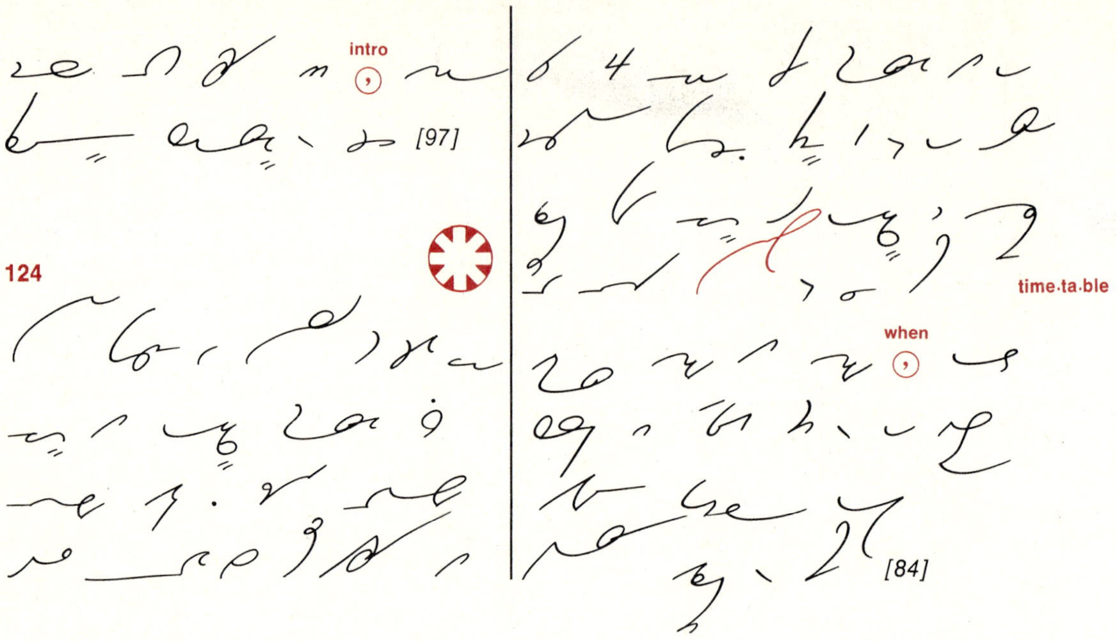

125 Transcription Quiz For you to supply: 5 commas—1 comma conjunction, 1 comma introductory, 1 comma *as* clause, 2 commas parenthetical; 2 missing words.

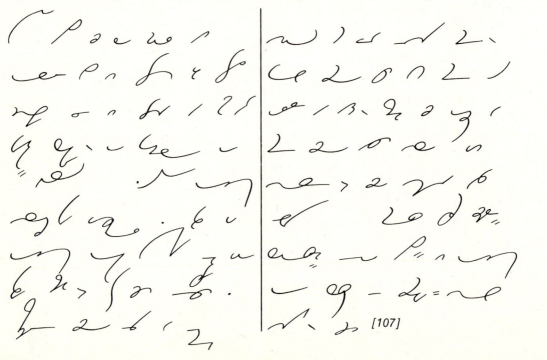

[107]

Developing Word-Building Power

126 SHORTHAND VOCABULARY BUILDER

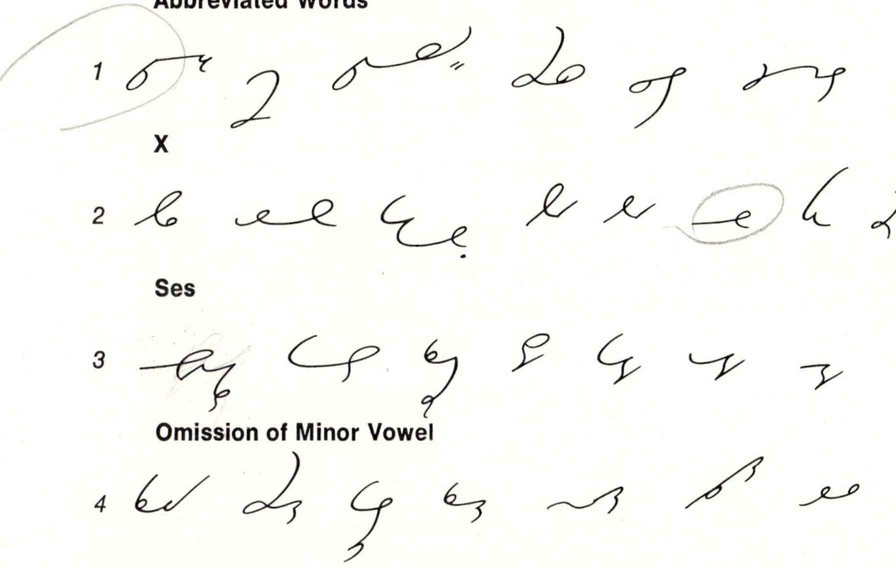

1 Atmosphere, convenient-convenience, Atlantic, variety, anniversary, significant-significance.

2 Taxi, relax, perplexing, taxed, text, mix, box, fix.

3 Masterpieces, places, services, assist, persist, resist, insist.

4 Period, various, previous, serious, courteous, tedious, theory.

Building Transcription Skills

127 Business Vocabulary Builder

derive To gain from.

media Means for conveying something.

congenial Harmonious; having similar tastes.

perplexing Puzzling.

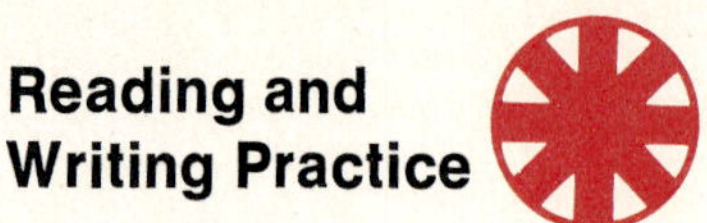

Reading and Writing Practice

128 A Trip to France

bud·gets

conj

de·scribed

zest

pre·vi·ous·ly

You can

sce·nic

nc

rev·el

ser

pag·eants

cos·tumes

when

fa·mil·iar

al·lure

fo·cal

and o

soars

com·pli·men·ta·ry

With the

con·ge·nial

intro

intro

taxi·ing

de·scent

par

francs

Perhaps

if

Seine

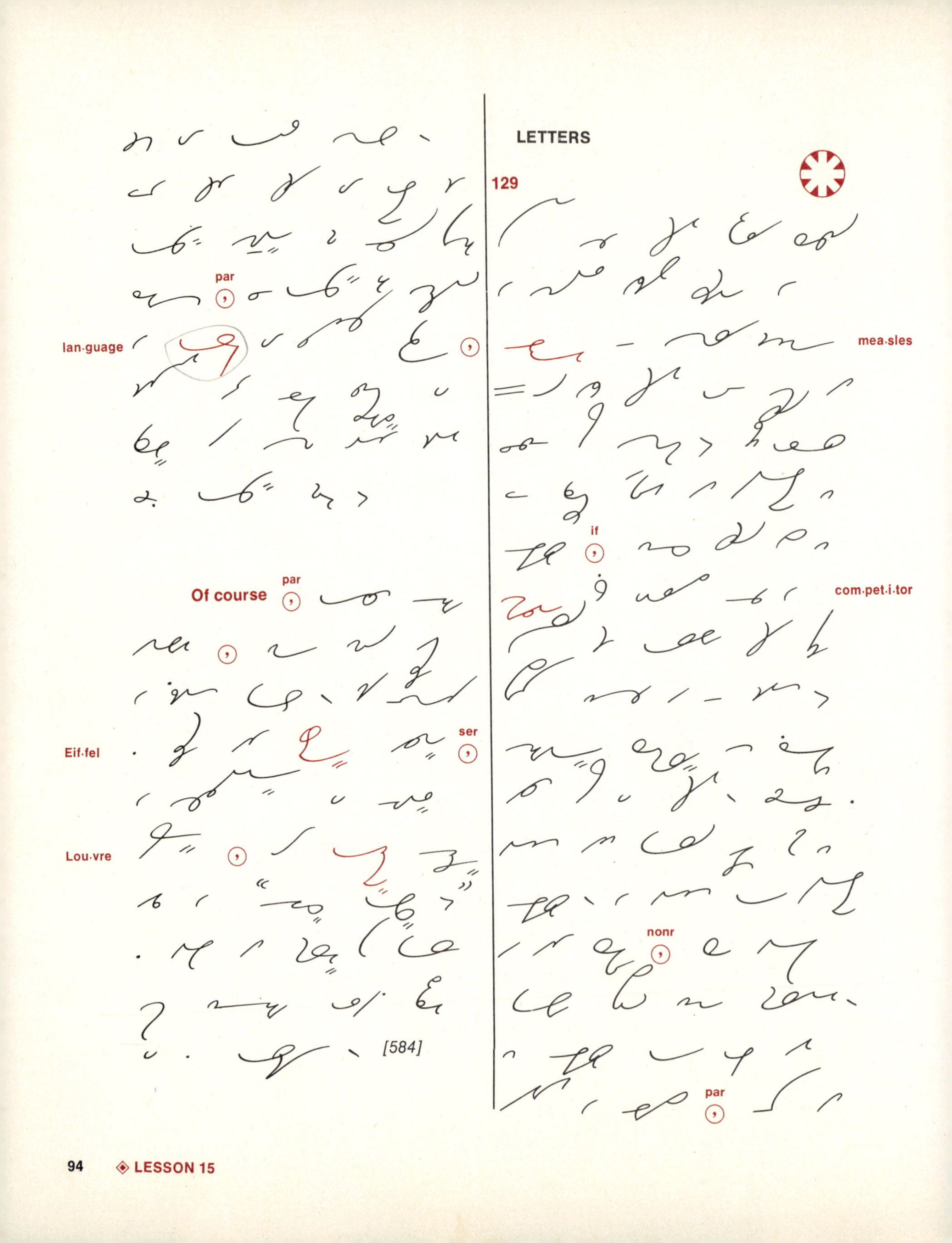

par

lan·guage

Of course par

Eif·fel ser

Lou·vre

[584]

LETTERS

129

mea·sles

if

com·pet·i·tor

nonr

par

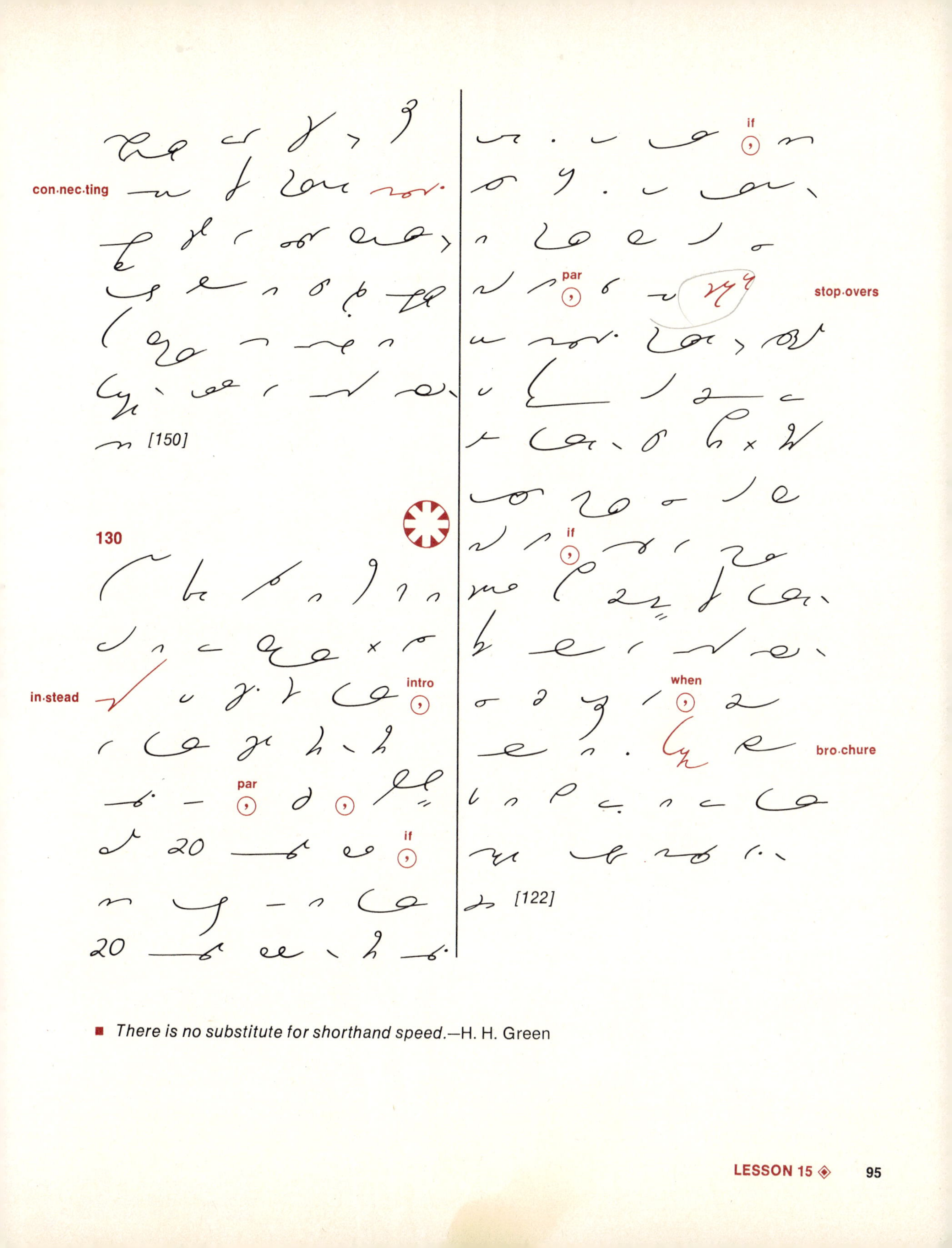

con·nec·ting

[150]

130

in·stead

intro

par

if

if

par

stop·overs

if

when

bro·chure

[122]

■ *There is no substitute for shorthand speed.*—H. H. Green

Banking

Developing Word-Building Power

131 BRIEF FORMS AND DERIVATIVES

Can you read these brief forms and derivatives in 40 seconds or less?

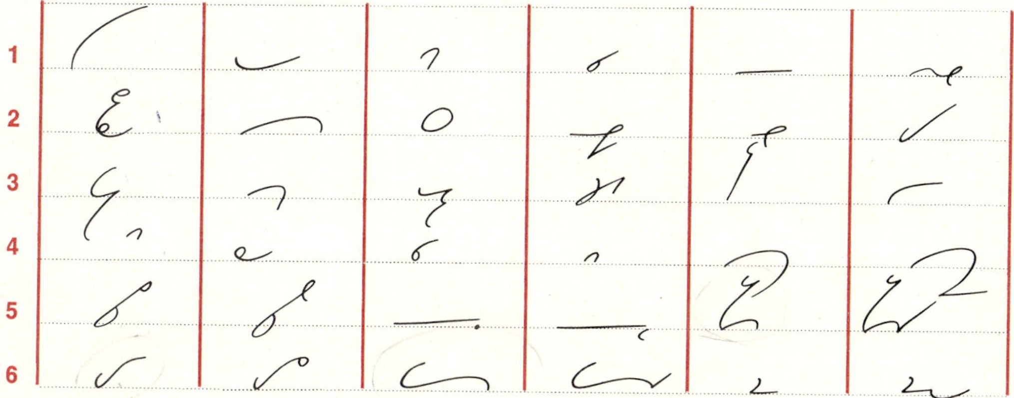

1 Time, will-well, wish, yet, am, correspond-correspondence.
2 Experience, good, I, merchant, next, order.
3 Probable, question, responsible, situation, subject, them.
4 Under, were-year, with, you-your, govern, government.
5 Idea, ideas; morning, mornings; object, objected.
6 Ordinary, ordinarily; progress, progressed; soon, sooner.

Building Transcription Skills

132 PUNCTUATION PRACTICE ■ . courteous request

Very often one businessman may wish to persuade another to take some definite action. He could make his request for action with a direct statement such as:

I want you to come to my office.

A direct statement of this type, however, might antagonize the reader. Many businessmen, therefore, prefer to make such a request in the form of a question.

May I ask that you come to my office.

This is how you can decide whether to use a question mark or a period:

1 When a question calls for definite action, a period is used at the end of the sentence.

2 When a question calls for a yes-or-no response, a question mark is used at the end of the sentence.

When a period is used in this situation in the Reading and Writing Practice, it will be indicated thus in the shorthand: cr

133 Business Vocabulary Builder

investment portfolio One's investment program.

securities Stocks and bonds.

hedge To protect oneself from losing.

semiannually Twice a year.

Reading and Writing Practice

134 Brief-Form Letter

busy

par

intro

fee

ser

su·per·vise

par

ac·cu·rate

sug·gest

par

cr

man·ag·er

ap

[174]

135

Wheth·er

intro

ser

hedge

cr

[102]

136

as

intro

shop·ping

intro

Transcribe:
1115
be·gin·ning

1115 15

intro

fa·cil·i·ties

build·ing

conj

won't

intro

[147]

137

don't

when

more·over

intro

nonr

intro

nonr

semi·an·nu·al·ly

[134]

138

conj

par

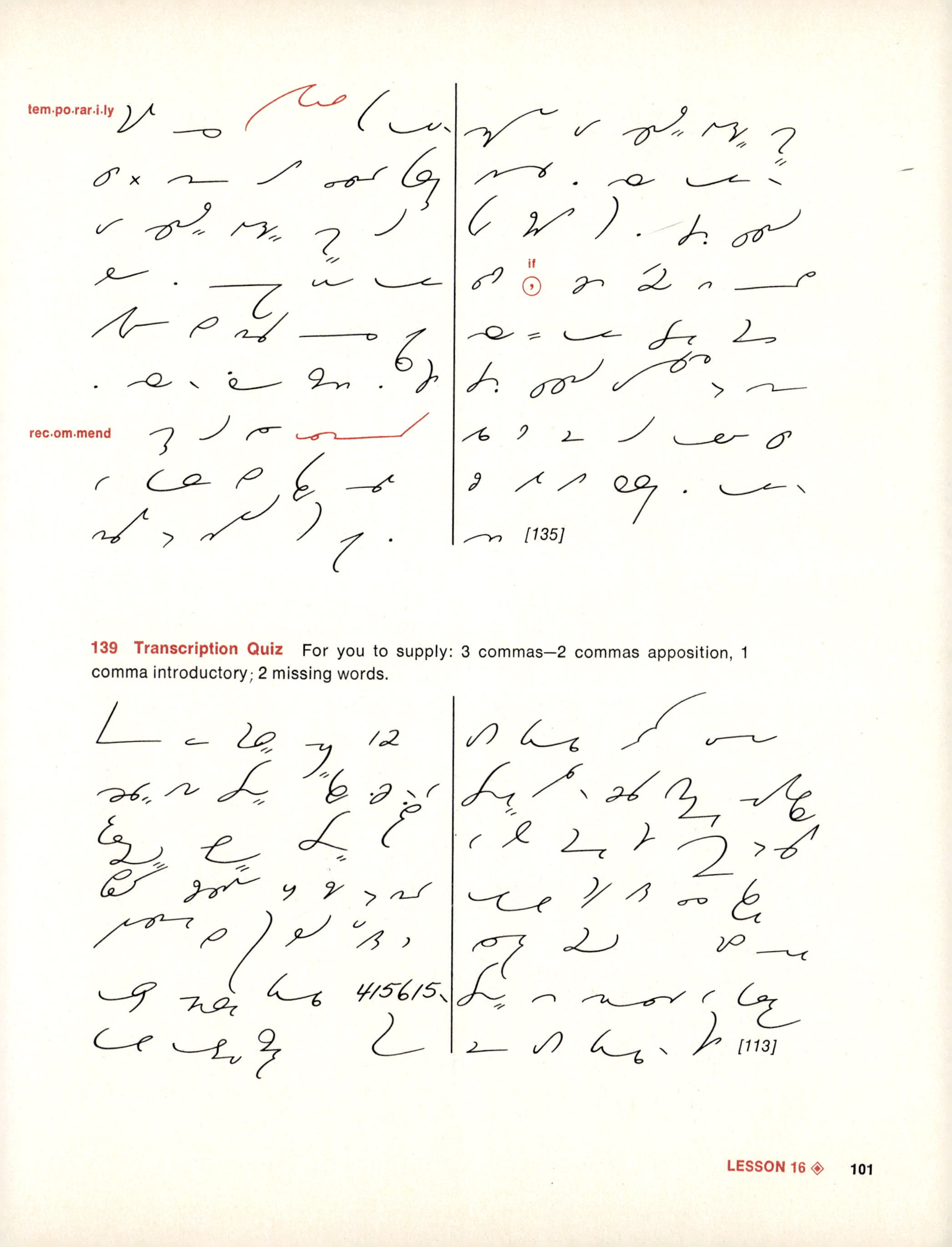

tem·po·rar·i·ly

rec·om·mend

if

[135]

139 Transcription Quiz For you to supply: 3 commas—2 commas apposition, 1 comma introductory; 2 missing words.

12

415615.

[113]

LESSON 

Building Phrasing Skill

140 USEFUL BUSINESS-LETTER PHRASES

The following groups contain a number of phrases. Can you read the entire list in 45 seconds?

I

1

Some

2

Hope

3

Omission of A

4

If

5

1 I am, I can, I cannot, I will, I will not, I will have, I will not have.

2 Some of the, some of them, some of that, some of our, some of these, some of those.

3 I hope, I hope you are, I hope you will, I hope that, we hope, we hope that, we hope you are, we hope you will be.

4 As a result, at a loss, for a few days, for a few minutes, in such a way, in a few months.

5 If you are, if so, if you want, if you need, if it is, if these, if the, if we can, if you have not.

141 GEOGRAPHICAL EXPRESSIONS

1 Charleston, Wilmington, Baltimore, Richmond, Columbus.

2 Delaware, North Carolina, South Carolina, Virginia, West Virginia, Georgia, Florida.

Building Transcription Skills

142 PUNCTUATION PRACTICE ■ hyphens

Hyphenated before noun

No noun, no hyphen

No hyphen after ly

You can decide whether to use a hyphen in compound expressions like *past due* or *well trained* by observing these rules:

1 If a noun follows the expression, use a hyphen.

We are concerned about your past-due *account* (noun).

Our well-trained *salesman* (noun) *will call you.*

When a hyphenated expression occurs in the Reading and Writing Practice, it will be called to your attention in the margin thus: well-trained
hyphenated
before noun

2 If no noun follows the compound expression, do not use a hyphen.

Your account is past due.

Our salesman is well trained.

Occasionally, these expressions in which a hyphen is not used will be called to your attention in the Reading and Writing Practice thus: well trained
no noun,
no hyphen

3 No hyphen is used in a compound modifier where the first part of the expression is an adverb ending in *ly*.

He made a carefully planned speech.

To be sure that you are not tempted to put a hyphen in expressions of this type, your attention will occasionally be called to them in the Reading and Writing Practice thus: care·ful·ly planned
no hyphen
after ly

143 Business Vocabulary Builder

inflation Reduction in buying power because of increased prices.

estate All property left by a person at his death.

shrink Become smaller.

Reading and Writing Practice

144 Phrase Letter

high·ly qual·i·fied *no hyphen after ly*

intro

and o

full-time *hyphenated before noun*

past

if

cr

[108]

up to date *no noun, no hyphen*

145

nc

ap·pre·ci·ate

par

four-page *hyphenated before noun*

well-sat·is·fied
hyphenated before noun

too

conj

pleas·ant

and o

[157]

146

as

pur·chas·ing

in·fla·tion

nonr

hard-pressed
hyphenated before noun

ser

well-trained
hyphenated before noun

ar·range·ments

intro

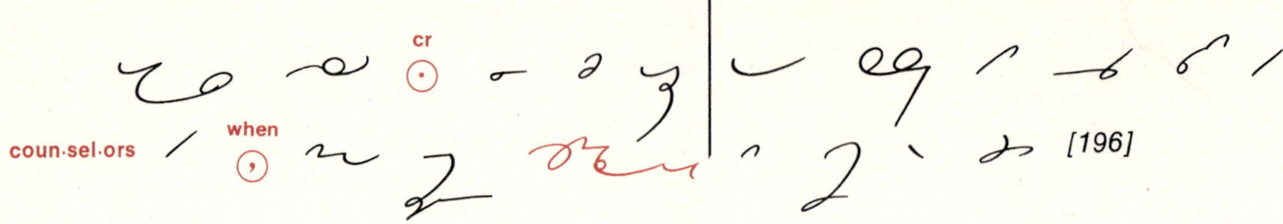

147 Transcription Quiz For you to supply: 5 commas—1 comma *if* clause, 2 commas introductory, 2 commas series.

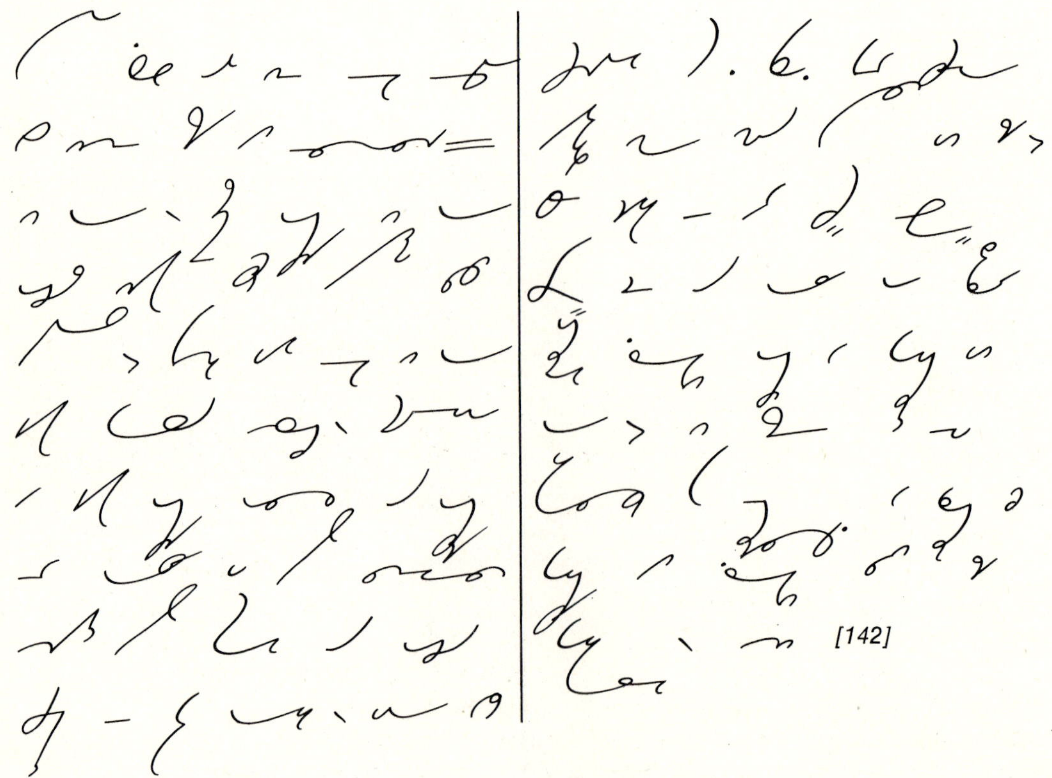

■ *The person who reads a good newspaper every day and who keeps up on what is going on in the world (and in town, too) can't help but be a more valuable employee as well as a more interesting person.*

LESSON 18

Developing Word-Building Power

148 WORD FAMILIES

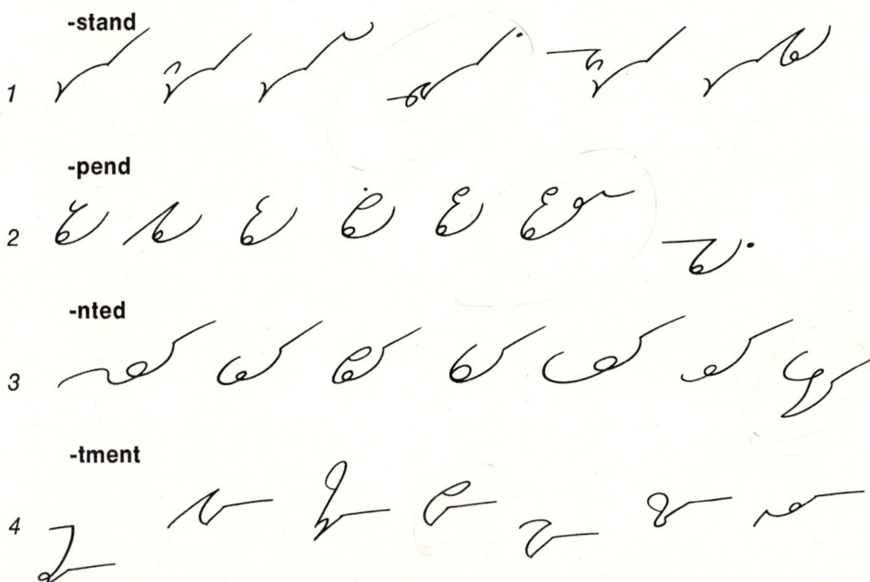

-stand

-pend

-nted

-tment

1 Stand, understand, standard, notwithstanding, misunderstand, standpoint.
2 Opened, depend, spend, happened, expend, expenditure, impending.
3 Granted, printed, appointed, painted, planted, rented, prevented.
4 Investment, department, adjustment, apartment, compartment, assortment, treatment.

Building Transcription Skills

149 PUNCTUATION PRACTICE ■ the apostrophe

1 A noun ending in an *s* sound and followed by another noun is usually a possessive, calling for an apostrophe *before* the *s* when the word is singular.

The salesman's *work was completed.*

Mr. Brown's *work will be finished in July.*

2 A plural noun ending in *s* calls for an apostrophe *after* the *s* to form the possessive.

Several employees' *records were lost.*

All students' *grades were good.*

3 An irregular plural calls for an apostrophe *before* the *s* to form the possessive.

We sell children's *clothing.*

He will open a men's *clothing store next month.*

4 The possessive forms of pronouns do not require an apostrophe.

You will be wasting your time as well as ours.

These books are theirs, *not* ours.

The company decided to update its *files.*

150 Business Vocabulary Builder

magnetic ink Ink which can be "read" by an optical scanner.

distributors Retail outlets for manufactured goods.

specialists Experts.

Reading and Writing Practice

151

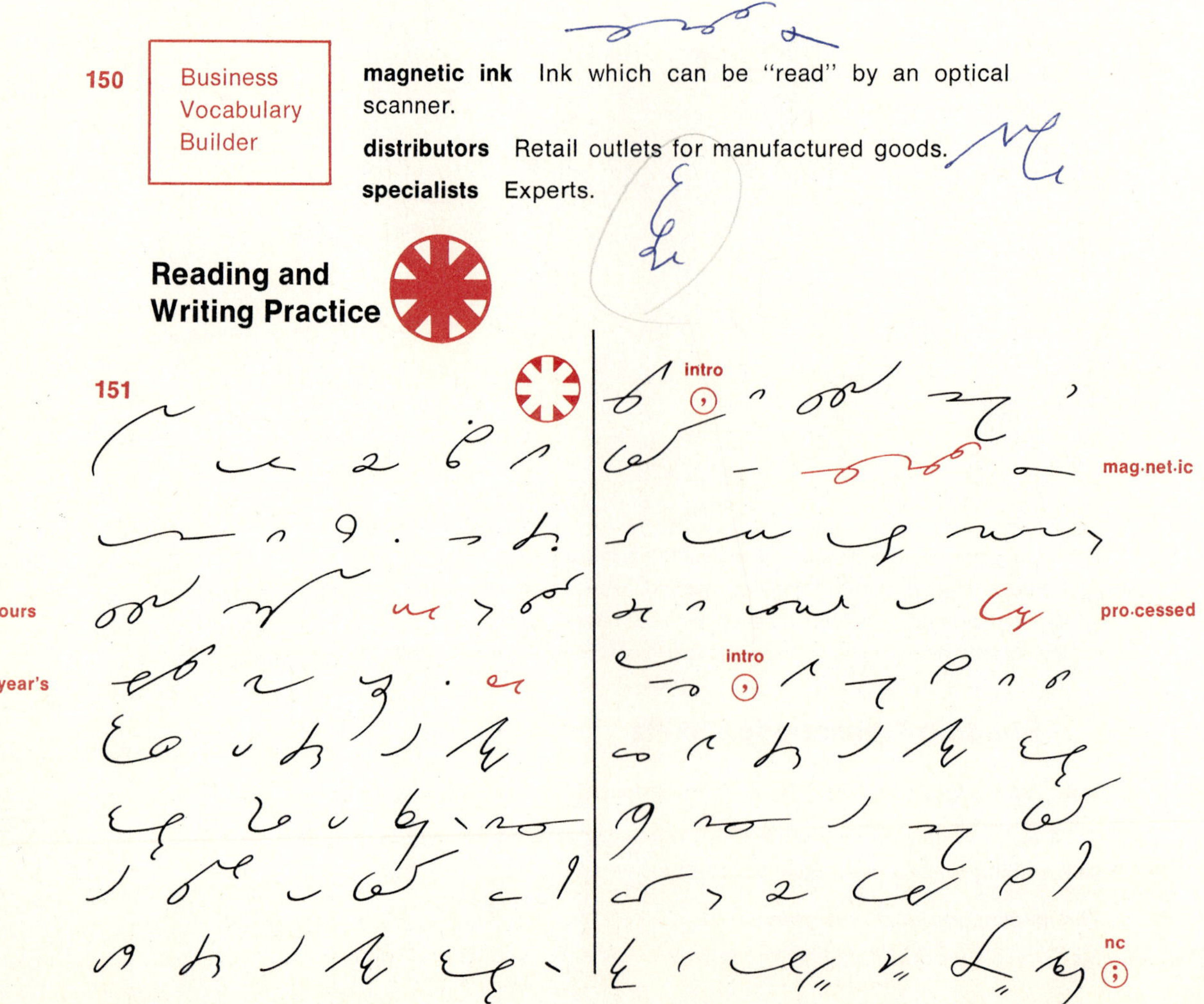

for·ward

[117]

fi·nan·cial

ser

when

[124]

152

ser

equip·ment

fleets

intro

dis·trib·u·tors

as

in·ven·to·ries

tai·lor-made *hyphenated before noun*

peo·ple's

153

con·fi·den·tial

Brown's

1968

bal·ances

1969

conj

Transcribe: **$1,000**

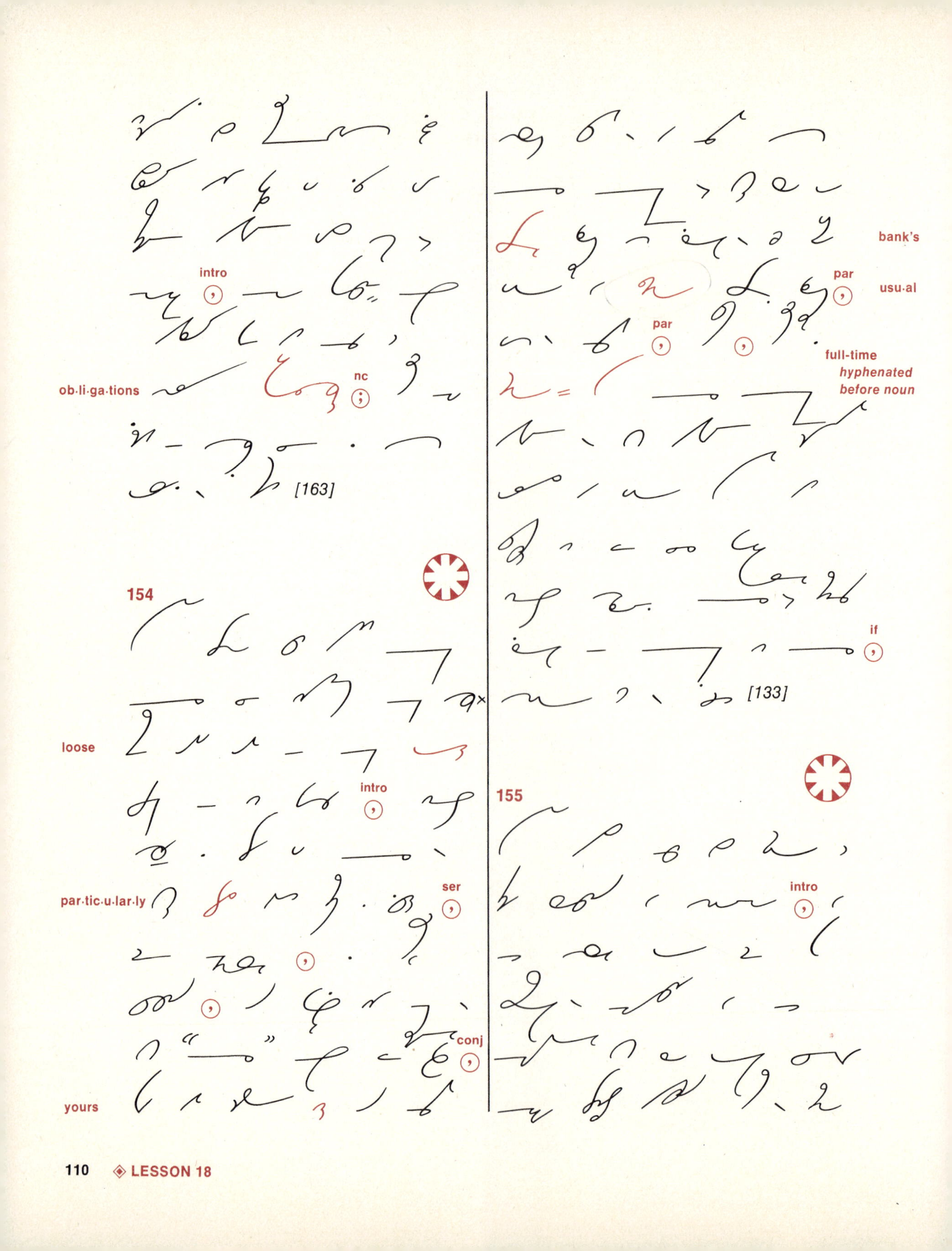

intro

ob·li·ga·tions

nc

[163]

154

loose

intro

par·tic·u·lar·ly

ser

conj

yours

bank's

par

usu·al

par

full-time

hyphenated before noun

if

[133]

155

intro

buy·ing

if

cr

low-cost
hyphenated before noun

intro

choose

[114]

156 Transcription Quiz For you to supply: 5 commas—1 comma introductory, 2 commas *if* clause, 2 commas series; 1 missing word.

[117]

Developing Word-Building Power

157 WORD ENDINGS

-tial

-lity

-ical

-ington

1 Initial, confidential, special, essential, residential, partial, official, social.
2 Facility, responsibility, ability, quality, personality, locality.
3 Practical, logical, chemical, medical, physical, musical.
4 Wilmington, Burlington, Harrington, Tarkington, Washington, Lexington.

Building Transcription Skills

158 SIMILAR-WORDS DRILL ■ some, sum

some A portion.

Some of the work is not finished.

sum Total; amount.

A check for this *sum* is enclosed.

159 Business Vocabulary Builder

discrepancy Disagreement in figures or terms.

withdrawals Amounts taken by check from a bank.

formerly Before; in the past.

Reading and Writing Practice

160

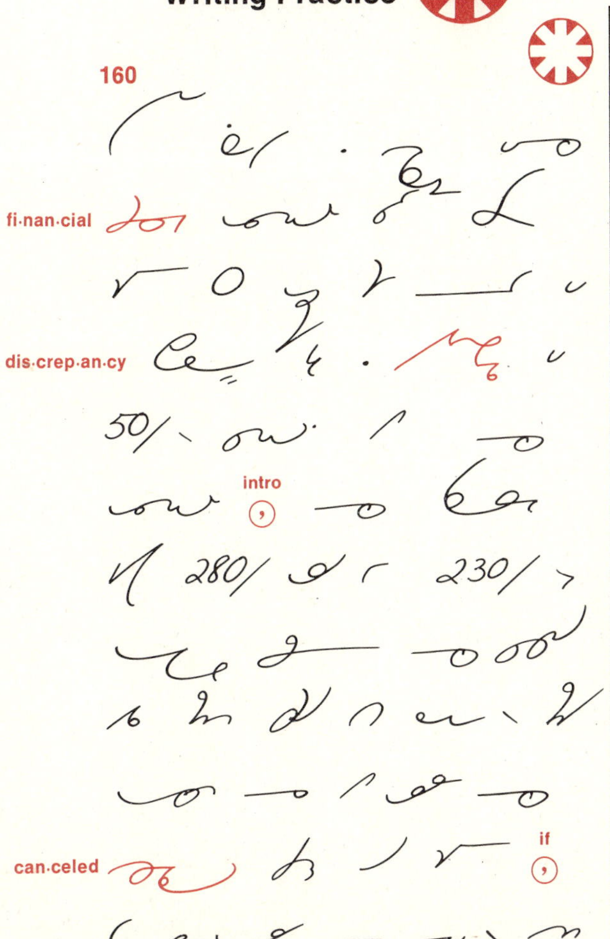

fi·nan·cial

dis·crep·an·cy

intro

can·celed

if

[81]

161

ours

conj

if

er·ror

nc

[72]

162

as

Transcribe: No. 11561

11561

intro

Transcribe: $1,115

1,115

sum

par

re·open

intro

[89]

163

un·for·tu·nate·ly

intro

conj

and o

pain·less

au·to·mat·ic·al·ly

cr

prac·ti·cal

and o

to·day's

ser

ini·tial

[143]

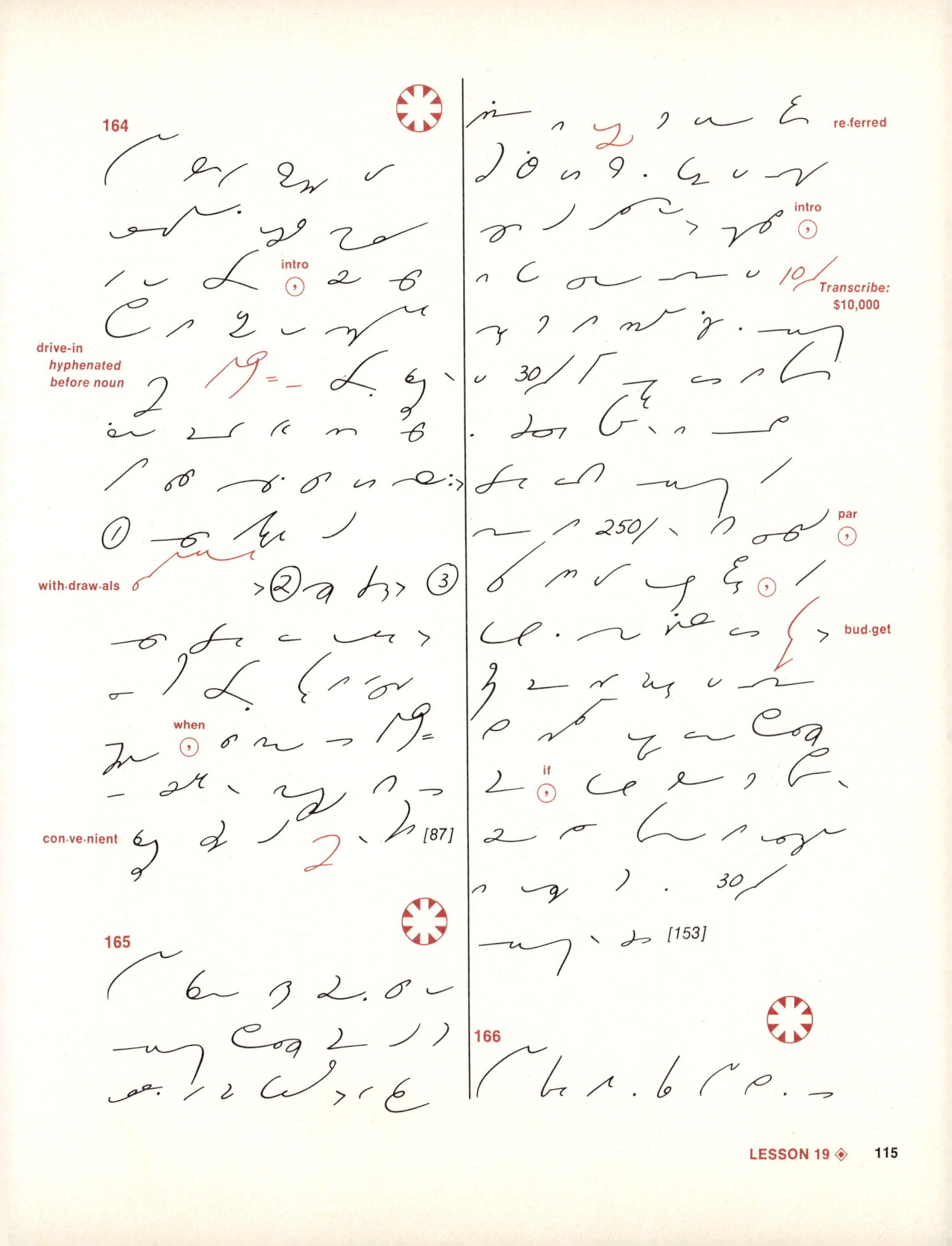

164

intro

drive-in *hyphenated before noun*

with·draw·als

when

con·ve·nient

[87]

re·ferred

intro

Transcribe: $10,000

par

bud·get

if

[153]

165

166

conj

intro

too

if

ser

home-im·prove·ment *hyphenated before noun*

pa·tio

intro

par

[124]

167 Transcription Quiz For you to supply: 6 commas—2 commas apposition, 4 commas parenthetical; 1 missing word.

[134]

Developing Word-Building Power

168 SHORTHAND VOCABULARY BUILDER

Tem, Dem

W

W Dash

Amounts

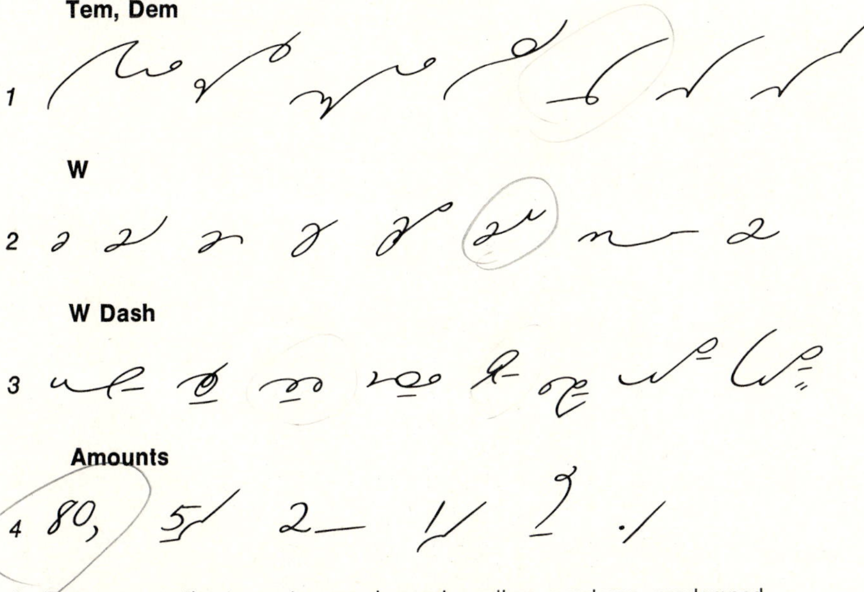

1 Temporary, estimate, customary, demand, medium, condemn, condemned.
2 We, went, week, wait, widely, window, woolen, wear.
3 Always, quiet, quickly, squarely, twice, equipped, roadway, Broadway.
4 80 percent; $500,000; 2,000,000; $1,000; several hundred, a dollar.

Building Transcription Skills

169 Business Vocabulary Builder

excavation Digging.
cascading Tumbling; falling.
currency Money.

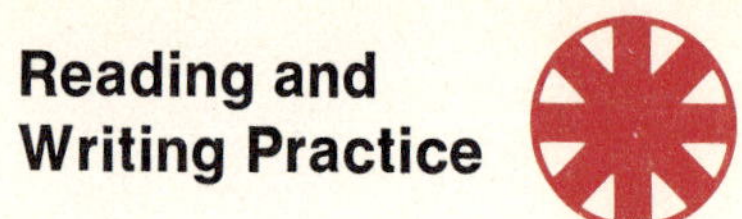

Reading and Writing Practice

170 Money

con·demned

their

intro

The "it"

fas·ci·nat·ing

intro

ac·cept·ed

sig·nif·i·cant

Demand Deposits.

nc

al·ways

intro

than

intro

coun·try's

read·i·ly

intro

rise

intro

plen·ti·ful

conj

re·verse

par

[274]

—Adapted from "Money . . . Its Care and Nourishment," *Senior Scholastic*, (April 21, 1967).

171 Where Does All the Money Go?

intro

bur·ied

Such secret

caches

dis·ap·pear·ing

1935

conj

prob·a·bly

1919

par

mint·ed

1946

1951 intro ,

Transcribe: 2,000,000

From ancient

Some coin

when ,

par ,

par·a·lyzed

nc ;

per·ma·nent·ly

nc ;

hoards

par·ents'

intro ,

dis·lodged

auc·tion

when ,

moth·er's

large-sized *hyphenated before noun*

par ,

23

sums

la·dy's

ser

intro

nev·er·the·less

[402]

intro

ar·ea

up to date
no noun, no hyphen

[112]

LETTERS

172

con·ver·sion

up-to-the-min·ute
hyphenated before noun

173

of·fi·cer's

if

118-6656

yours

[92]

DICTATION SUGGESTIONS

By this time you have no doubt been taking dictation on unfamiliar material, that is, material that you have not previously practiced. As you have probably discovered by this time, developing skill in the writing of unfamiliar material presents some problems, problems that every shorthand writer encounters at one time or another. Here are some suggestions that will help you meet those problems.

Poor Outlines Every shorthand writer, no matter how skillful he may be, will occasionally write a poor outline during dictation. When this happens to you, don't make the mistake of scratching out that outline and writing a better one. The dictator will not stop while you are patching up your notes, and you may find yourself hopelessly behind as a result. Once you have written an outline, leave it. Even though you may have written it poorly, the chances are that, with the help of context, you will be able to read it.

Unfamiliar Words No matter how experienced a stenographer or secretary may be, no matter how long she has been writing shorthand, she will often have to write an unfamiliar word. In your practice work and in your dictation on the job, hardly a day will pass that you will not encounter a new word. When this happens, try to write it in full; write all the sounds that you hear. If this is not possible, try to write at least the beginning of the word. Often this beginning, with the help of context, will help you find the word in the dictionary.

If the word completely escapes you, leave a space in your notes—perhaps skip a line—and continue writing. Don't spend so much time trying to construct an outline that the dictation gets too far ahead of you. You will be surprised, when you transcribe, how frequently you will be able to fill in the word or supply an acceptable substitute.

Hearing There will be times in your dictation that you will not hear—or mishear—a word because the dictator did not enunciate clearly or because some noise interfered with your hearing. If you do not hear a word, leave a space in your notes. When you transcribe, you may be able to determine from the context the meaning of the word you did not hear.

If you *think* you heard a word but know from the context that it could not possibly be the correct one, write the word that you *think* you heard and encircle it. If you are too pressed for time to encircle it, skip a line. Often the outline for the word you *thought* you heard will help you supply the correct one.

Sometimes the word you did not hear—or misheard—will occur to you later during dictation. Do not take the time to insert it in the proper place. Instead, try to hold the word in your mind, and immediately upon the completion of the dictation, fill it in.

Phrasing Well-learned phrases are a great help to the writer in his efforts to develop shorthand speed. Remember, however, that the dictator may not always say a phrase as one piece. He may say one word in a phrase and then pause before he says the remaining words. When that occurs, you will probably have the first word written before you hear the rest of the phrase. Do not stop to scratch out the word you have written and substitute the phrase. This takes time, and time is precious in speed development. Rather, write the remaining words of the phrase as though no phrase were involved.

These suggestions, of course, apply to your work on speed development. On the job, you would stop the dictator tactfully when one of these situations arises rather than risk the possibility of turning in an inaccurate transcript.

Data Processing

LESSON 21

Developing Word-Building Power

174 BRIEF FORMS AND DERIVATIVES

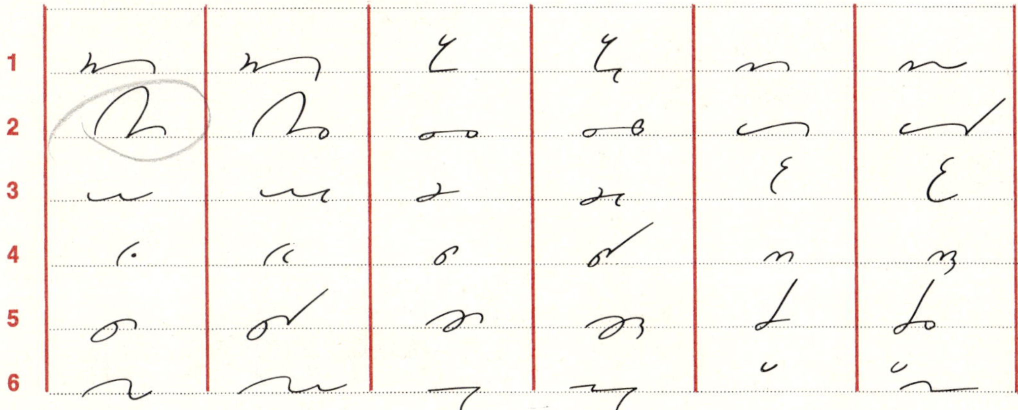

1 Suggest, suggestion; opinion, opinions; work, worker.

2 Difficult, difficulty; immediate, immediately; organize, organized.

3 Railroad, railroads; send, sends; speak, speaker.

4 Thing-think, things-thinks; use, used; world, worlds.

5 Acknowledge, acknowledged; character, characters; general, generally.

6 Great, greater; important-importance, unimportant; over, overcome.

Building Transcription Skills

175 TYPING STYLE STUDY ■ dates

1 If the name of the month precedes the day, do not use *th, st,* or *d* after the number.

On June 13, 1972, *he was transferred to Chicago.*

When a date is expressed in this way, there is a comma both *before* and *after* the year.

2 If the day precedes the month, *th, st,* or *d* should be included.

On the 25th *of July he will visit the factory.*

When dates appear in the Reading and Writing Practice, they will be called to your attention in the margin thus: *Transcribe:* February 25 *Transcribe:* 25th

176 Business Vocabulary Builder

seminar Conference; meeting.

simulation Activity similar to another.

real-time Time actually used by a computer in solving a problem.

Reading and Writing Practice

177 Brief-Form Letter

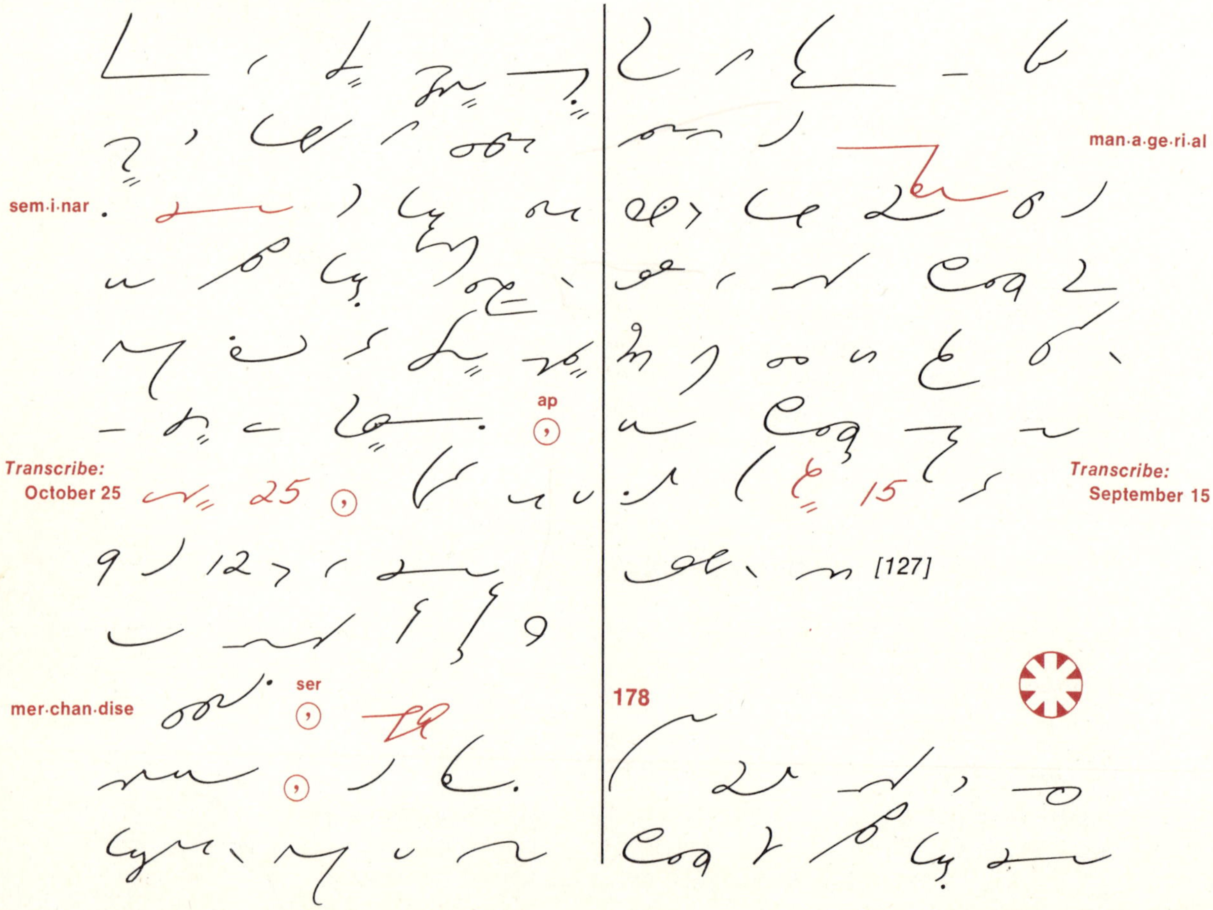

sem·i·nar

ap

Transcribe: October 25

mer·chan·dise

ser

man·a·ge·ri·al

Transcribe: September 15

[127]

178

Transcribe: 25th

25

as

re·ceiv·ing

5

[90]

179

low-cost *hyphenated before noun*

15

nonr

in·stalled

4601

mod·el

real-time on-line *hyphenated before noun*

and o

fur·ther

if

[148]

180

if

hard·ware

and o

Transcribe:
January 20

20

[137]

181

15

Transcribe:
June 15, 1973,

1973

nc

30

conj

busi·nesses

ser

intro

un·for·tu·nate·ly

off-cam·pus
hyphenated before noun

par

if

[140]

182

re·ferred

[76]

183 Transcription Quiz Beginning with this lesson the transcription quizzes will be a greater challenge to you. Thus far you have had to supply only commas and missing words; hereafter, you will also have to supply semicolons.

For you to supply: 4 commas—1 comma apposition, 1 comma introductory, 2 commas *if* clause; 1 semicolon no conjunction; 1 missing word.

1515

18

[114]

■ *In meeting the public, your best approach is a polite, interested manner, and your best technique is to smile. A smile has an amazing effect, even over the phone.*

Fairplay Industries

9962 NORTH STATE STREET CHICAGO, ILLINOIS 60604

April 1, 197-

Mr. Robert D. Grace
680 Fifth Avenue
Los Angeles, California 90015

Dear Mr. Grace:

While I was attending the meeting of computer manufacturers in Boston last week, I had lunch with a mutual friend of ours, Harry C. Barnes. Mr. Barnes told me you had recently resigned your position with the Eastern Business Machines Company and that you are looking for a new connection. He said it would be all right for me to mention that I am getting in touch with you at his suggestion.

We are now working on plans to organize a West Coast sales office to promote our electronic equipment in the western area, where we have never had representation before. We feel that the West Coast has great potential for our products, and it offers a wonderful opportunity for a man like yourself who has had experience in electronic data processing.

Would you consider representing us in the states of California and Washington on a salary and commission basis? If you have not yet made a new connection and this offer appeals to you, please call me so that I can arrange an interview for you with the officers of the company.

As we are anxious to begin our sales efforts on the West Coast as soon as possible, I hope you will let me know of your interest, or lack of it, within a few days.

Very truly yours,

Arthur D. Johnson

Arthur D. Johnson
Sales Manager

ADJ:JG

Long Letter
Indented Style
Standard Punctuation

LESSON 22

Building Phrasing Skill

184 USEFUL BUSINESS-LETTER PHRASES

In

1

Been

2

Which

3

Yet

4

Time

5

1 In the, in that, in this, in these, in them, in those, in which, in our, in time, in the past.

2 Have been, I have been, I have not been, I have not been able, has been, has been able, has not been able, we have been, who have been, you have been able.

3 By which, in which, in which the, to which, to which you are, for which, on which, of which, upon which.

4 As yet, has not yet, have not yet, I have not yet, has not yet been, we are not yet, we have not yet.

5 At this time, any time, next time, since that time, at the time, for some time.

185 GEOGRAPHICAL EXPRESSIONS

1 Phoenix, Madison, Lexington, Philadelphia, Birmingham, Providence.

2 Alabama, Arizona, Wisconsin, Rhode Island, Arkansas, Tennessee, Vermont.

Building Transcription Skills

150 TYPING STYLE STUDY ■ addresses

1 Use figures to designate house numbers.

She works at 300 (*not* three hundred) *Canal Street.*

2 Spell out numbers below 11 in street names.

He works at 250 Fourth *Avenue.*

3 Use figures for street names above ten.

Her new address is 27 West 83 *Street, New York, New York 10037.*

◈ Note 1: Spell out *Street, Avenue, Road,* etc.

◈ Note 2: Omit *th, st,* and *d* from numbered street names. The omission of these endings makes numbered street names easier to read.

When street addresses occur in the Reading and Writing Practice, they will occasionally be called to your attention in the margin of the shorthand thus:

Transcribe:
18 West 61 Street

186 Business Vocabulary Builder

competence Sufficiency; ability.

advent Coming or arrival.

hard copy Printed for reading by the eyes.

Reading and Writing Practice

187 Phrase Letter

stu·dent's

in·struc·tor's

[166]

par

188

plan·ning

odds

par

of·fered

conj

available

when

fur·ther

if

lo·cal

Transcribe:
Fourth Street

nonr

if

[149]

189

ad·vent

intro

and o

in·stan·ta·neous

cus·tom·er's

nonr

via

if

Transcribe:
18 West 61 Street

if

sim·ply

[133]

190

and o

com·put·er-fast
hyphenated before noun

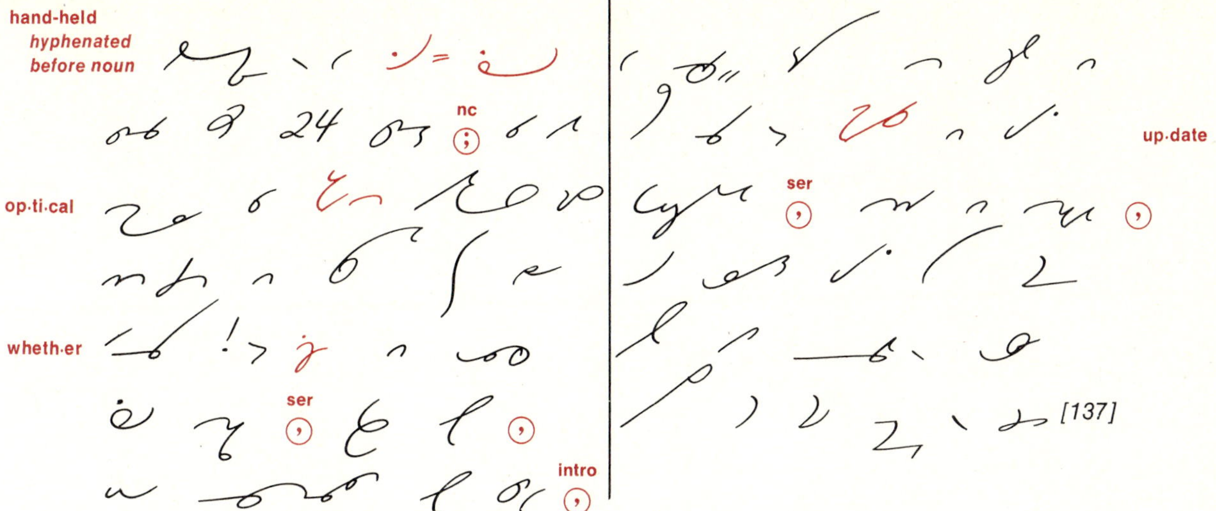

191 Transcription Quiz For you to supply: 4 commas—1 comma introductory, 1 comma apposition, 2 commas *if* clause; 1 missing word.

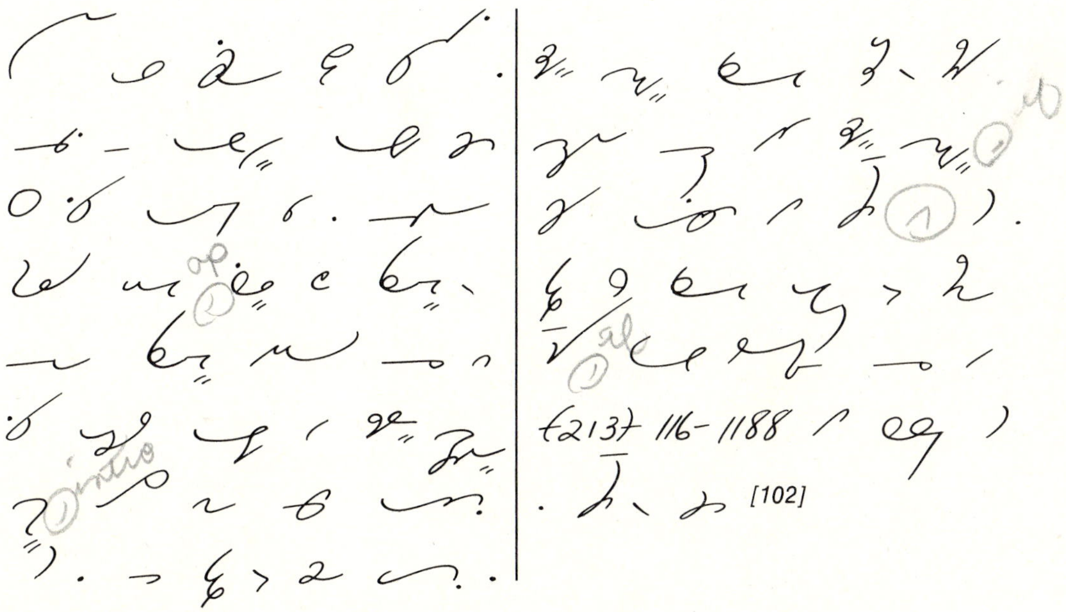

[102]

■ *Get your day off to a good start by wishing everyone a cheery "Good morning."*

LESSON 23

Developing Word-Building Power

192 WORD FAMILIES

-tional

1

-ware

2

-ous

3

-man

4

1 Traditional, additional, educational, exceptional, instructional.
2 Software, hardware, beware, silverware, flatware.
3 Tedious, various, serious, studious, courteous, instantaneous.
4 Businessman, salesman, salesmanship, foreman, workmanship.

Building Transcription Skills

193 TYPING STYLE STUDY ■ amounts of money

1 In business letters transcribe whole dollar amounts without adding a decimal or following zeros.

The check for $152 (*not* $152.00) *was mailed yesterday.*

2 In business letters use the word *cents* in amounts under $1.

The pen costs only 19 cents (*not* $.19).

When amounts such as those above appear in the Reading and Writing Practice, they will occasionally be called to your attention in the margin of the shorthand thus: *Transcribe:* $225

194 Business Vocabulary Builder

traditional Standard.

exceptional Outstanding.

license (*verb*) To grant official permission.

simultaneously At the same time.

Reading and Writing Practice

195

its

ac·com·mo·date

par

cus·tom

when

adapt

par

to·day

[163]

196

intro

Transcribe:
$500
$300

busi·ness·man's

nc

conj

conj

[124]

prompt·ly

197

par

re·cent

qual·i·fi·ca·tions

intro

usu·al

up to date
no noun, no hyphen

here

if

[145]

198

an·swer·ing

ap

nc

raised

cer·ti·fi·ca·tion

rec·og·ni·tion

li·cense

cer·ti·fy·ing

nc

de·grees

[154]

199

as

and o

ac·cu·rate

ser

par

ex·pen·sive

ser

if

[129]

200 Transcription Quiz For you to supply: 8 commas—2 commas introductory, 1 comma *and* omitted, 2 commas series, 2 commas apposition, 1 comma conjunction.

[180]

Developing Word-Building Power

201 WORD BEGINNINGS AND ENDINGS

Inter-, Intro-

-ful

-ble

Tern, Term

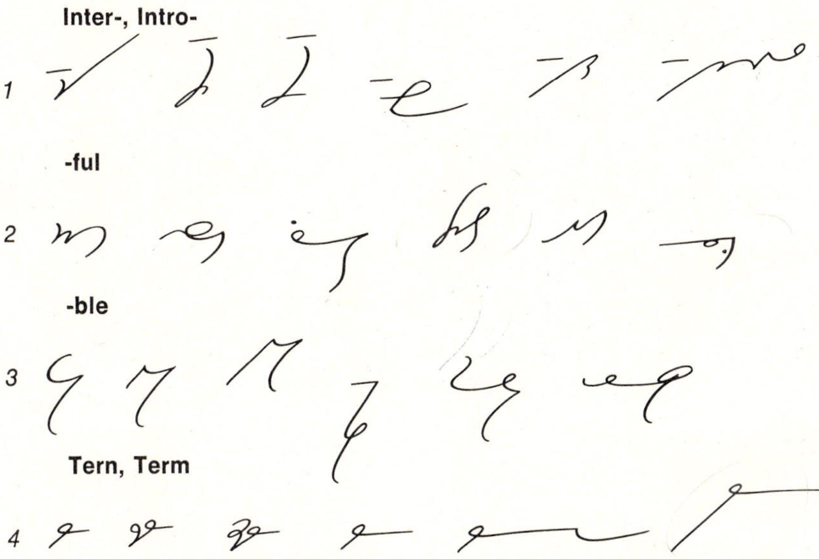

1 Interested, interview, intervene, international, introduce, introductory.
2 Successful, careful, helpful, beautiful, thoughtful, meaningful.
3 Probable, trouble, durable, enjoyable, flexible, reliable.
4 Turn, eastern, western, term, terminal, determine.

Building Transcription Skills

202 TYPING STYLE STUDY ■ time

1 Use figures to express time with the word *o'clock.* (Remember the apostrophe!)

He arrived at 10 o'clock (*not* ten o'clock, *unless formality is required*).

2 Use figures to express time with *a.m.* and *p.m.*

She left at 10:15 *a.m. and returned at* 9:45 *p.m.*

◈ Note: Type *a.m.* and *p.m.* with small letters and no space after the first period.

Occasionally these expressions of time will be called to your attention in the margins of the shorthand in the Reading and Writing Practice thus: *Transcribe:* 9 a.m. *Transcribe:* 2 o'clock

203 Business Vocabulary Builder

defective Out of order; broken.

jeopardy Danger.

Reading and Writing Practice

204

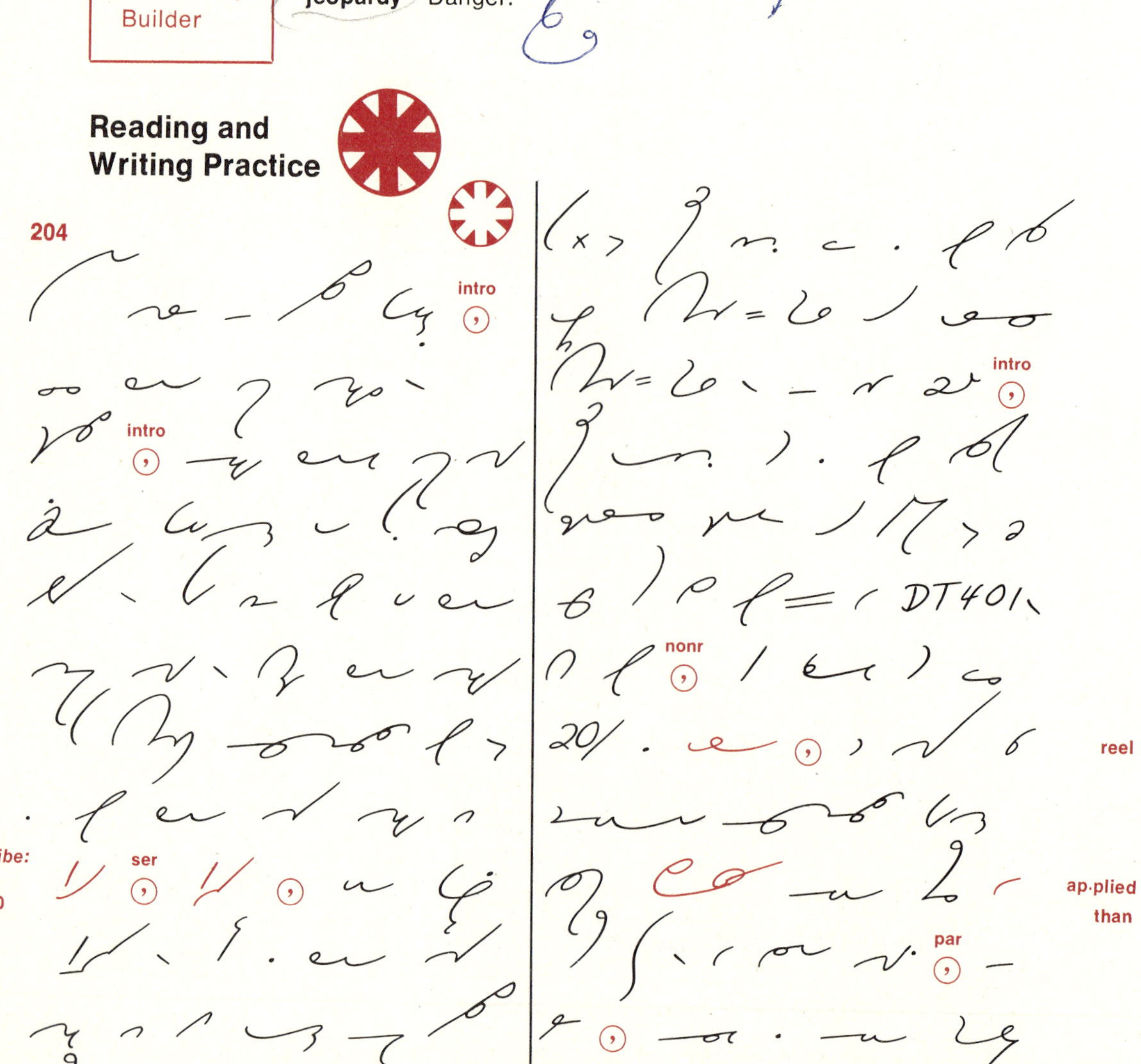

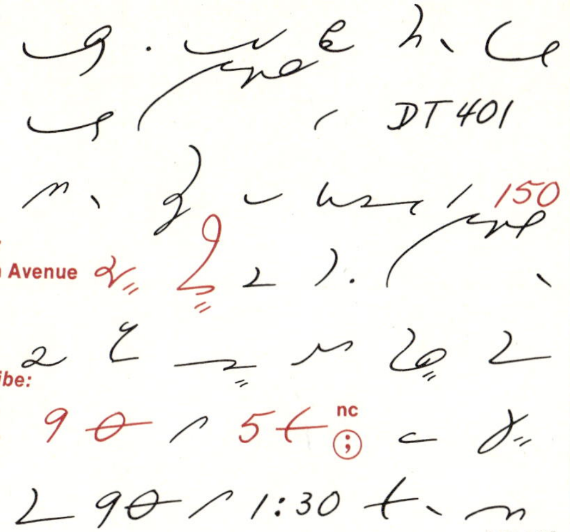

DT 401

150

Transcribe: 150 Sixth Avenue

Transcribe: 9 a.m. 5 p.m.

nc

1:30

[218]

205

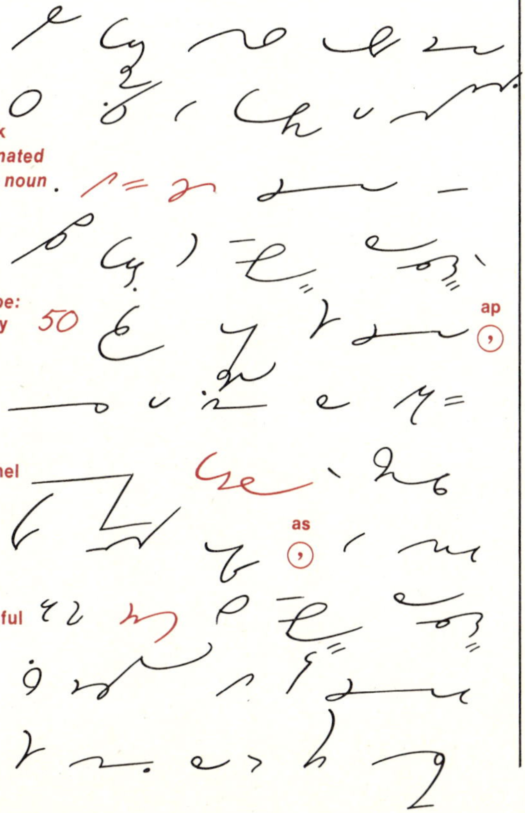

two-week hyphenated before noun

Transcribe: Fifty 50

ap

per·son·nel

as

suc·cess·ful

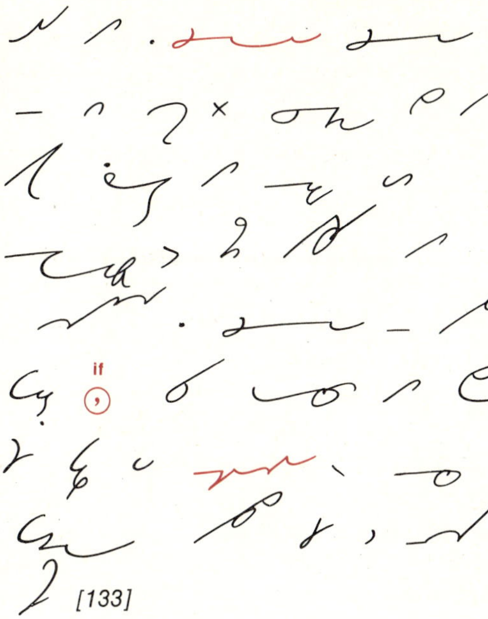

sim·i·lar

if

in·struc·tor

[133]

206

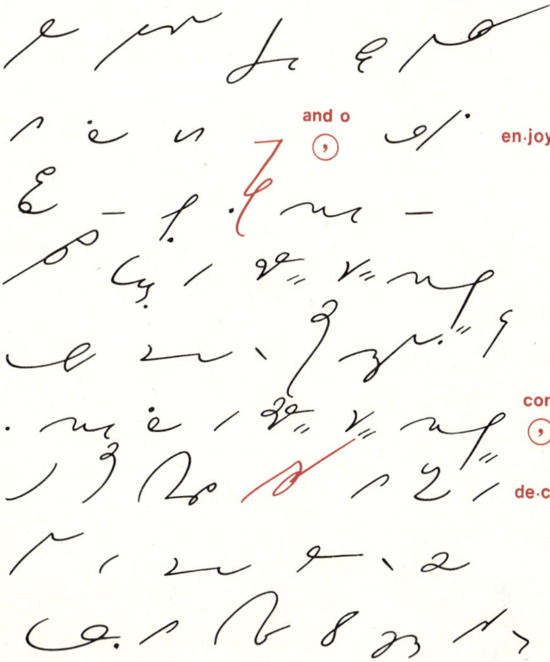

and o

en·joy·able

conj

de·cid·ed

if

ses·sion

Transcribe: 10 o'clock

[129]

to·day's

of·fer·ings

full-time hyphenated before noun

ap

Transcribe: 3 o'clock

intro

[130]

207

ac·cept

judg·ment

intro

208

easy-to-un·der·stand hyphenated before noun

and o

par

ser

aware·ness

fa·mil·iar·ize

intro

intro

[135]

209 Transcription Quiz For you to supply: 5 commas—2 commas conjunction, 1 comma introductory, 2 commas *if* clause; 1 missing word.

10:30

[142]

Developing Word-Building Power

210 SHORTHAND VOCABULARY BUILDER

-ld

1

Tem

2

Nt

3

Nd

4

1 Installed, filled, shareholders, skilled, mailed, called.
2 Customers, automatically, automation, temperature, temper, contemporary.
3 Central, century, account, accounts, invent, inventory.
4 Thousand, trained, handle, find, lined, bindery, kindly.

Building Transcription Skills

211 Business Vocabulary Builder

revolution Sudden change; turn around.
shunted Pushed away.
consultants Persons who give advice.

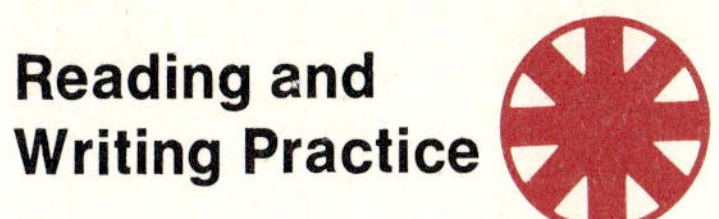

212 Revolution in Office Work

in·stalled

par

All this

ser

er·rors

cler·i·cal

conj

nonr

be·gin·ning

na·tion's

1953

intro

ser

pay·rolls

ser

em·ploy·ees

Today

com·pa·nies

intro

qual·i·fies

whiz·zing

well-trained *hyphenated before noun*

and o

A large

its

safe·ty

ser

growth

when

fill·ing

Chain stores

track

sup·plies

conj

flight

nonr

con·sul·tants

par

intro

[540]

LETTERS

213

ser

soft·ware

intro

Transcribe:
No. 1161

1161

conj

intro

six-page *hyphenated before noun*

[160]

214

fi·nan·cial

ser

intro

suc·cess·ful

conj

[91]

215

ap

book·keep·ing

and o

par

intro

nc

bear

[110]

Education

Developing Word-Building Power

216 BRIEF FORMS AND DERIVATIVES

1 Recognize, recognized; state, states; thank, thanked.
2 Value, values; where, wherever; worth, worthy.
3 Advantage, advantages; enclose, enclosed; gentlemen, gentleman.
4 One (won), ones; part, parts; purpose, purposes.
5 Street, streets; which, whichever; advertise, advertisement.
6 Circular, circulars; envelope, envelopes; glad, gladly.

Building Transcription Skills

217 Business Vocabulary Builder

eliminates Does away with.
leisure Ease; freedom from hurry.
honorarium Money paid to a person in appreciation.

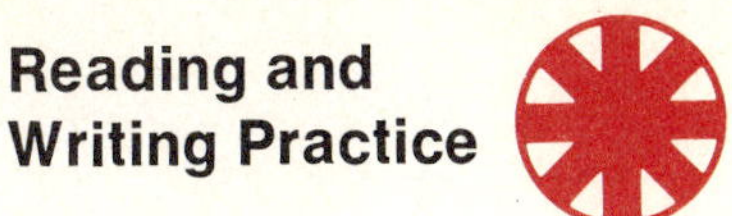

Reading and Writing Practice

218 Brief-Form Letter

re·al·ize

conj

day's

year's

conj

as·sis·tance

ques·tion·naire

and o

re·sponses

when

if

when

par

[158]

219

ad·vance-or·der *hyphenated before noun*

nonr

sched·ule

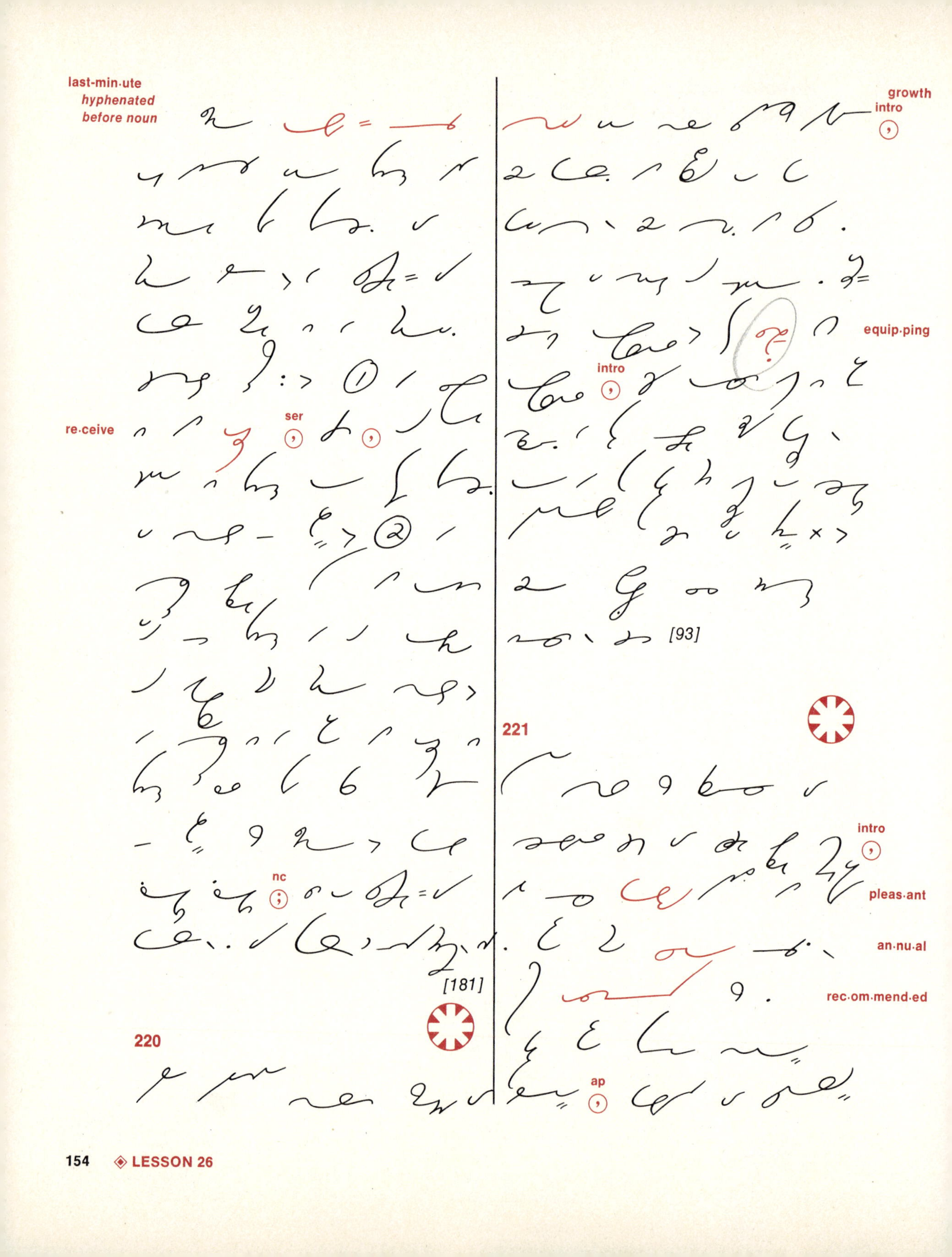

last-min·ute
hyphenated before noun

re·ceive

ser

nc

[181]

220

growth

intro

equip·ping

intro

[93]

221

intro

pleas·ant

an·nu·al

rec·om·mend·ed

ap

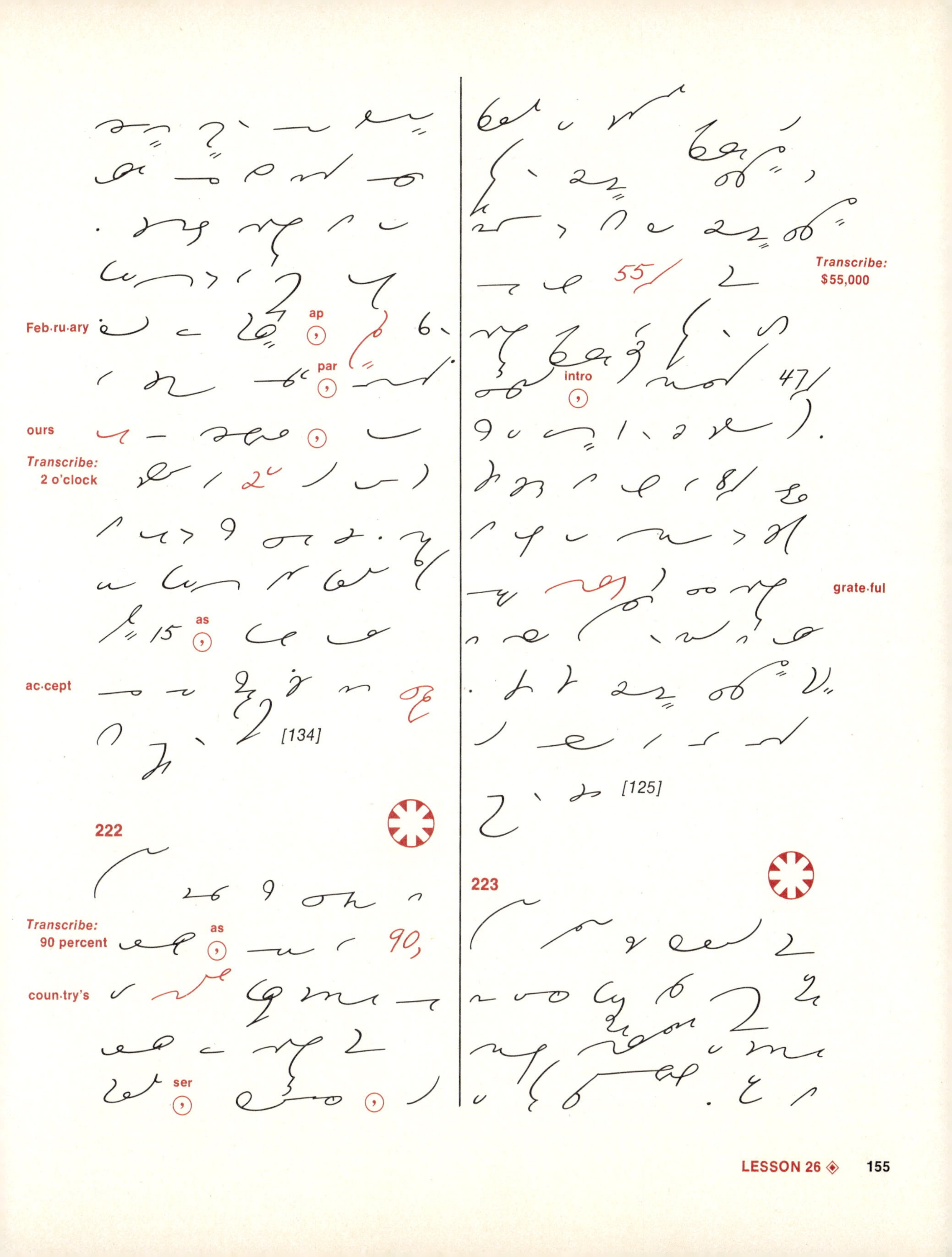

Feb·ru·ary

ap

par

ours

Transcribe:
2 o'clock

as

ac·cept

[134]

222

Transcribe:
90 percent

as

coun·try's

ser

Transcribe:
$55,000

intro

grate·ful

[125]

223

for·eign

224

el·i·gi·ble

nc ; intro , intro ,

[100]

[80]

225 Transcription Quiz For you to supply: 4 commas—1 comma apposition, 1 comma *when* clause, 1 comma introductory, 1 comma *if* clause.

[102]

LESSON 27

Building Phrasing Skill

226 USEFUL BUSINESS-LETTER PHRASES

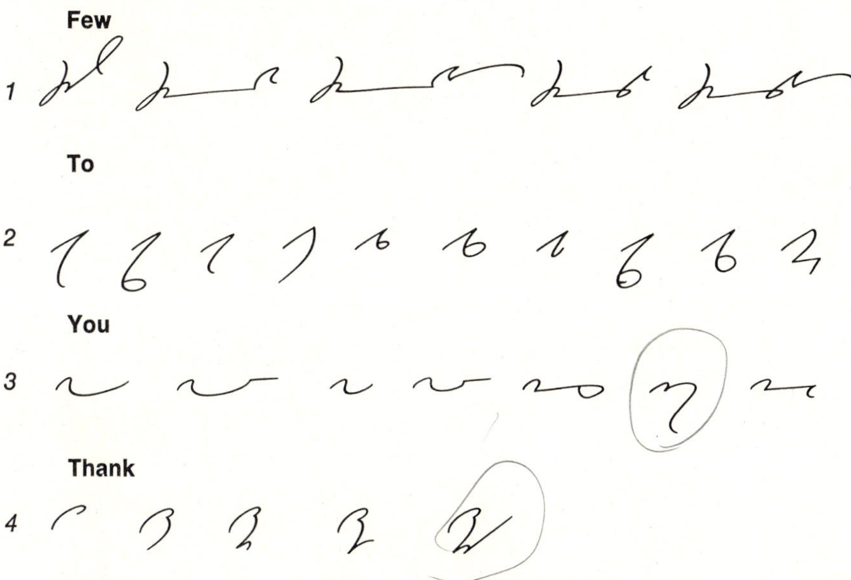

1 Few days, few months, few months ago, few minutes, few minutes ago.
2 To be, to be able, to put, to have, to see, to say, to show, to buy, to pay, to furnish.
3 You will, you will not, you are, you are not, you may, you can be, you must.
4 Thank you, thank you for, thank you for your, thank you for the, thank you for your order.

227 GEOGRAPHICAL EXPRESSIONS

1 Plattsburg, Pittsburgh, Harrisburg, Newburg, Hamburg.
2 America, American, Canada, Canadian, England, English, United States.

Building Transcription Skills

228 SIMILAR-WORDS DRILL ■ choose, chose

choose To select.

You should investigate several colleges before you *choose* one.

chose (past tense of *choose*) Selected.

The students *chose* the quarter system.

229 Business Vocabulary Builder

visiting lecturer Temporary teacher.

counselors Advisors.

liberal arts Subjects of a general nature.

Reading and Writing Practice

230 Phrase Letter

grad·u·at·ing

intro

par

conj

choose

nonr

lib·er·al

as

and o

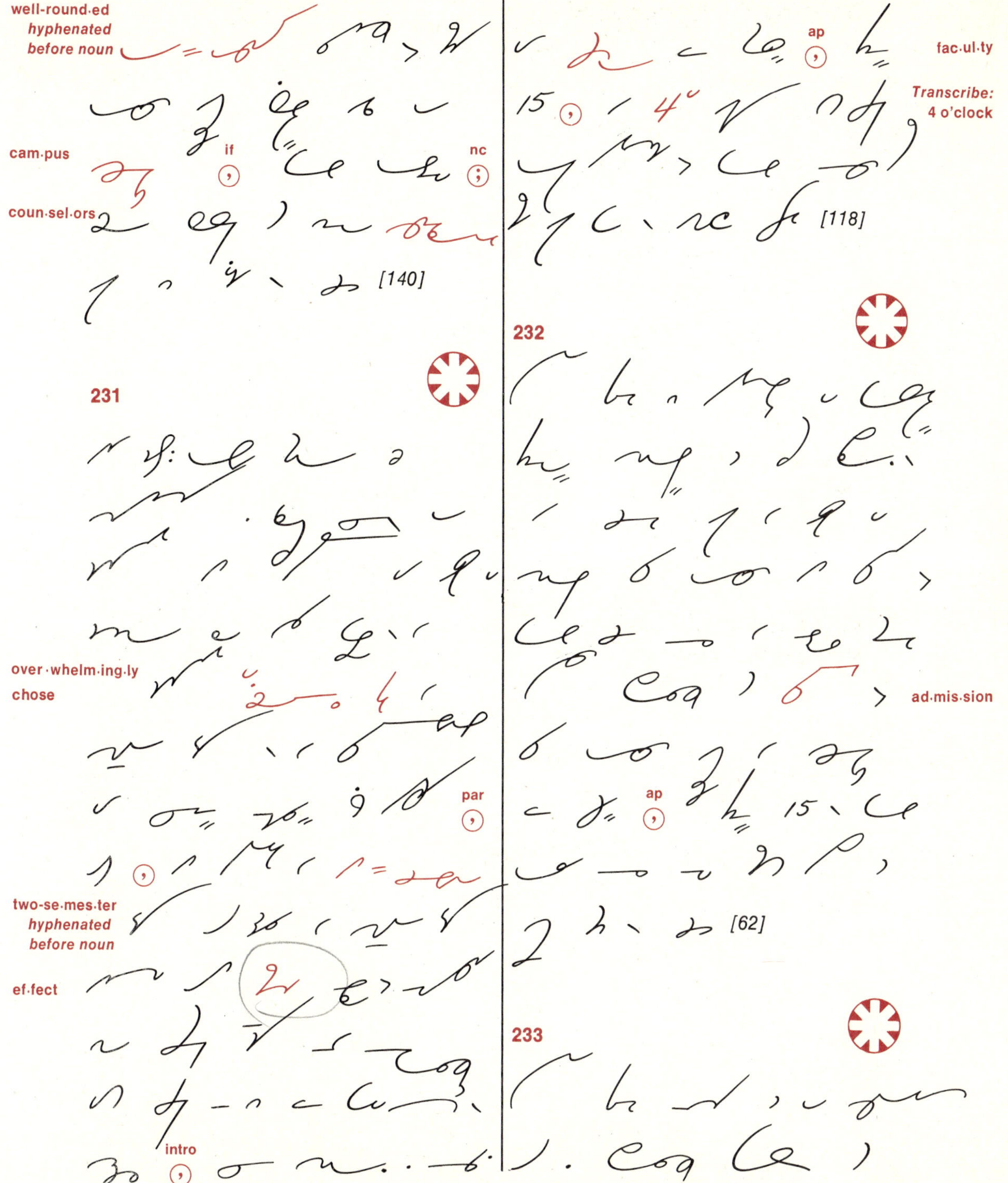
well-round·ed
hyphenated
before noun
cam·pus
if
nc
coun·sel·ors
[140]
231
over·whelm·ing·ly
chose
par
two-se·mes·ter
hyphenated
before noun
ef·fect
intro
ap
fac·ul·ty
15
4
Transcribe:
4 o'clock
[118]
232
ad·mis·sion
ap
15
[62]
233

if

tu·ition

fees

conj

trust·ees

choose

if

ser

chal·leng·ing

[108]

234

well-qual·i·fied
hyphenated before noun

par

ser

eight-week
four-week
two-day
hyphenated before noun

intro

if

agree·ment

par

nc

de·light·ful

[154]

235 Transcription Quiz For you to supply: 3 commas—1 comma *if* clause, 2 commas introductory; 1 semicolon no conjunction; 1 missing word.

[108]

REVIEW TIP

Beginning on page 438 you will find complete lists of the word beginnings and endings, phrases, and brief forms of Gregg Shorthand.

You are already familiar with the words and phrases in those lists, but to be sure that they do not become hazy in your mind, you should review them frequently.

Consequently, plan to set aside a few minutes each day to read from those lists. Time spent on those lists will be time well spent.

After you have read all the lists from left to right, read them again from right to left.

At this stage of your shorthand course, you should be able to read the lists very rapidly.

LESSON 28

Developing Word-Building Power

236 WORD FAMILIES

-come

1 [shorthand outlines]

-us

2 [shorthand outlines]

-side

3 [shorthand outlines]

-ish

4 [shorthand outlines]

1 Welcome, become, come, outcome, income, overcome.
2 Us, just, campus, gracious, discuss, ambitious, precious, spacious.
3 Side, reside, aside, inside, beside, preside, sideline.
4 Spanish, establish, furnish, accomplish, cherish, embellish, finish, varnish.

Building Transcription Skills

237 SPELLING FAMILIES ■ for-, fore-

Be careful when you transcribe a word beginning with the sound of *for.* The beginning of the word will sometimes be spelled *for* and other times *fore.*

Words Beginning with For-

for·ward	**for·bid**	**for·get**
for·mal	**for·gave**	**for·give**

Words Beginning with Fore-

fore·cast	**fore·word**	**fore·tell**
fore·ground	**fore·close**	**fore·sight**

◈ Be sure to spell the number *four* correctly.

four	**four·teen**	**fourth**

but

for·ty

238 Business Vocabulary Builder

graduate level College studies beyond the baccalaureate level.

reside To live.

residence Living quarters.

master's degree College degree granted after graduate study.

Reading and Writing Practice

239

Phoe·nix

intro

grad·u·ate

par

conj

ser

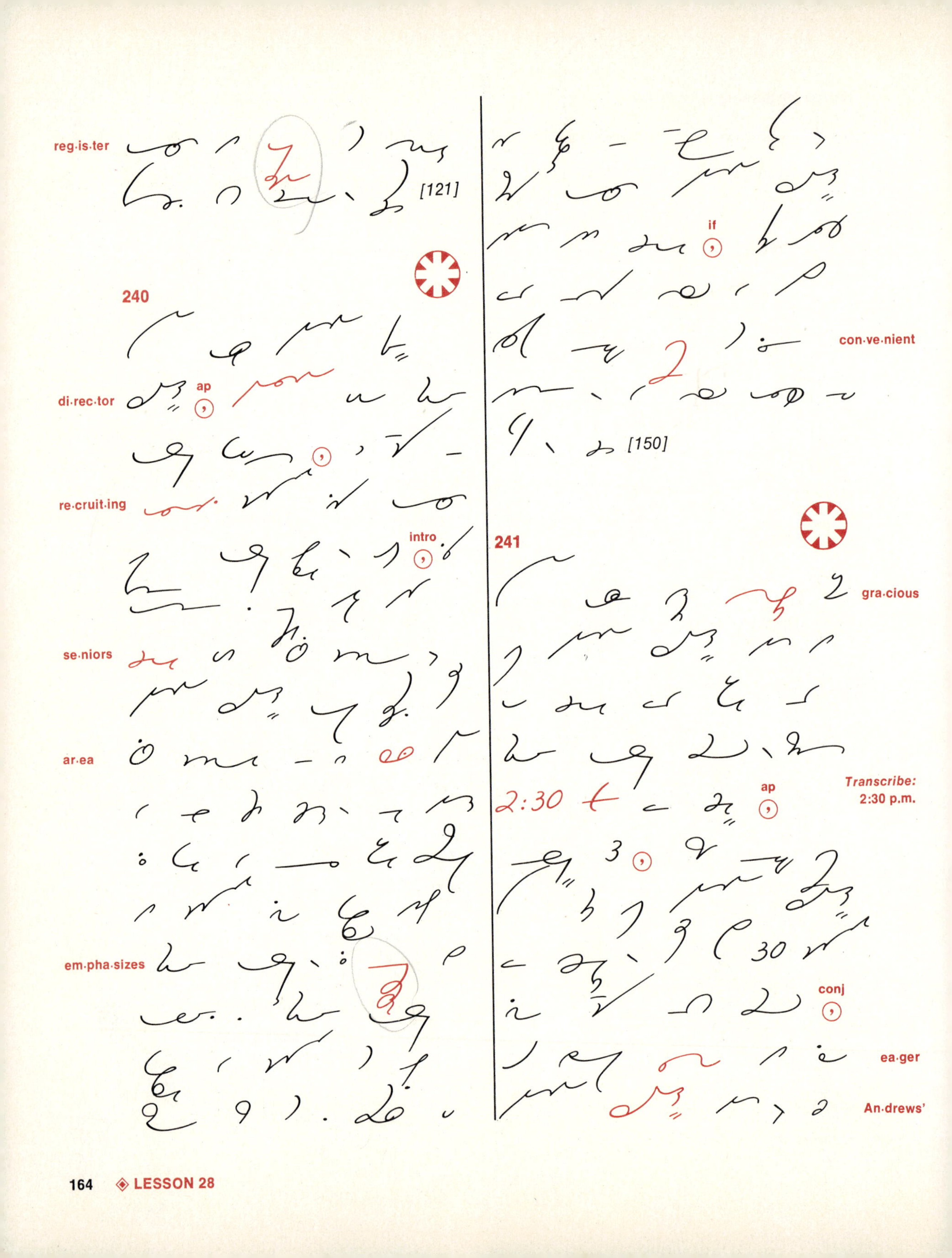

reg·is·ter

[121]

240

di·rec·tor

ap

re·cruit·ing

intro

se·niors

ar·ea

em·pha·sizes

if

con·ve·nient

[150]

241

gra·cious

Transcribe:
2:30 p.m.

2:30

ap

3

30

conj

ea·ger

An·drews'

[80]

242

as

de·scrib·ing

of·fered

ma·jor

ser

1912

conj

intro

pro·gres·sive

and o

ap

if

ques·tions

[135]

243

dor·mi·to·ry

ap

res·i·dence

ap

14

ap

16

ser

tow·els

per·mit·ted

par

when

Transcribe: Fourth

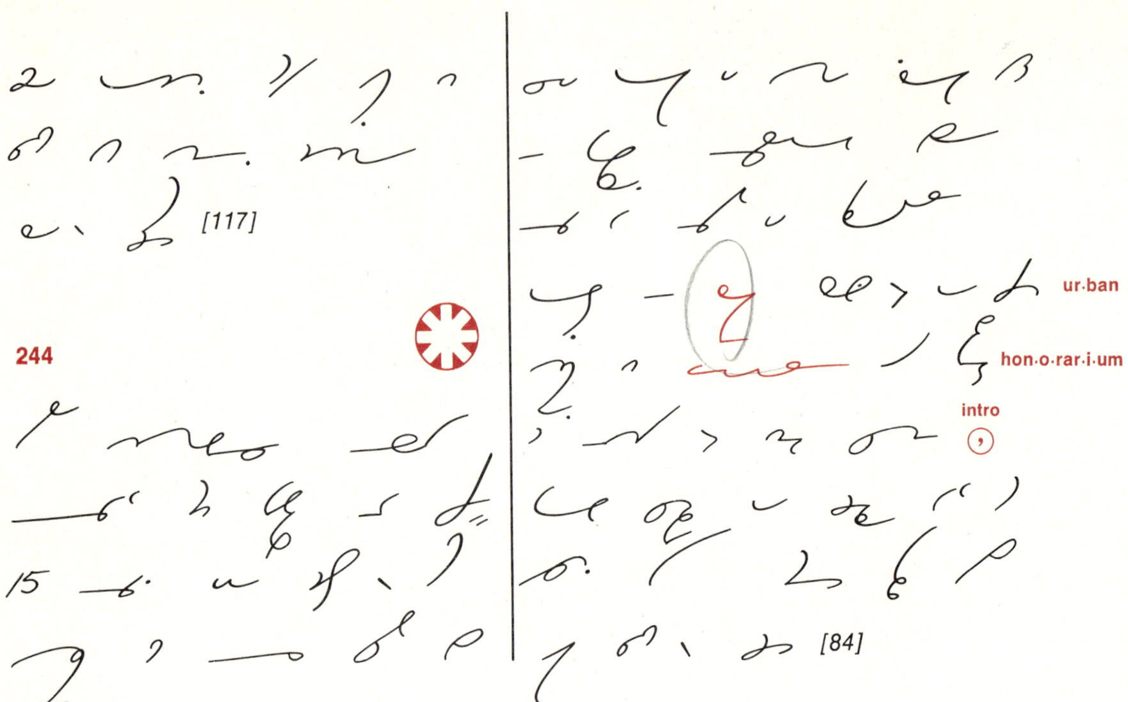

245 Transcription Quiz For you to supply: 5 commas—1 comma *as* clause, 4 commas parenthetical; 2 missing words.

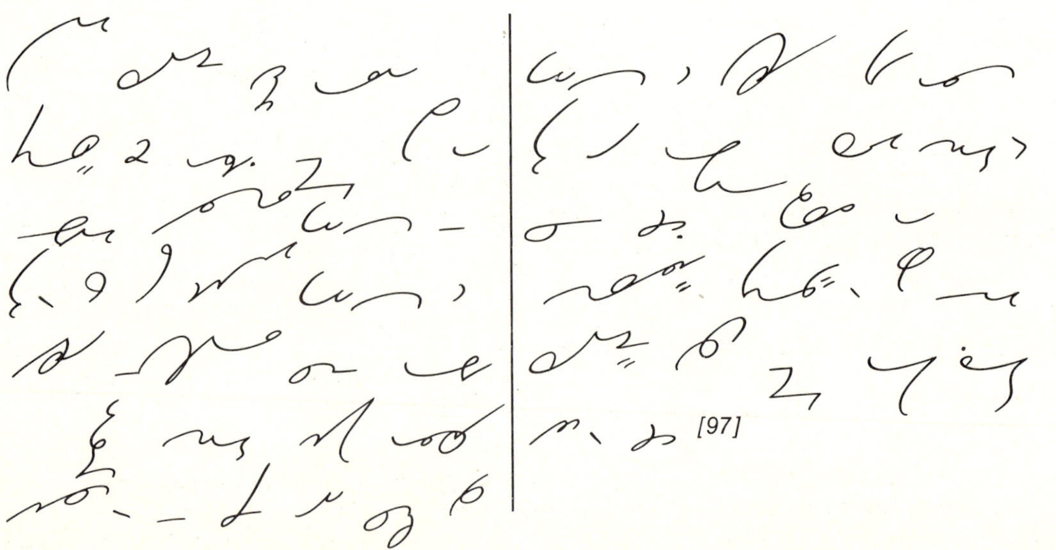

Developing Word-Building Power

246 Word Beginnings and Endings

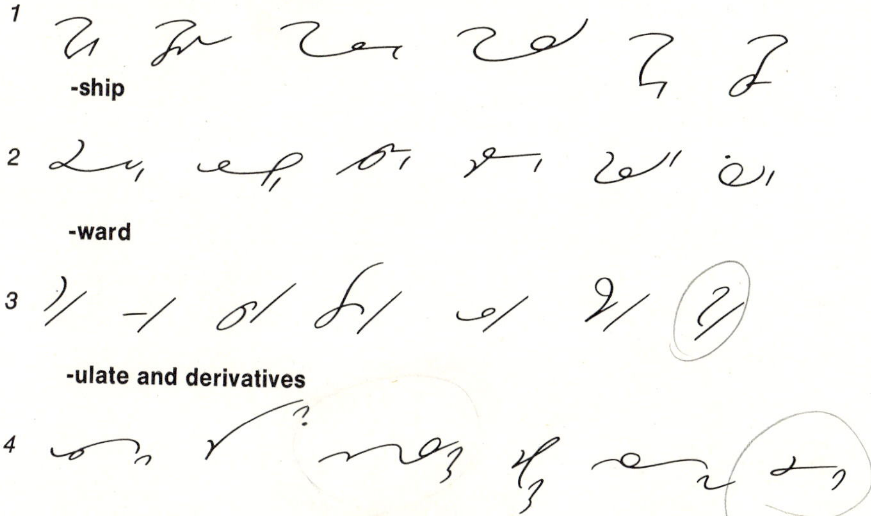

1 Competition, computer, compliments, complaint, combination, combine.
2 Fellowship, relationship, township, steamship, friendship, hardship.
3 Forward, inward, outward, backward, reward, afterward, upward.
4 Regulate, stimulating, congratulations, stipulations, calculator, simulates.

Building Transcription Skills

247 COMMON PREFIXES ■ in-

A knowledge of the meaning of the more common prefixes is of great value in helping you increase your command of the English language.

In Volume One you studied a number of common prefixes; in Volume Two you will learn somewhat more advanced prefixes.

Read the definition of each prefix and then study the illustrations that follow.

in- as a prefix, *in* frequently has the meaning "not."

incapable Not able.

incompetent Not proficient.

incomplete Not finished; partially finished.

inconvenient Not suitable.

indisposed Not well.

informal Not formal; casual.

248 **Business Vocabulary Builder**

fellowships Grants to graduate students for teaching or laboratory work.

thesis A graduate research project typed and bound as a book.

duplicators Machines for copying—spirit, stencil, or photocopy.

stimulating Causing excitement.

Reading and Writing Practice

249

intro ,

coun·try

sec·ond·ary

par

spe·cial·ized

nc

intro

nc

[142]

250

conj

priv·i·lege

Transcribe: $500

ma·jor

ap

par

stim·u·lat·ing

and o

[119]

251

as

pre·lim·i·nary

conj

full time
no noun
no hyphen

conj

as·sis·tance

[101]

252

cour·te·sy

intro

sep·a·rate·ly

com·pli·ments

tech·ni·cal

us·age

nc

if

ap

ar·range

687-
8101

[158]

253

one-hour
hyphenated before noun
well-equipped
hyphenated before noun

and o

Transcribe:
8:30 a.m.
4 p.m.

8:30 4 ser per·son·nel if ac·cept intro nc 451-4111 [115]

254 Transcription Quiz For you to supply: 7 commas—2 commas series, 1 comma *and* omitted, 1 comma introductory, 2 commas apposition, 1 comma *if* clause; 2 missing words.

13 116-1117 8 3 [118]

■ *People are judged to a large degree by their ability to work with other people*—Robert F. Black

Developing Word-Building Power

255 SHORTHAND VOCABULARY BUILDER

Omission of Minor Vowel

1

Ī

2

Div, Dev

3

Ŭ

4

1 Bondholder, stockholder, shareholder, landholder.
2 High, higher, buy, buyer, rice, price, private, realize.
3 Dividend, individual, diversify, devise, develop, developed.
4 Us, conduct, suffer, up, adjust, trust, enough, luck.

Building Transcription Skills

256 Business Vocabulary Builder

bonds Loans to companies.

dividend Profit declared in a business.

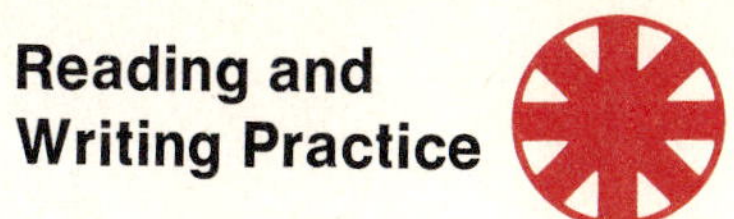

Reading and Writing Practice

257 The Stock Market

raise

ba·si·cal·ly

Shares of

par

busi·ness

if

prof·it·able

intro

cor·po·ra·tion's

if

if

re·ceive

than

cap·i·tal

intro

10 25/ if 50/

par long-term *hyphenated before noun*

par

like·ly

par

fac·tors

First

when its

con·verse·ly intro

los·ing

when

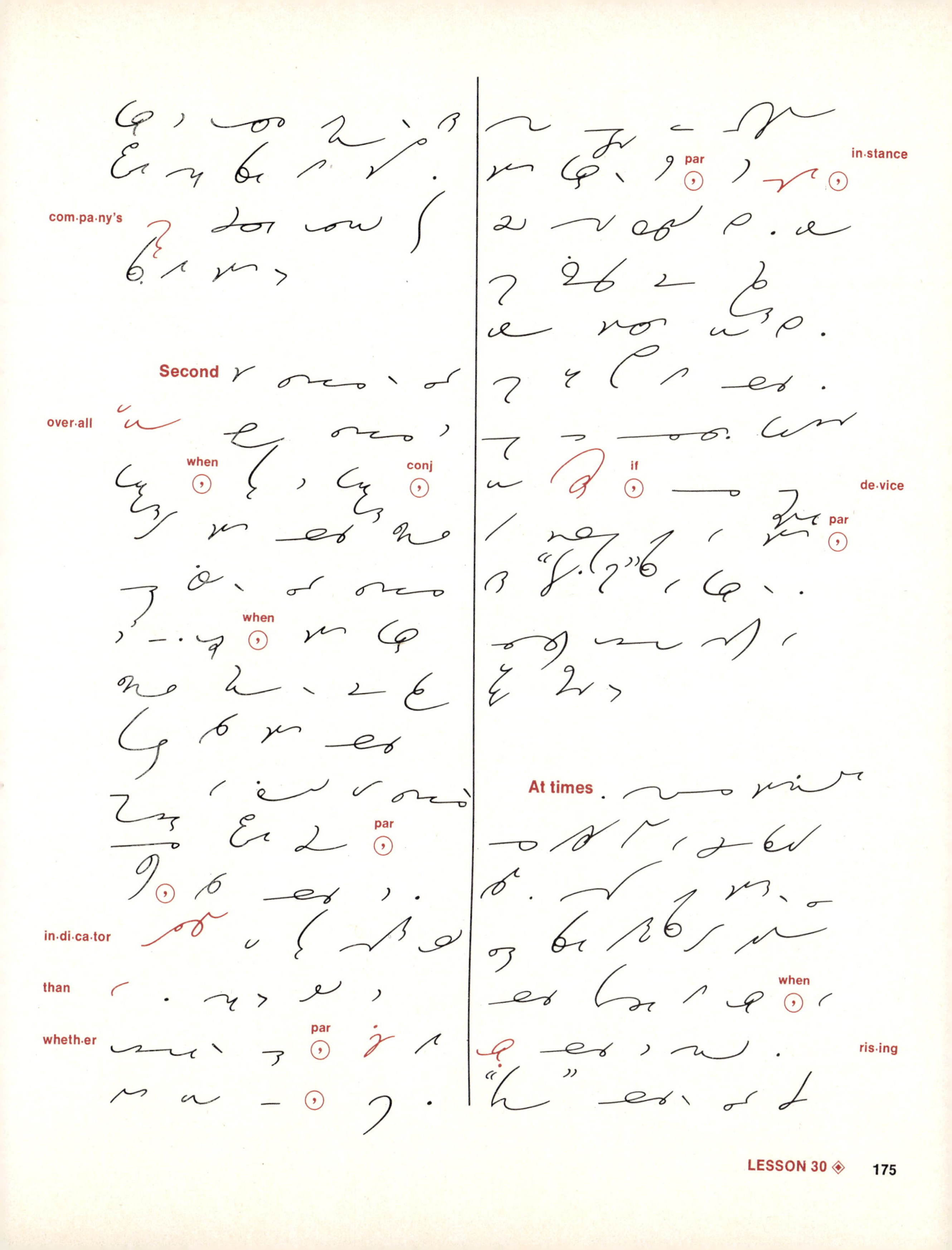

com·pa·ny's

Second

over·all

when

conj

when

par

in·di·ca·tor

than

par

wheth·er

par

in·stance

if

de·vice

par

At times

when

ris·ing

par

de·clin·ing

bear

in·ge·nu·ity

bear·ish

ring·er

conj

[727]

—Adapted from "Investment: The Lure of Wall Street," *Senior Scholastic*, May 9, 1968, pp. 14-16.

LETTERS

258

ser

equiv·a·lent

if

train·ee

if

ap

116- 1818

118 2 [173]

Ex·ten·sion

7 Hotels

Developing Word-Building Power

259 BRIEF FORMS AND DERIVATIVES

1 Manufacture, manufactured; opinion, opinions; particular, particularly.

2 Put, puts; regard, regarded; short, shorter.

3 Subject, subjected; yesterday; after, afternoon, aftermath.

4 Big, bigger; company, companies; ever-every, everyone.

5 Merchandise, merchandising; newspaper, newspapers; opportunity, opportunities.

6 Present, represent; quantity, quantities; request, requested.

Building Transcription Skills

260 Business Vocabulary Builder

accessible Easy to reach.

ample Adequate.

memorable Worth remembering.

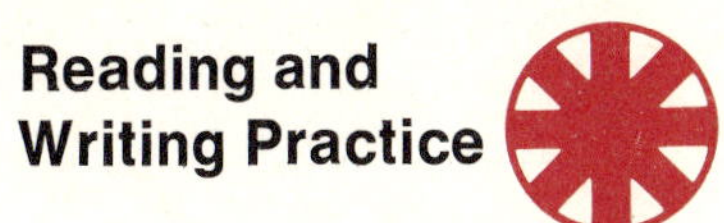

Reading and Writing Practice

261 Brief-Form Letter

re·ferred

be·gin·ning

ap

if

nonr

[112]

262

and o

low-cost
hyphenated before noun

[70]

263

par

Transcribe:
$100

its

dai·ly nc intro

[90]

264

ap

com·mit·tee

as

of·fer·ing

ex·hib·i·tor's

if

[104]

265

par

Chi·ca·go

am·ple

intro

fur·ther·more

ac·ces·si·ble

na·tion's

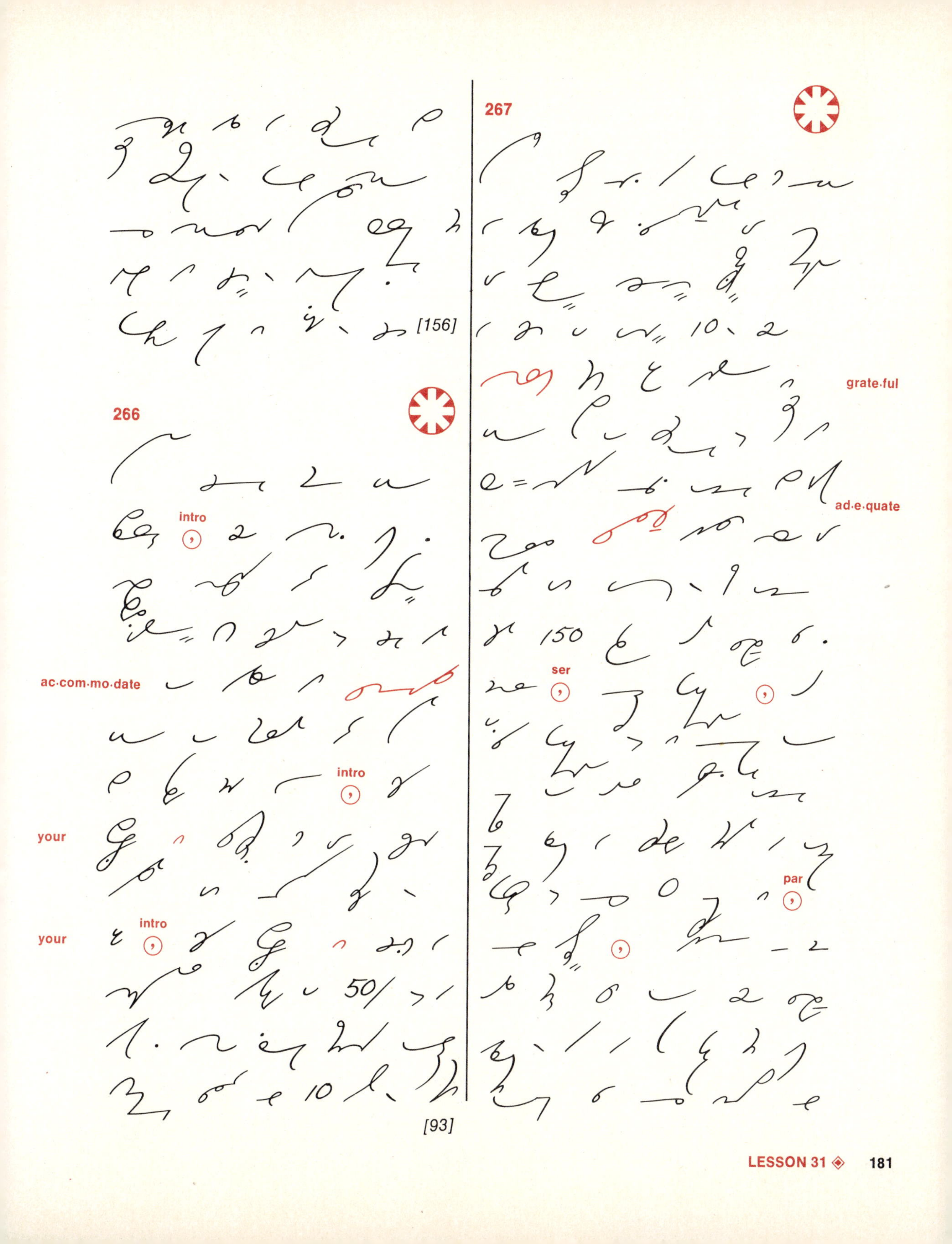

[156]

266

intro

ac·com·mo·date

intro

your

your

intro

50/

10

[93]

267

10

grate·ful

ad·e·quate

150

ser

par

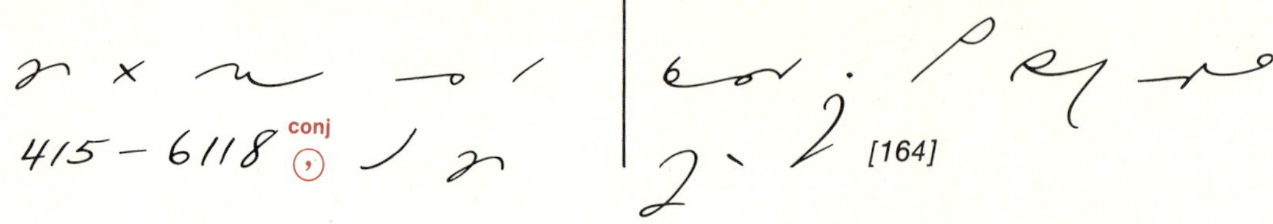

268 Transcription Quiz In the Transcription Quizzes in previous lessons you have had to supply missing words that were obvious, as only one possible word made sense in the sentence. From now on, several words will make sense, and it will be your responsibility to supply the word you think fits best in the sentence.

For example:

Where there has been an omission, any one of the following words could be considered correct: *happy, delighted, glad.*

If you decide that the word *happy* makes the best sense, you would write it in your shorthand notebook thus:

Be sure that the word you choose makes good sense in the sentence.

For you to supply: 5 commas—1 comma conjunction, 2 commas parenthetical, 2 commas series; 1 missing word.

[101]

LESSON 

Building Phrasing Skill

269 USEFUL BUSINESS-LETTER PHRASES

For

Sure

To in Phrases

Miscellaneous

1 For me, for my, for his, for the, for that, for it, for some time, for us.

2 Be sure, being sure, to be sure, I am sure, you are sure, if you are sure, I feel sure.

3 To be, is to be, to see, to plan, to fill, to finish, to bear, to put.

4 As soon as, as soon as possible, to me, to know, to make, to us, to do, let us, we hope you will.

270 GEOGRAPHICAL EXPRESSIONS

1 Philadelphia, Salem, Dover, Bedford, Richmond, Grand Rapids.

2 Pennsylvania, Massachusetts, Delaware, Michigan, Illinois, North Carolina.

Building Transcription Skills

271 SIMILAR-WORDS DRILL ■ suite, suit

suite (pronounced *swēt*) A group of rooms occupied as a unit.

We know you will be pleased with the *suite* of rooms.

suit (*verb*) To meet the requirements of.

I hope the time will *suit* you.

suit (*noun*) An article of clothing.

He bought a new *suit*.

272 Business Vocabulary Builder

deduct Take away from; withdraw from total.

minimum Least possible.

site Location.

verified Checked the correctness of.

Reading and Writing Practice

273 Phrase Letter

par

head·quar·ters

re·mod·el·ing

past

intro

and o

mod·ern

suite

yours

ac·com·mo·date

nc

guest

par

suit

and o

well-planned
hyphenated before noun

[176]

274

as

oc·cu·pied

suite

when

Transcribe:
$200

par

hur·ry

oc·curred

conj

su·perb

[130]

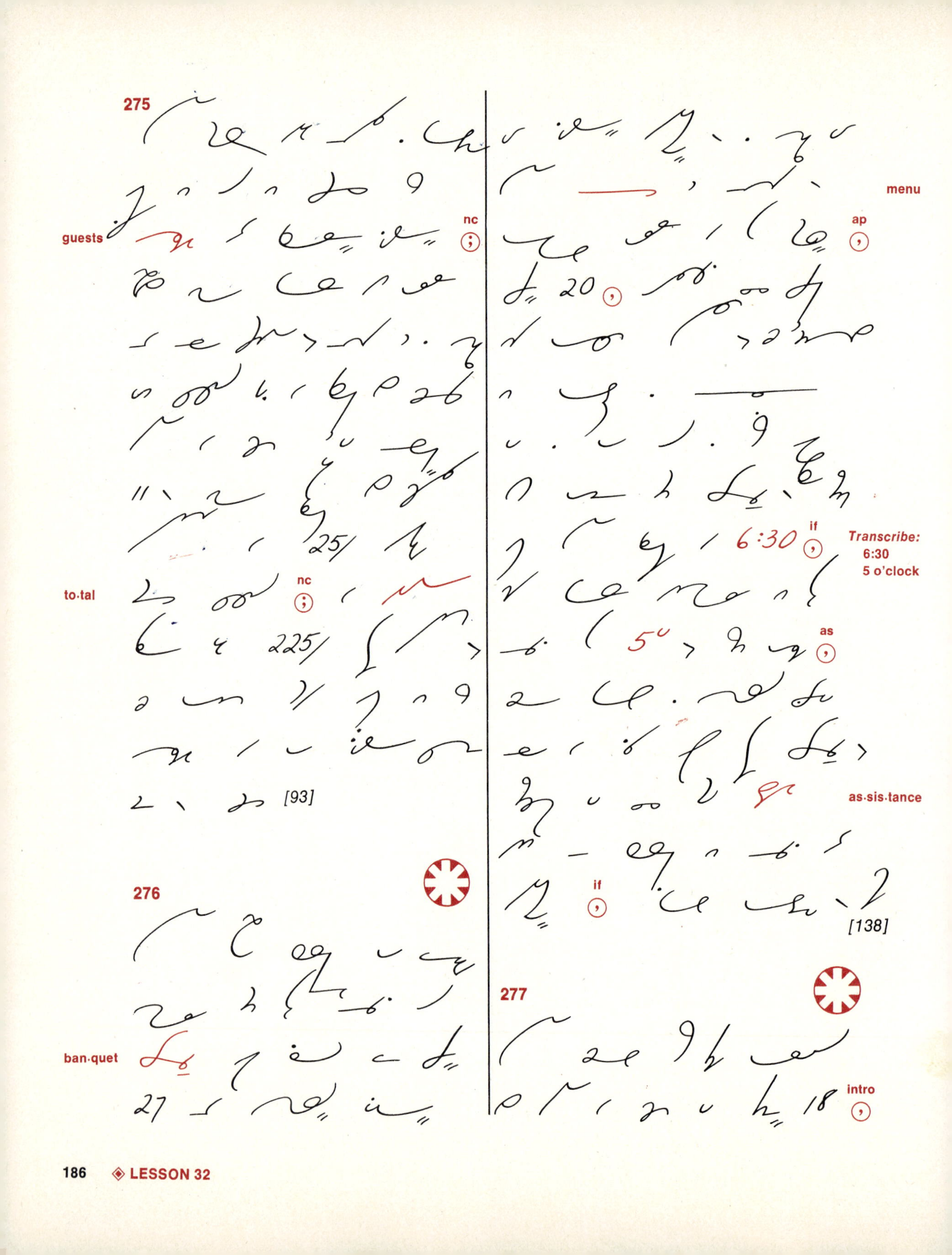

275

guests

nc ;

25

to·tal

nc ;

225

[93]

276

ban·quet

27

menu

ap ,

20 ,

if

6:30 ,

Transcribe:
6:30
5 o'clock

5

as ,

as·sis·tance

if ,

[138]

277

18

intro ,

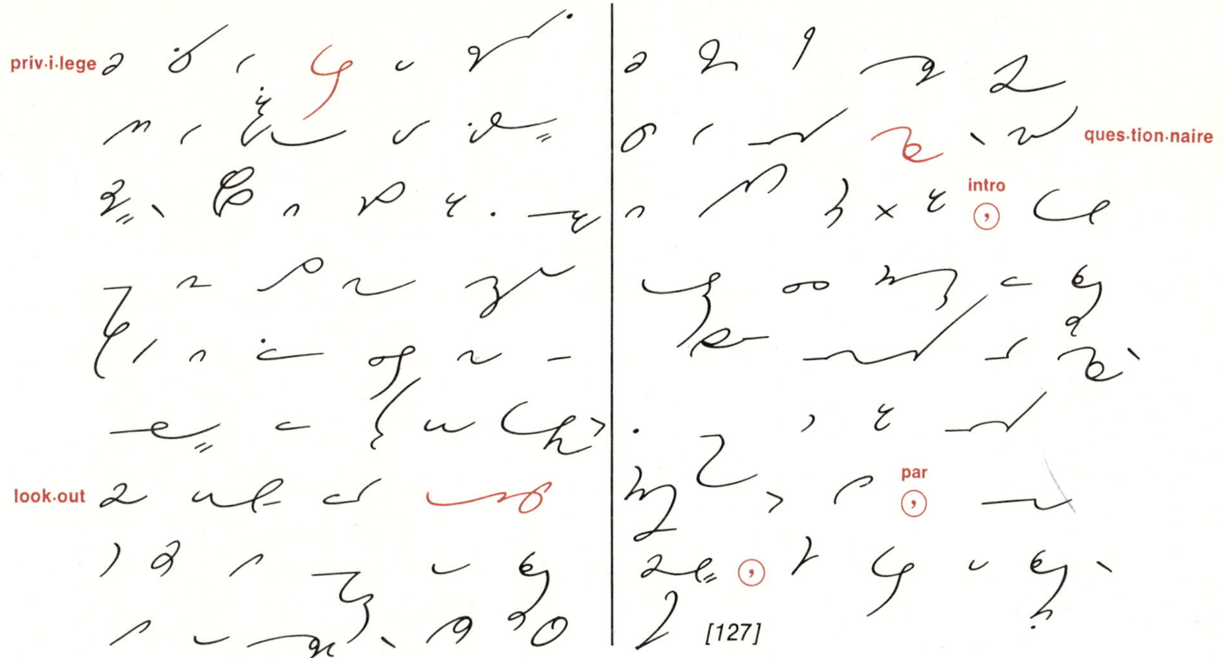

278 Transcription Quiz For you to supply: 5 commas—2 commas series, 1 comma *if* clause, 2 commas apposition; 1 missing word.

[120]

Developing Word-Building Power

279 WORD FAMILIES

-age

-ger

-val, -vel

-less

-duct

1 Package, luggage, manage, baggage, average, mileage.
2 Larger, manager, passenger, messenger, endanger, merger.
3 Arrival, approval, naval, marvel, travel, level, shovel.
4 Thoughtless, needless, peerless, unless, spotless, valueless.
5 Conduct, product, induct, deduct, abduct, by-product.

Building Transcription Skills

280 SPELLING FAMILIES ■ -ight

In some languages a vowel sound is always spelled the same way. In English, however, a vowel sound may be spelled a number of different ways. Below you will find common words in which *i* is spelled *igh.*

-ight

height	**bright**	**right**
sight	**might**	**slight**
night	**de·light**	**fright**

281 Business Vocabulary Builder

parcel post Fourth-class mail.

capacity Measure of ability to contain.

spacious Large.

lectern Reading desk.

reconsiliation

Reading and Writing Practice

282

ap

night

intro

if

your

[77]

han·dling

283

ap

Feb·ru·ary

its

par

to·day's

well-equipped
hyphenated before noun

and o

whether

intro

and o

if

if

flight

intro

[141]

284

as

ma·jor

conj

re·al·ize

when

than

par

too

intro

if

available

and o

spa·cious

Chi·ca·go's

intro

intro

nc

[129]

ma·jor

285

heart

In·di·a·nap·o·lis

intro

ap

intro

[161]

ap

286

trav·els

ar·riv·al

intro

ser

Transcribe: 5 p.m.

intro

de·layed

intro

20

[77]

287

mid·town

18

intro

intro

(415) 216-1881

[97]

288 Transcription Quiz For you to supply: 5 commas—4 commas series, 1 comma *if* clause; 1 missing word.

11 12 13

80

5

[86]

Developing Word-Building Power

289 Word Beginnings and Endings

-ings

En-

Un-

Al-

1 Meetings, evenings, buildings, dealings, mornings, furnishings, recordings.
2 Enjoy, enjoyable, endeavor, engage, engagement, envy, enlarged.
3 Until, unless, undisturbed, unfilled, unpaid, untimely, unpacked.
4 Almost, also, Albany, alter, alteration, although, altogether.

Building Transcription Skills

290 GRAMMAR CHECKUP ■ don't, doesn't

Use *doesn't* in the third person singular, not *don't.*

She *doesn't* (not *don't*) live in Chicago.
He *doesn't* have a telephone in his office.
That *doesn't* seem logical.

Few people use *doesn't* when they should use *don't*—you seldom hear anyone say, "I *doesn't*," but you often hear people incorrectly say, "he *don't*" and "that *don't*." Be careful not to make that mistake.

291 **Business Vocabulary Builder**

elegant Splendid; choice.

sauna Steam bathhouse.

discriminating (*adjective*) Carefully selective.

Reading and Writing Practice

292

intro

con·ve·nience

en·deav·ors conj

cities

par

nc intro

ser

un·dis·turbed

night's

intro

(400) 134-2593

en·joy·able

par

[149]

293

ap

10

ap

el·e·gant

lux·u·ry

par

nice·ly fur·nished *no hyphen after ly*

and o

suites

par

sau·na

ser

par

mag·nif·i·cent

ap

Chef

sand·wich

when

[157]

294

as

ac·cept

par

can·cel·la·tions

if

[62]

295

menus

Transcribe: $20

20/

high-qual·i·ty hyphenated before noun

60/

[93]

[113]

296

ap

Ho·tel's

12

10

12

297

when

par

ser

intro

one-day hyphenated before noun

guar·an·tee

intro

intro

(116) 118-2222 [155]

298 Transcription Quiz For you to supply: 5 commas—1 comma conjunction, 1 comma introductory, 2 commas parenthetical, 1 comma *as* clause; 1 missing word.

[134]

LESSON 35

Developing Word-Building Power

299 SHORTHAND VOCABULARY BUILDER

X

1 [shorthand outlines]

Ū

2 [shorthand outlines]

Ēa, Ĭa

3 [shorthand outlines]

Ted

4 [shorthand outlines]

1 Deluxe, relax, luxury, maximum, mixed, taxation.
2 Units, utilize, usually, unique, uniform, review, fuse.
3 Area, create, recreation, appreciate, appreciation, depreciate, initiate.
4 Operated, limited, rated, greeted, seated.

Building Transcription Skills

300 Business Vocabulary Builder

deluxe Of special elegance or luxury.

forerunners Things that come before.

frustration Discouragement.

Spartan Barren; not luxurious.

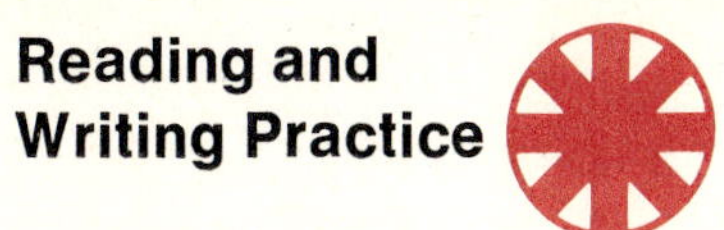

Reading and Writing Practice

301 The Motel Business

ap

fore·run·ners

par·al·leled

1920's

pres·ent-day hyphenated before noun

edge

conj

The term

1930's

conj

of·fered

ser

res·tau·rant

intro

kennels

enterprises

intro

The convenience

one's

and o

multistory

accommodations

With the

bowling

ser

intro

occupancy

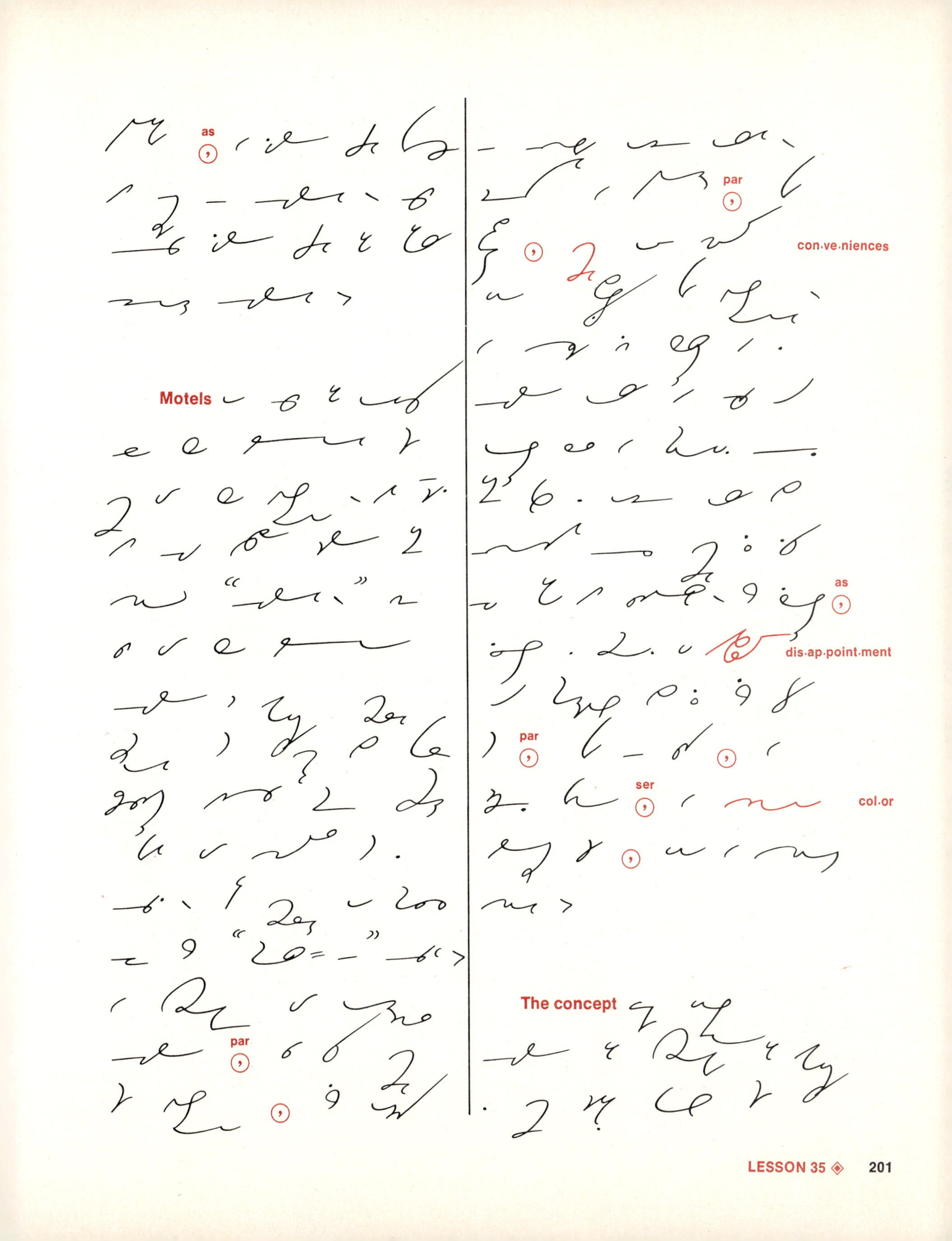

as

Motels

par

par

con·ve·niences

as

dis·ap·point·ment

par

ser

col·or

The concept

night's

intro

par

luxuries

conj

intro

intro

[827]

■ *Many young people who have special talents or interest in drama, music, art, journalism, politics, and so on have found that secretarial training works almost like magic in gaining entrance to these areas of work.*—John Robert Gregg

WORLD INDEMNITY COMPANY
A New York Corporation
New York N.Y.
A COMPANY OF THE
WORLD
A MEMBER
OF T
COMBINATION POLICY
Policy No. GDH 93 17 32
DECLARATIONS
ITEM 1 NAMED INSURED AND ADDRESS
F.R. BOYLE AND JAMES NEIL
3906 SAN FELICIANO DR.
BOYLE
CALIF.
PACIFIC DEPT.
ITEM FROM 6/5/73 to 6/5/74
STANDARD TIME

8 Insurance

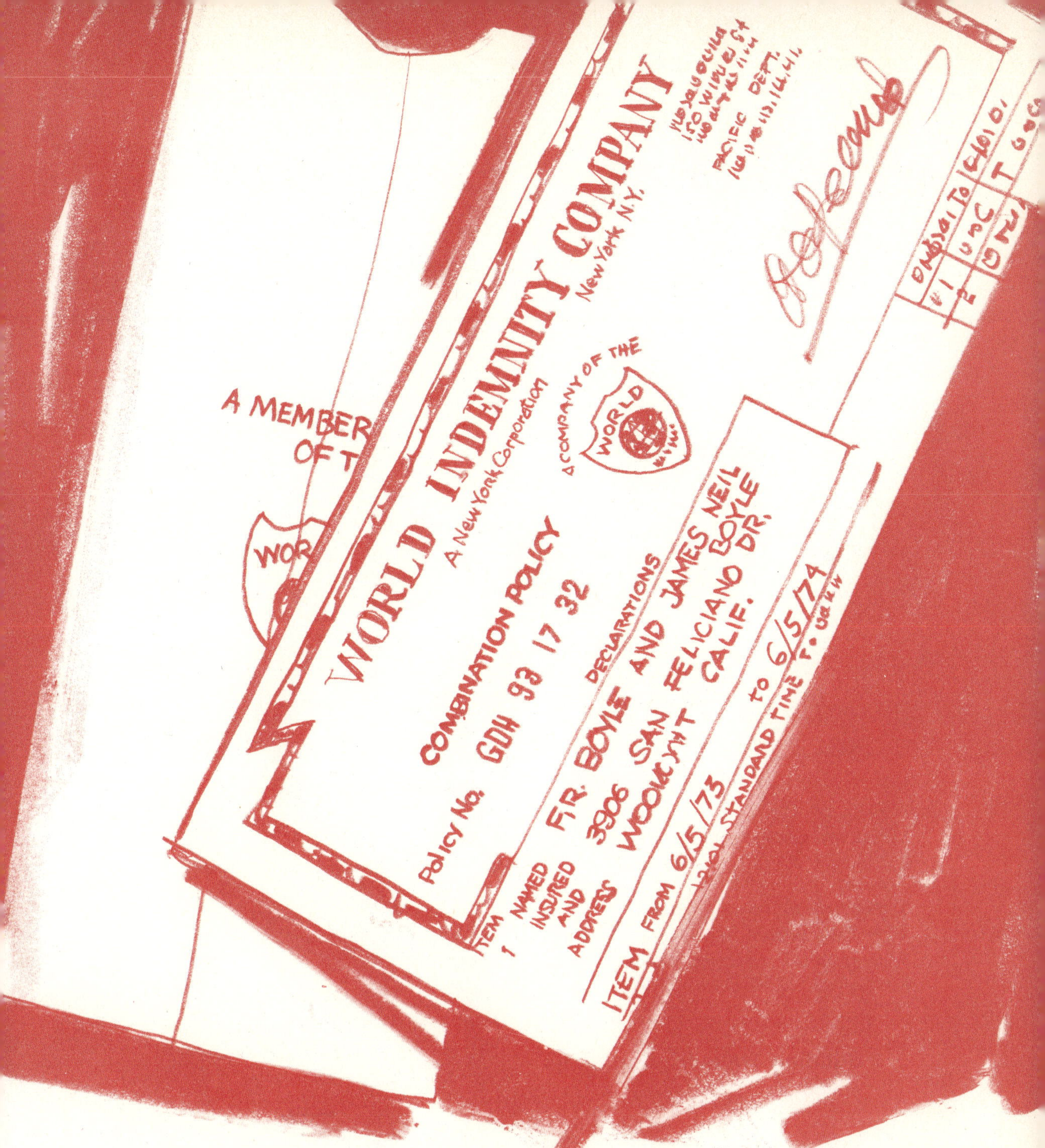

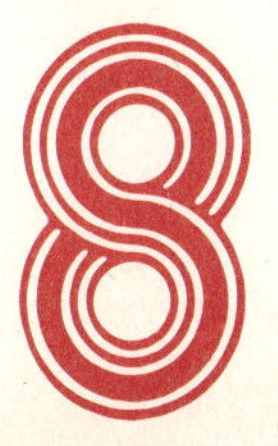

Developing Word-Building Power

302 BRIEF FORMS AND DERIVATIVES

1 Success, successive; time, untimed; wish, wishful.

2 Business, businesses; correspond-correspondence, correspondents; experience, experienced.

3 Good, goods; merchant, merchants; order, disorder.

4 Probable, probably; question, unquestioned; responsible, responsibility.

5 Situation, situations; them, themselves; under, underneath.

6 Were-year, years; you-your, yourself; govern, government.

Building Transcription Skills

303 Business Vocabulary Builder

imperative Necessary; commanding.

catastrophe Tragic event.

involuntary Done without choice; compulsory.

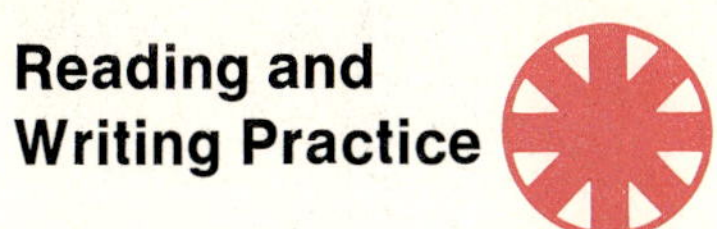

Reading and Writing Practice

304 Brief-Form Letter

im·per·a·tive

par

Transcribe:
9 a.m.
5 p.m.

if

[127]

305

com·pa·nies

ser

buy

nc

thou·sands

nonr

ca·tas·tro·phe

par

loss

dis·cuss

mind

[173]

306

spur

wheth·er

in·vol·un·tary

ap

conj

par

when

all-time *hyphenated before noun*

intro

ur·gent

its

post·age-paid *hyphenated before noun*

nc

[158]

307

re·spon·si·ble

and o

oc·curred

years'

if

grate·ful

and o

keen

en·ve·lope

[149]

308 Transcription Quiz For you to supply: 6 commas—2 commas series, 1 comma *if* clause, 2 commas parenthetical, 1 comma introductory; 2 missing words.

[121]

Building Phrasing Skill

309 USEFUL BUSINESS-LETTER PHRASES

As

About

Few

We

1 As good, as well, as you, as you are, as you will see, as you can, as you know.
2 About the, about the time, about which, about my, about that, about this, about your.
3 Few days, few minutes, few minutes ago, few months, few moments.
4 We can, we may, we have, we might, we will, we may be, we maintain.

310 GEOGRAPHICAL EXPRESSIONS

1 Nashville, Ashville, Omaha, Lincoln, Wichita, Tulsa.
2 North Dakota, South Dakota, Nebraska, Kansas, Oklahoma, Montana.

Building Transcription Skills

311 SIMILAR-WORDS DRILL ■ advice, advise

advice (*noun*) Recommendations; suggestions; guidance.

These people look to our agents for *advice* when they need financial help.

advise (*verb*) To guide; to suggest; to inform.

We *advise* you to pay your overdue premium without delay.

312 Business Vocabulary Builder

supplementing Adding to; completing.

phase Part; area.

evacuate To leave; to remove; to make empty.

Reading and Writing Practice

313 Phrase Letter

ad·vice

choose

intro

fur·ther·more

phase

ad·vise

conj

[154]

314

if

safe·ly

conj

trapped

evac·u·ate

if

ad·vise

intro

and o

of·fer·ing

routes

whole

intro

con·ve·nient

if

when

[157]

315

15

112156

ap

18

intro

conj

intro

par

if

month's

[133]

316

to·day's

par

too

year's

ser

bank·rupt·cy

conj

[118]

317

if

intro

dis·hon·es·ty

ser

lose

nc

[122]

318 Transcription Quiz For you to supply: 8 commas—2 commas nonrestrictive, 1 comma introductory, 1 comma apposition, 2 commas parenthetical; 1 comma *as* clause, 1 comma *if* clause; 2 missing words.

30 30 10 10 28

[127]

LESSON 38

Developing Word-Building Power

319 WORD FAMILIES

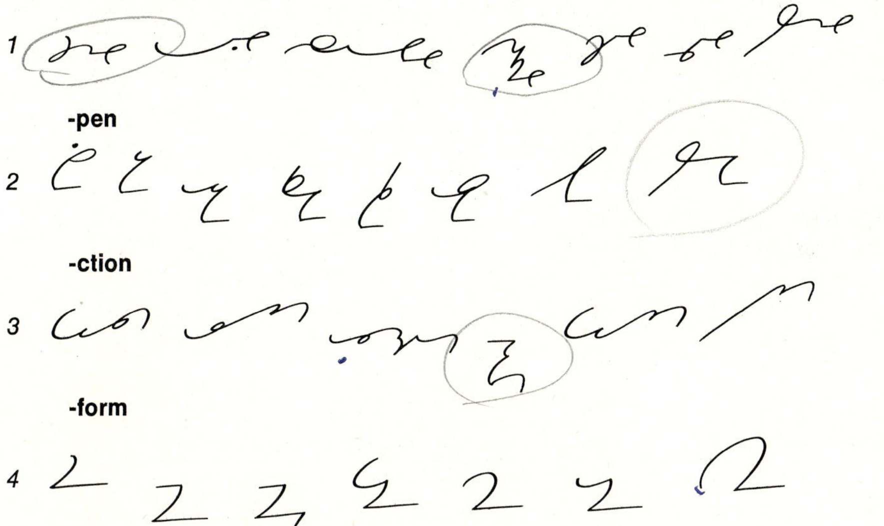

1 Sickness, willingness, carelessness, cautiousness, witness, neatness, darkness.
2 Happen, open, reopen, sharpen, cheapen, ripen, deepen, dampen.
3 Protection, reduction, reconstruction, inspection, production, deduction.
4 Form, inform, information, perform, conform, reform, deform.

Building Transcription Skills

320 COMMON PREFIXES ■ dis-

dis- in many English words, the prefix *dis-* means *not* or *the opposite of* or *in the absence of.*

dislike The opposite of *like;* to have an aversion to.

disregard The opposite of *regard;* to pay no attention to.

disloyal Not *loyal;* unfaithful.

disagreeable Not *agreeable;* taking a different point of view.

discomfort The opposite of *comfort;* uneasiness.

discontented The opposite of *contented;* not satisfied.

disapprove The opposite of *approve;* not agree to.

321 Business Vocabulary Builder

immune Protected against.

appraised Set a value on.

no-fault insurance Automobile insurance in which a person's own company pays for a loss without regard to which person caused the accident.

survive To remain alive; to exist after.

Reading and Writing Practice

322

nonr

well-trained hyphenated before noun

intro

in·qui·ries

no-fault hyphenated before noun

ser

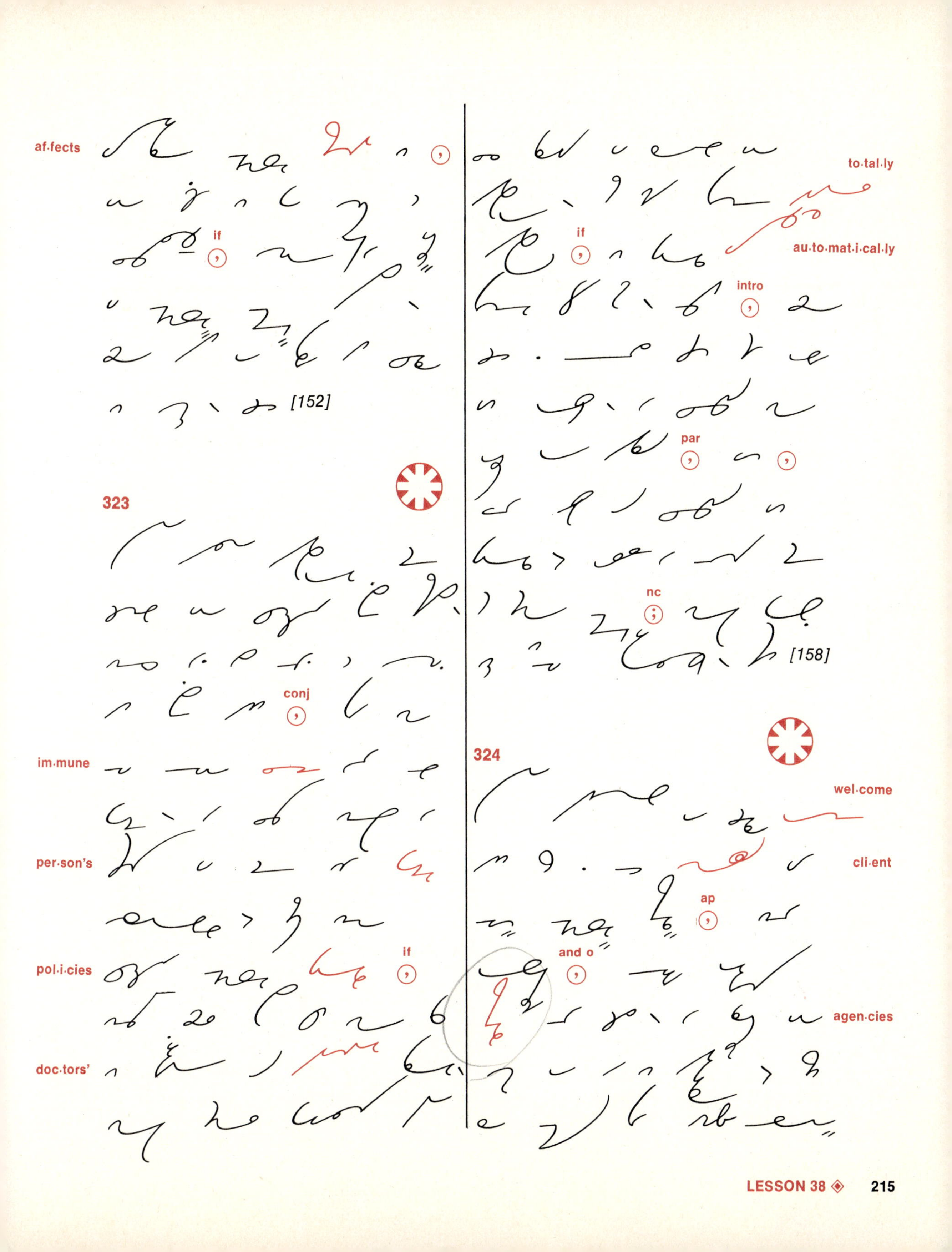

af·fects

if

[152]

323

conj

im·mune

per·son's

pol·i·cies

if

doc·tors'

to·tal·ly

if

au·to·mat·i·cal·ly

intro

par

nc

[158]

324

wel·come

cli·ent

ap

and o

agen·cies

as

nonr

ca·su·al·ty

ap·praised

ap·prais·al

if

if

nc

intro

[167]

325

conj

pur·chase

no-fault
hyphenated before noun

par

ap·pre·ci·ate

par

Transcribe:
6 o'clock

[103]

326

highs

cus·tom·er's

owes

bad-debt *hyphenated before noun*

when

intro

[87]

327 Transcription Quiz For you to supply: 7 commas—4 commas series, 2 commas introductory, 1 comma parenthetical; 2 missing words.

40,

[167]

LESSON 

Developing Word-Building Power

328 WORD BEGINNINGS AND ENDINGS

Be-

1

-ure

2

-ther

3

Dis-, Des-

4

1 Before, beginning, become, betray, below, besides, beneath.

2 Future, feature, miniature, expenditure, picture, procedure.

3 Weather, other, either, rather, bothered, gathered, together, altogether.

4 Distract, disappoint, disregard, distinction, described, description, despite.

Building Transcription Skills

329 Business Vocabulary Builder

options Alternatives; rights to change.

reimbursed Paid back in money.

versatility Quality of having many skills or abilities.

Reading and Writing Practice

330

per·ma·nent

if

op·tions

conj

intro

re·ceive

if

when

fact-filled

45-page

hyphenated before noun

45=

ap

[120]

331

par

ap·pre·ci·ate

ap·praise

116-1185

[70]

332

ap

15

com·mit·tee

par

wheth·er

ap

[98]

333

em·ploy·ees

intro

re·im·bursed

28

4

3

[135]

334

dis·tin·guished

ver·sa·til·i·ty

fea·tures

if

par

[147]

335 Transcription Quiz For you to supply: 5 commas—1 comma conjunction, 2 commas nonrestrictive, 2 commas parenthetical; 2 missing words.

[137]

LESSON 

Developing Word-Building Power

336 SHORTHAND VOCABULARY BUILDER

Mon, Min, Etc.

1 [shorthand outlines]

W Dash

2 [shorthand outlines]

Compounds

3 [shorthand outlines]

Omission of E in Ū

4 [shorthand outlines]

1 Monthly, common, examination, minimum, minute, manage.
2 Quite, quarterly, breadwinner, liquidation, quietly, Broadway.
3 Someone, however, withstand, worthwhile, anywhere, everyone, whenever, everybody.
4 New, continue, education, issue, numerous, duties, avenue, manuscript.

Building Transcription Skills

337 Business Vocabulary Builder

contingencies Possibilities.

conceivable Possible; thinkable.

liquidation Settlement; discharging of debts.

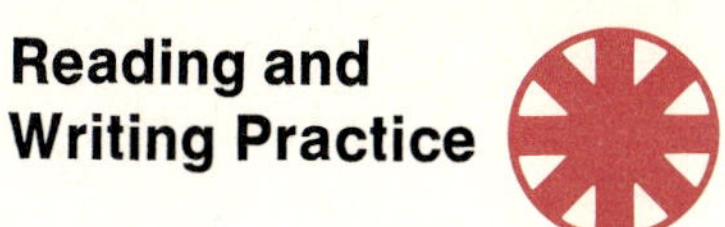

338 Planning Insurance

par

re·al·ize

par

par

bur·den

intro

de·pen·dents

arise

Insurance planning

par

ser

in·stall·ment

par

ne·ces·si·tate

and o

un·hur·ried

sur·vi·vors

if

fur·ther

chil·dren's

The ideal

par

intro

[354]

—Adapted from *Insurance for Credit Unions*

339 Ordinary Life Insurance

con·ceiv·able

stake

die

par

intro

grown

chil·dren's

intro

of·ten

par

People

liq·ui·da·tion

As you

as

sum

ser

semi·an·nu·al·ly

in·di·vid·u·al

intro

[377]

Advice From a Champion

When Martin J. Dupraw won the world's shorthand championship, he established some remarkable records for accuracy. On a speech dictated at 200 words a minute for five minutes, he made only one error. On court testimony dictated at 280 words a minute for five minutes, he made only two errors. These and many other records that he has established are the result, in large measure, of the amazing legibility of his shorthand notes.

When you examine Mr. Dupraw's shorthand notes on the opposite page, one thing will immediately impress you—the careful attention to proportion.

Notice, for example, how large he makes the *a* circles and how small he makes the *e* circles. Notice, too, how much larger his *l's* are than his *r's.*

Another thing that will strike you is the way he rounds off angles. He does not consciously do this; rounding angles comes naturally to him as a result of his high speed. As your speed increases, you, too, will find that you will naturally round off angles.

In the page that Mr. Dupraw has written in his beautiful shorthand, he discusses the size of notes. Note that he has a fairly large shorthand style, just as he has a large longhand style.

Don't try to imitate Mr. Dupraw's style of writing; take the advice he gives in his article, "How Big Should My Shorthand Be?"

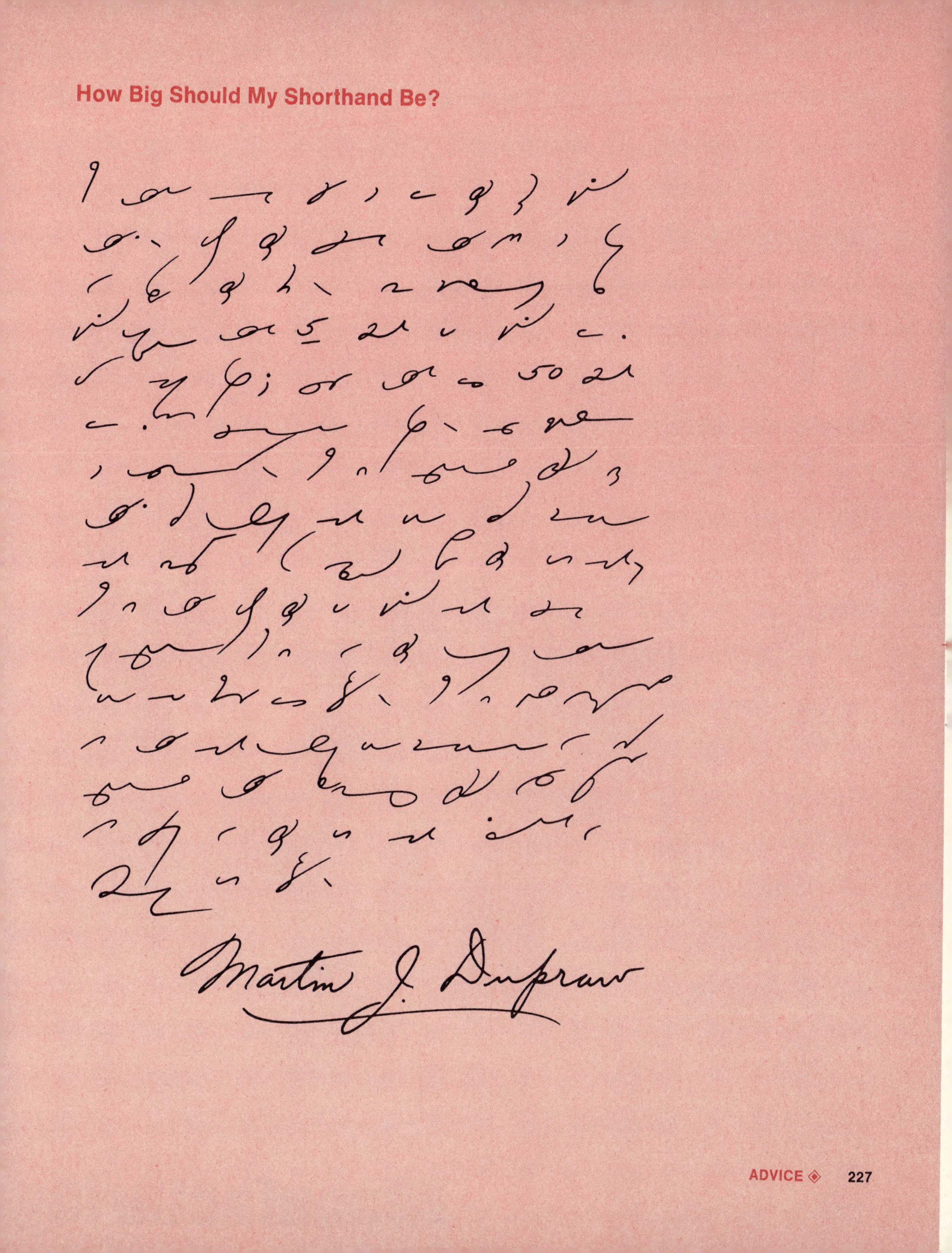

How Big Should My Shorthand Be?

Martin J. Dupraw

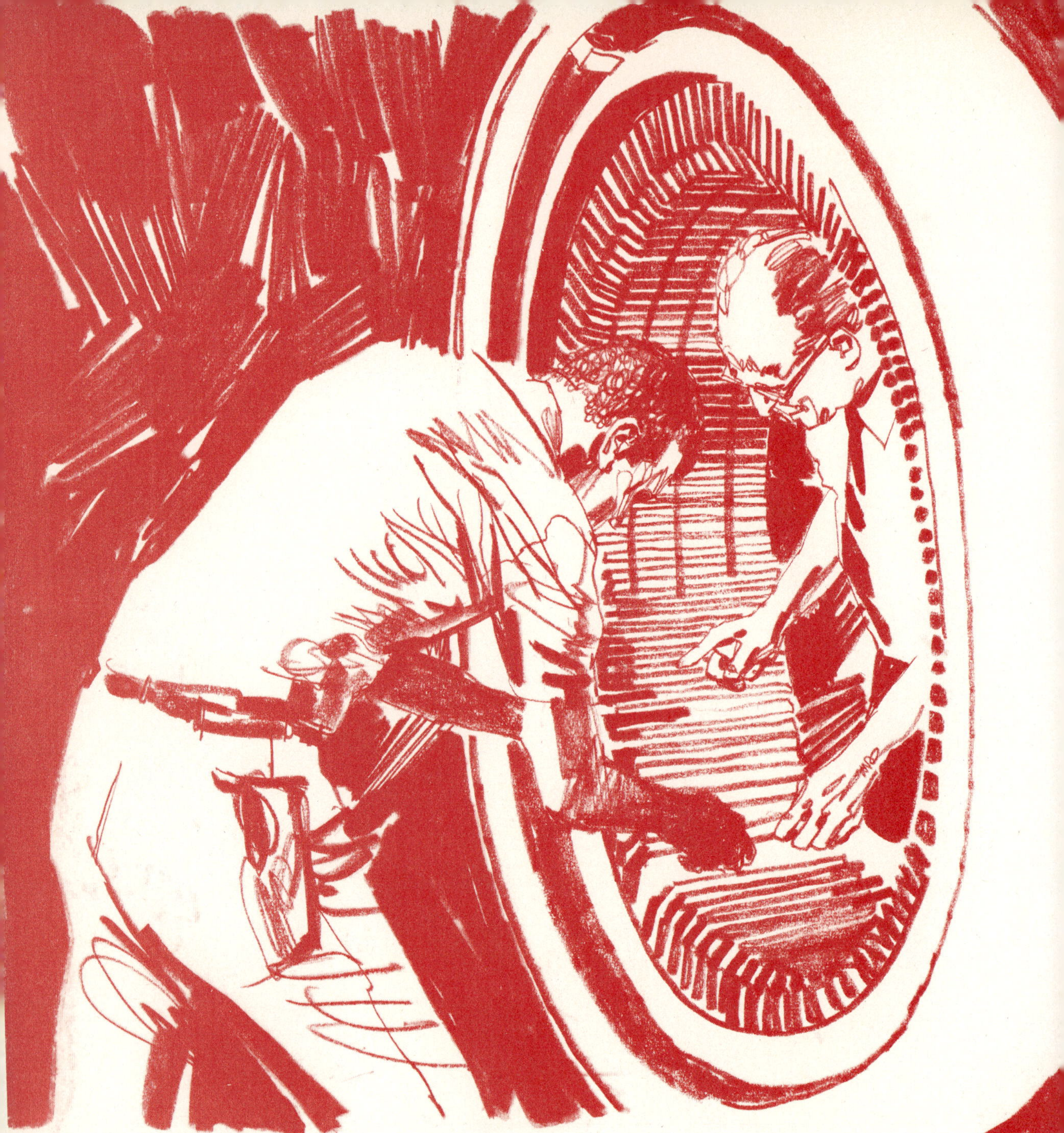

Manufacturing

LESSON 41

Developing Word-Building Power

340 BRIEF FORMS AND DERIVATIVES

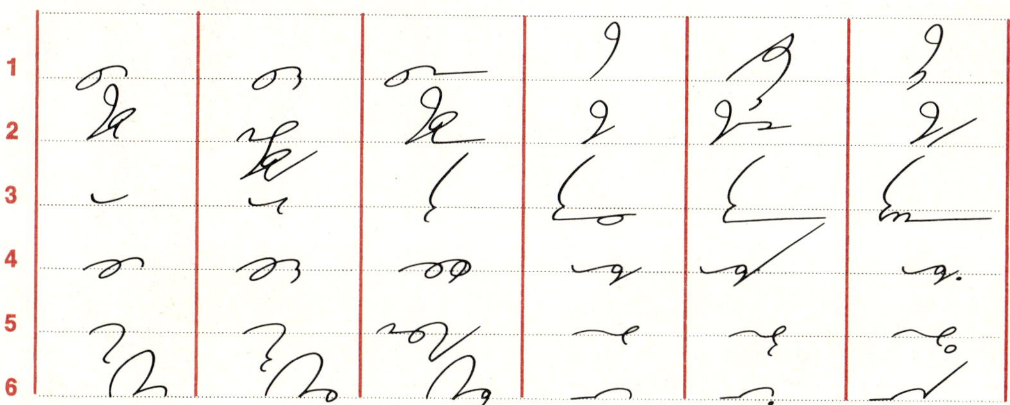

1 Acknowledge, acknowledges, acknowledgment; advantage, disadvantages, advantageous.

2 Advertise, unadvertised, advertisement; after, afternoon, afterward.

3 Are-our-hour, ours-hours; business, businessman, businessmen, businesswoman.

4 Character, characters, characterize; request, requested, requesting.

5 Company, companies, unaccompanied; correspond-correspondence, corresponds, correspondingly.

6 Difficult, difficulty, difficulties; enclose, enclosing, enclosed.

Building Transcription Skills

341 Business Vocabulary Builder

Common Market Group of European nations bonded together by agreement to conduct international trade as a single nation.

gateway International route of entry.

striving Working diligently.

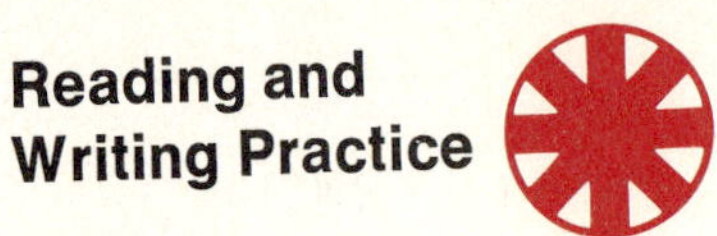

Reading and Writing Practice

342 Brief-Form Letter

healthy

intro

suc·cess·ful

and o

ar·ea

intro

de·scrib·ing

if

nc

prompt·ly

[140]

343

mod·ern

intro

ser

intro

eco·nom·i·cal

and o

well-trained

hyphenated before noun

[123]

[90]

344

ap

Transcribe: July 15

15

as

striv·ing

won

intro

vi·cin·i·ty

when

ges·ture

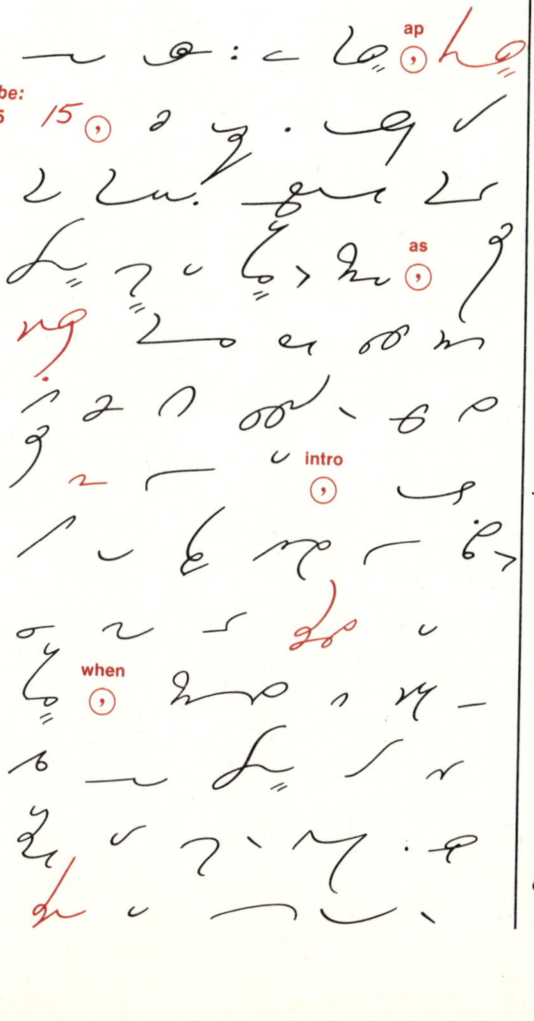

345

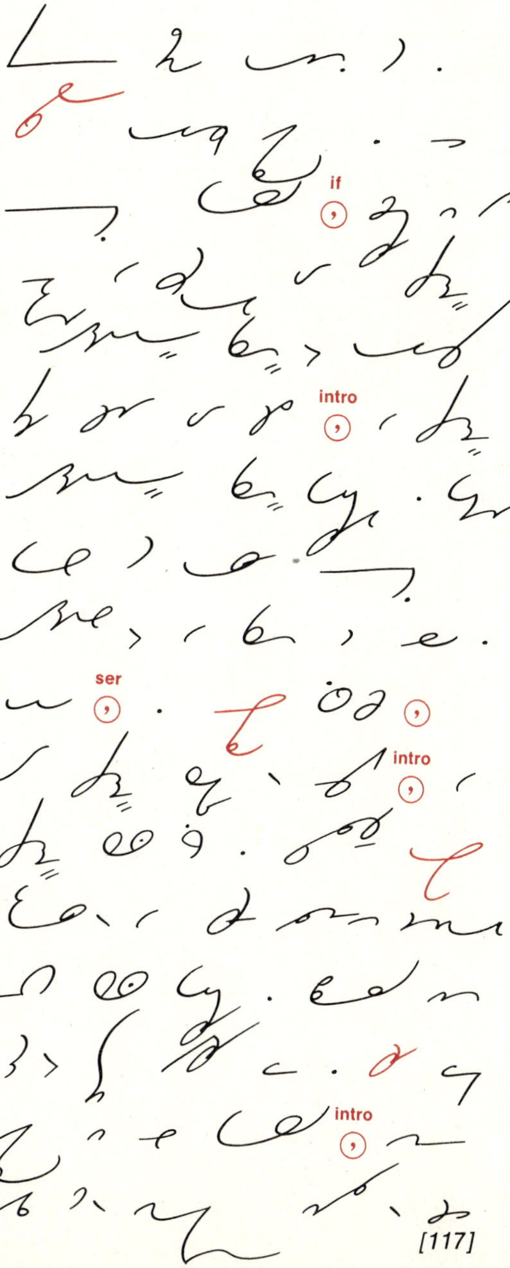

ide·al

if

intro

ser

ma·jor

intro

la·bor

site

intro

[117]

346

qual·i·ty

par

,

,

pol·lu·tion

intro

,

if

,

fur·ther

[141]

347 **Transcription Quiz** For you to supply: 5 commas—1 comma *as* clause, 1 comma introductory, 2 commas parenthetical, 1 comma *if* clause; 1 missing word.

25

[109]

interoffice memorandum

To	Richard W. Macy	From	James T. Barnes
Dept. or Pub.	Editorial	Dept. or Pub.	Sales
Floor or Branch	25	Floor and Ext. or Branch	25
Subject	Manuscript Evaluation	Date	October 7, 197-

When I was in New York recently, I learned of a manuscript for a modern, up-to-date book entitled <u>Self-Teaching Course in Typing</u>. It occurred to me that <u>Self-Teaching Course in Typing</u> would be a fine addition to our self-improvement and self-study series. Under the circumstances I asked the author to submit the manuscript to us, which he has done.

I assume you will want to examine this manuscript yourself to see whether it meets our specifications. Accordingly, I am transmitting it to you along with the author's letter, which is self-explanatory.

J. T. B.

JTB:CS
Enclosure

Interoffice Memorandum

LESSON 

Building Phrasing Skill

348 USEFUL BUSINESS-LETTER PHRASES

If

One of

Ago

Miscellaneous

1 If you, if you are, if you can, if we, if we are, if we can, if you will, if it is, if this is.
2 One of the, one of them, one of our, one of those, one of the most, one of the best.
3 Days ago, weeks ago, months ago, minutes ago, years ago, hours ago.
4 I hope, I hope you are, we hope you will, to me, to do, to make, your order.

349 GEOGRAPHICAL EXPRESSIONS

1 Cincinnati, Princeton, Allentown, Jackson, Tampa, Orlando.
2 Mississippi, Maine, Kansas, Kentucky, Hawaii, Alaska.

Building Transcription Skills

350 SIMILAR-WORDS DRILLS ■ past, passed

past (*noun*) A former time.

He worked here in the *past.*

past (*adjective*) Just gone; just elapsed.

The *past* year was a good one.

passed Moved along; went by; transferred.

He *passed* your request on to me.

351 Business Vocabulary Builder

distressed Worried.

crating Packing in wooden cases.

depot Transportation or shipping terminal.

Reading and Writing Practice

352 Phrase Letter

when

ap

crates

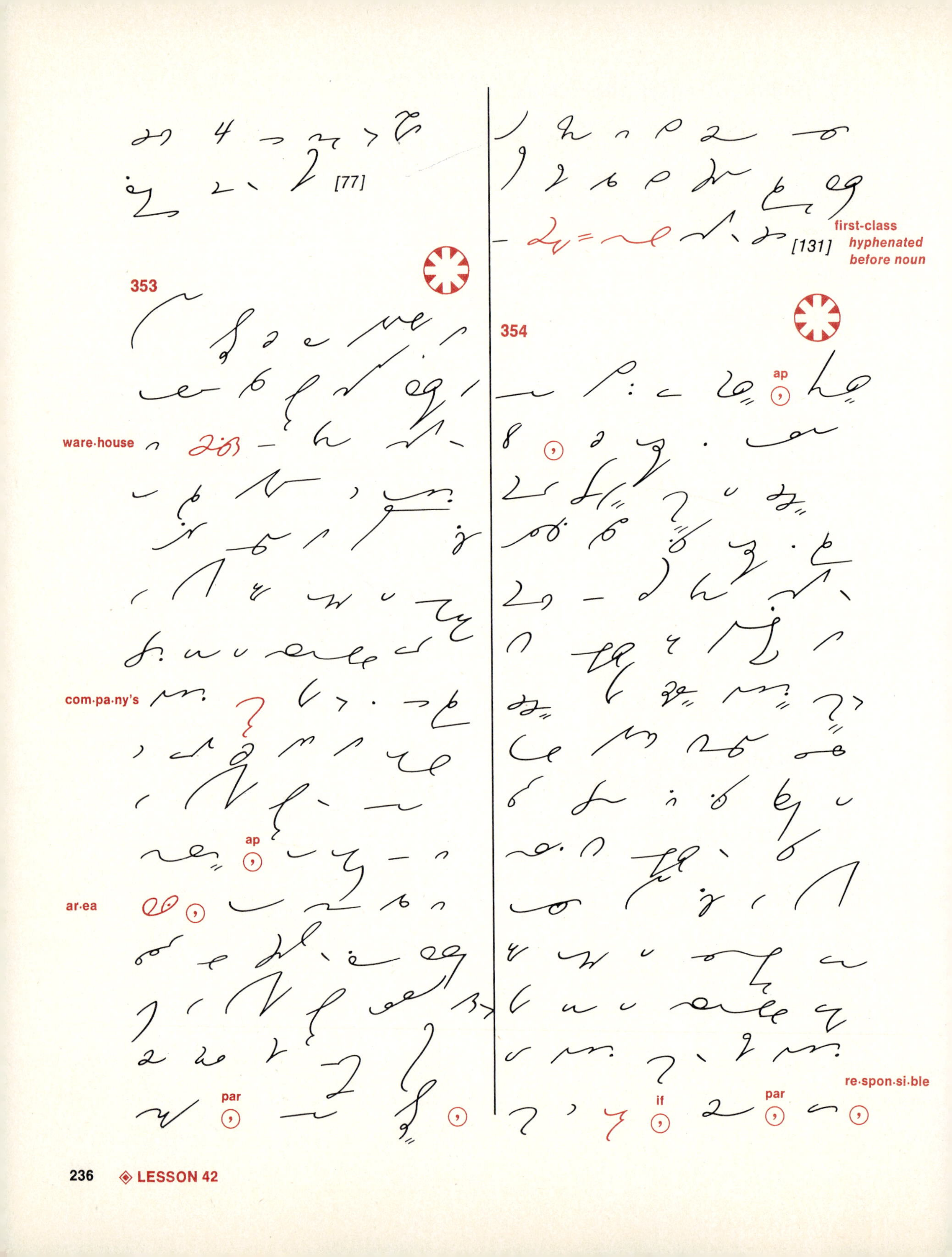

[77]

[131]

first-class hyphenated before noun

353

ware·house

com·pa·ny's

ap

ar·ea

par

354

ap

if

par

re·spon·si·ble

[144]

355

ap

passed

conj

past

due

intro

oc·ca·sions

Transcribe: 2 percent

if

and o

co·op·er·a·tive

if

fur·ther

nc

[150]

356

2543

Transcribe: No. 2543

as

intro

re·or·der

[67]

357 Transcription Quiz For you to supply: 4 commas—1 comma introductory, 1 comma conjunction, 2 commas series; 2 missing words.

[107]

■ *The girl who stands out head and shoulders above the drones is the one who shows that she can assume responsibility—that she can think for herself and that she possesses the initiative to work out problems on her own.*

Developing Word-Building Power

358 WORD FAMILIES

-ic

1

-lution

2

Ind-

3

-rence

4

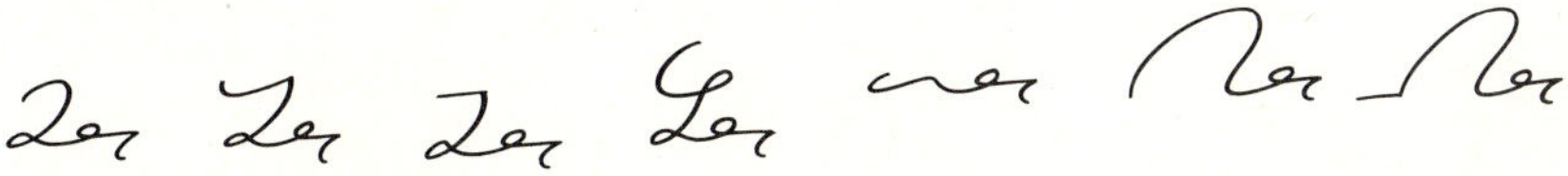

1 Topic, basic, specific, graphic, logic, magic, classic.
2 Solution, pollution, disillusion, revolution, evolution, resolution.
3 Industry, indication, independent, indecision, induce, indispensable, index.
4 Conference, reference, inference, preference, occurrence, difference, indifference.

Building Transcription Skills

359 SPELLING FAMILIES ■ -ious, -eous

Another spelling trap is the ending that is pronounced *e-ous.* In most words in the English language, this combination of sounds is spelled *ious,* but there are just enough words in which it is spelled *eous* that you should stop to think each time you transcribe a word ending with that sound.

Words Ending in -ious

var·i·ous	**te·dious**	**stu·di·ous**
se·ri·ous	**gra·cious**	**in·dus·tri·ous**
ob·vi·ous	**pre·vi·ous**	**cu·ri·ous**

Words Ending in -eous

cour·te·ous	**spon·ta·ne·ous**	**si·mul·ta·neous**
ad·van·ta·geous	**gor·geous**	**mis·cel·la·neous**

360 Business Vocabulary Builder

biannual Occurring twice a year.

literature Pamphlets, booklets, etc.

graciously Warmly; courteously.

Reading and Writing Practice

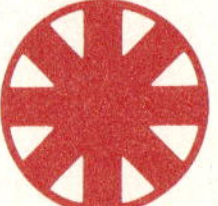

361

var·i·ous

as

bi·an·nu·al

nonr

conj

ser

prin·ci·ples

best-known *hyphenated before noun*

and o

intro

ad·van·ta·geous·ly

if

[200]

362

guide·lines

intro

ap

As·so·ciates

as

se·ri·ous

intro

Ecol·o·gy

if

fur·ther

[123]

363

en·vi·ron·ment

intro

ref·er·ence

ap

avail·able

if

[109]

ap

gra·cious·ly

ap·pli·ca·tion

if

[124]

364

conj

365

when

nc

intro

mod·el

when

Transcribe:
$18

ap

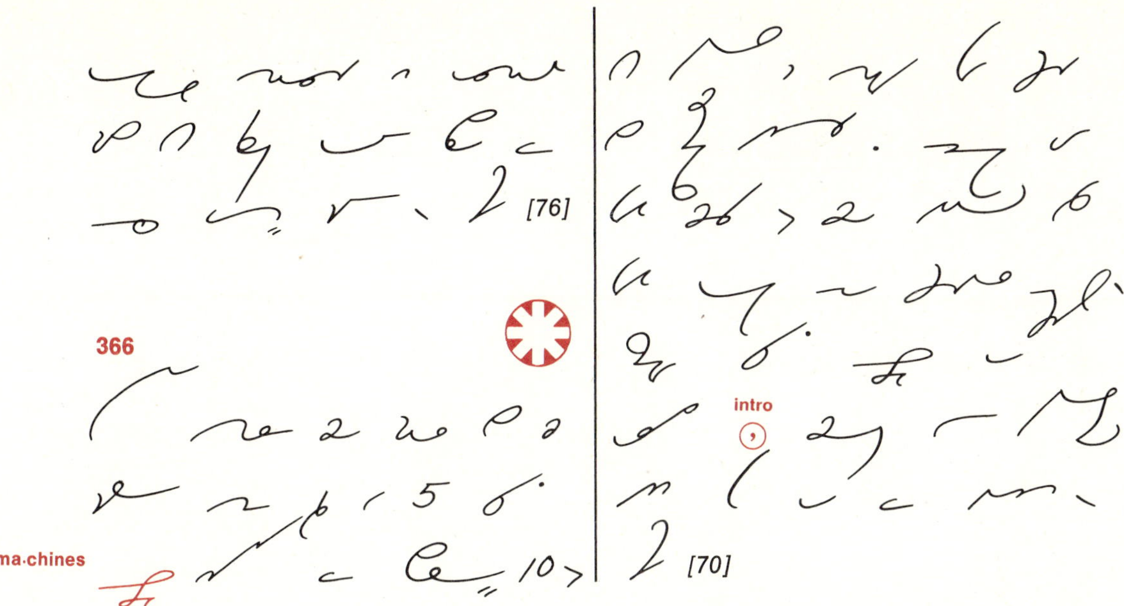

367 Transcription Quiz For you to supply: 7 commas—4 commas parenthetical, 2 commas apposition, 1 comma *and* omitted; 1 missing word.

[125]

LESSON 

LESSON 44

Developing Word-Building Power

368 WORD BEGINNINGS AND ENDINGS

-cal, -cle

Circum-

Sub-

-sume, -sumption

1 Practical, critical, radical, chemically, article, particle.

2 Circumstance, circumstances, circumstantial, circumnavigate, circumscribe, circumscribed, circumvent.

3 Subscriber, submitting, substantially, subway, sublet, sublease, suburban.

4 Consume, consumer, consumption, presume, presumption, presumed, resume.

Building Transcription Skills

369 GRAMMAR CHECKUP ■ preposition at the end of a sentence

It is considered good practice to avoid ending a sentence with a preposition.

not good

Please give me the address of the building you work in.

better

Please give me the address of the building in which you work.

However, if the application of this general rule would result in an awkward or stilted construction, the sentence may end with a preposition.

He was an easy person to work with.
What is this for?

370 **Business Vocabulary Builder**

summarized Abridged; summed up.

deadline Closing date.

depict Represent in a picture; describe.

Reading and Writing Practice

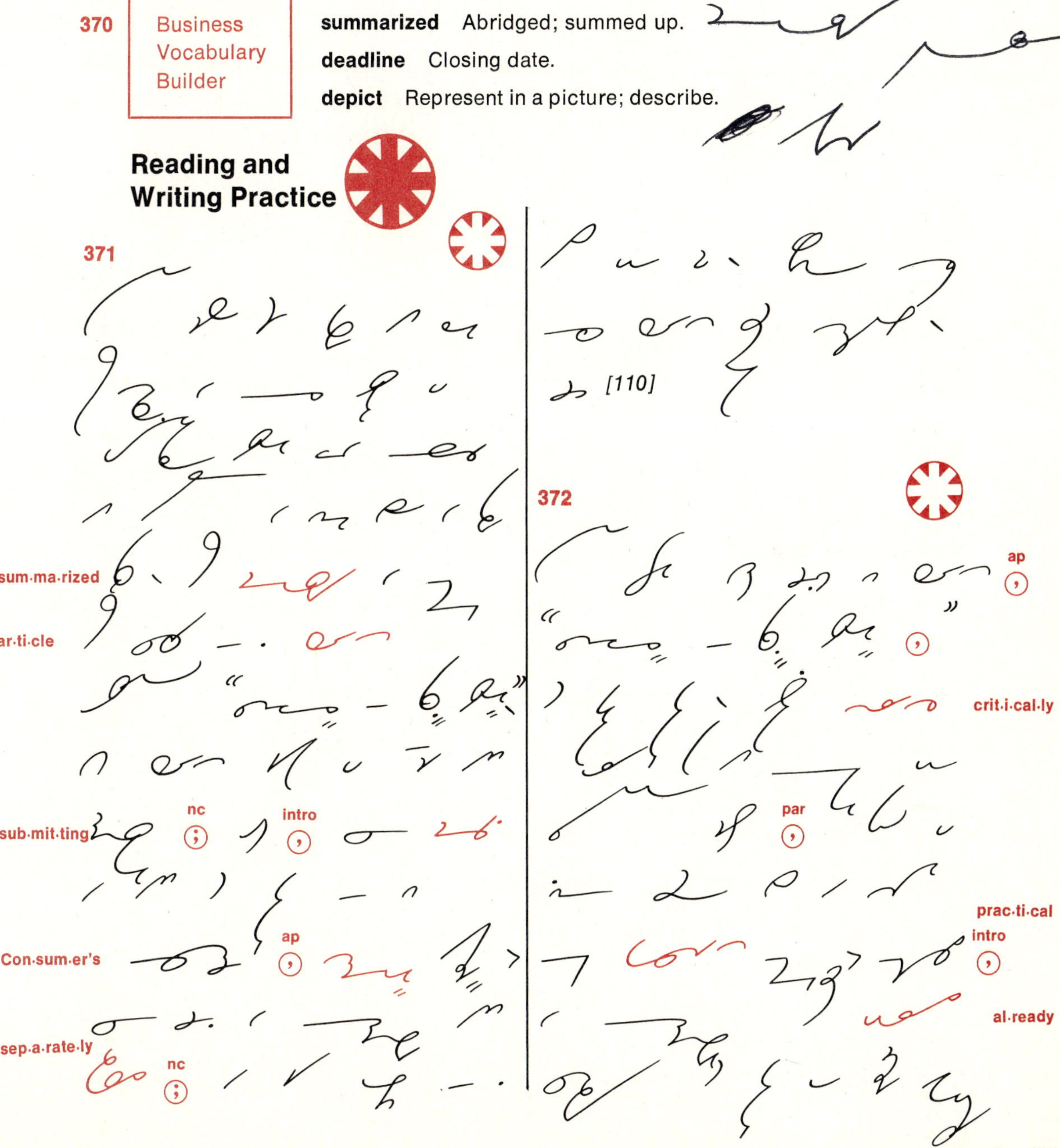

intro

par

when

sub·scrib·ers

[153]

373

Col·i·se·um

ser

conj

intro

cloth·ing

post·age-paid *hyphenated before noun*

[146]

374

intro

conj

year's

[110]

375

safe·ty

conj

aids

intro

won

and o

col·or·ful

de·pict

if

[143]

376

ap

ap

Transcribe: No. 1181

if

intro

conj

[93]

377 Transcription Quiz For you to supply: 8 commas—4 commas parenthetical, 2 commas apposition, 1 comma *if* clause, 1 comma conjunction; 1 missing word.

[127]

LESSON 

Developing Word-Building Power

378 SHORTHAND VOCABULARY BUILDER

W, Sw

Wh

Ng

Md, Mt

1 Widespread, walls, Washington, west, swamped, sweat, swimmer, swear.
2 White, whale, wheat, whether, whisper, wheel, whim, overwhelm.
3 Single, along, wing, long, strong, length.
4 Boomed, named, famed, blamed, framed, promptly, empty.

Building Transcription Skills

379 Business Vocabulary Builder

alterations Changes.
acoustics Quality of sound.
adorned Decorated.
motifs Themes; styles.

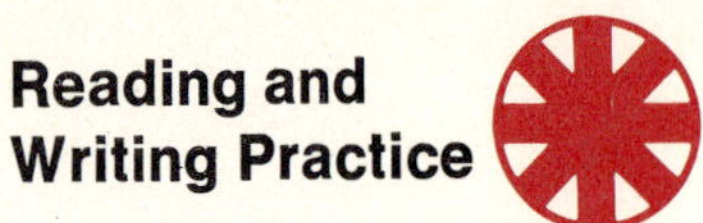

Reading and Writing Practice

380 History of the Capitol Building

Cap·i·tol

par

ea·gle

coun·cils

con·cep·tion

intro

Designs for the

sum

par

par

nonr

to·ward

ap

Hal·let

Thorn·ton

su·per·vise

com·ple·tion

The Capitol

par

un·fore·seen

shin·gle

ser

chan·de·lier

ceil·ing

1812

par

be·fit·ted

era

Then war

1814

par

sur·prise

when

peace

nonr

La·trobe

mo·tifs

Not long

re·al·ized

intro

13

par

1851

ser

jos·tled

seams

conj

nonr

busy

par

[590]

LETTER

381

18

10

when

[47]

10 Office Equipment and Supplies

LESSON 46

Developing Word-Building Power

382 BRIEF FORMS AND DERIVATIVES

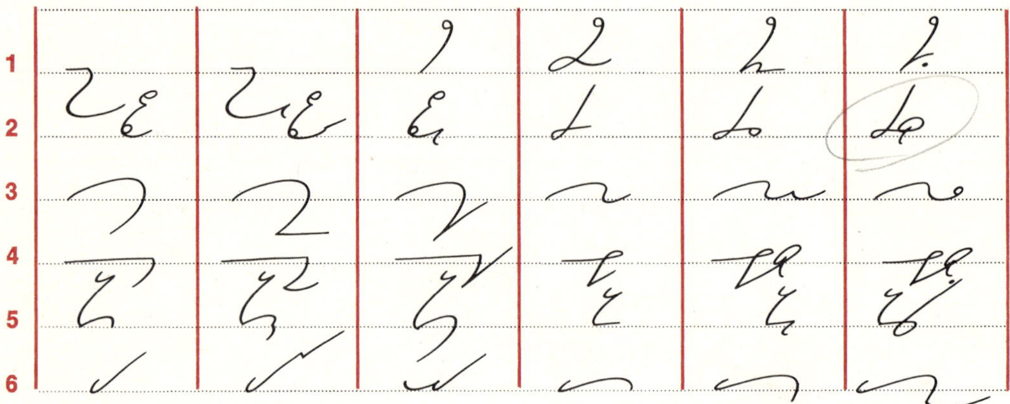

1 Envelope, envelopes; ever-every, everywhere, everyone, everything.

2 Experience, experienced, experiences; general, generally, generalize.

3 Govern, government, governed; great, greater, greatly.

4 Manufacture, manufacturer, manufactured; merchant, merchandise, merchandising.

5 Object, objects, objective; opinion, opinions, opinionated.

6 Order, ordered, reorder; organize, organization, organizational.

Building Transcription Skills

383 Business Vocabulary Builder

diverted Directed away from.

disrupted Put into disorder.

descends Comes down.

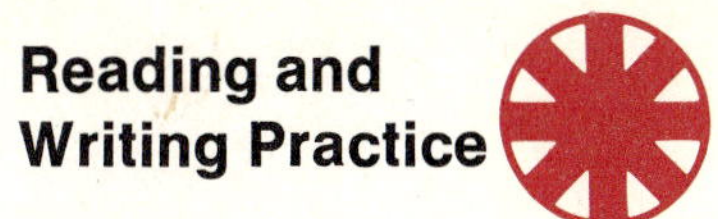

Reading and Writing Practice

384 Brief-Form Letter

out·put

par

par

Transcribe: 5 o'clock

de·scends

piece

par

if

weight

intro

[124]

385

ser

pre·par·ing

top-qual·i·ty *hyphenated before noun*

par

than

max·i·mum

and o

qual·i·ty

if

[141]

386

intro

conj

dis·rupt·ed

par

161

ser

pieces

Transcribe: 5,000

40

161

10

ten-day *hyphenated before noun*

intro

sim·ply

[171]

387

Transcribe: $200

wor·ries

par

simply

nc

re·pair

if

cr

[155]

388

re·lieved

com·pa·ny's

if

ser

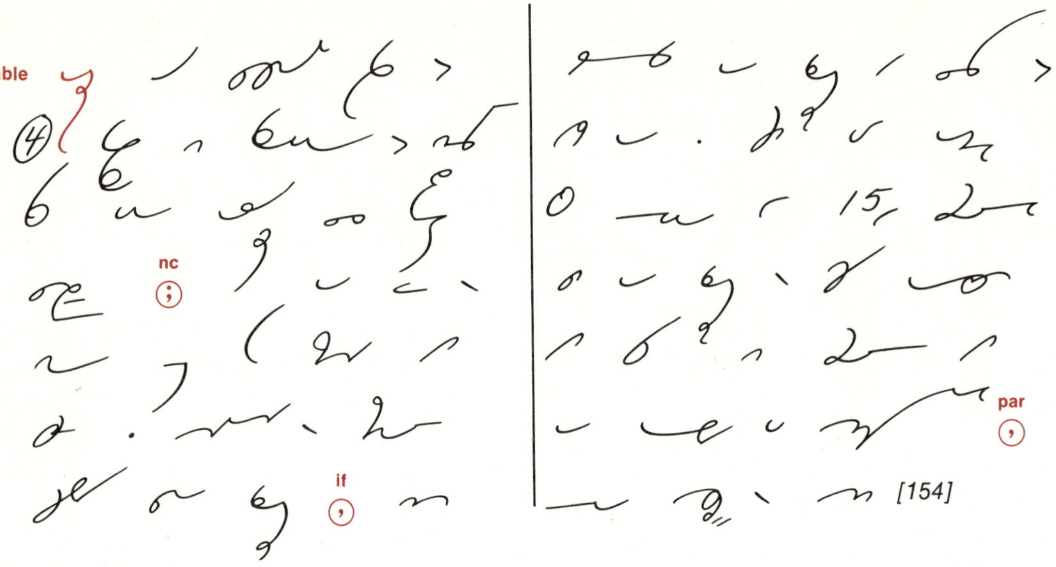

re·ceiv·able

(4)

nc ;

if ,

par ,

[154]

389 Transcription Quiz For you to supply: 6 commas—2 commas series, 2 commas *when* clause, 2 commas *if* clause; 2 missing words.

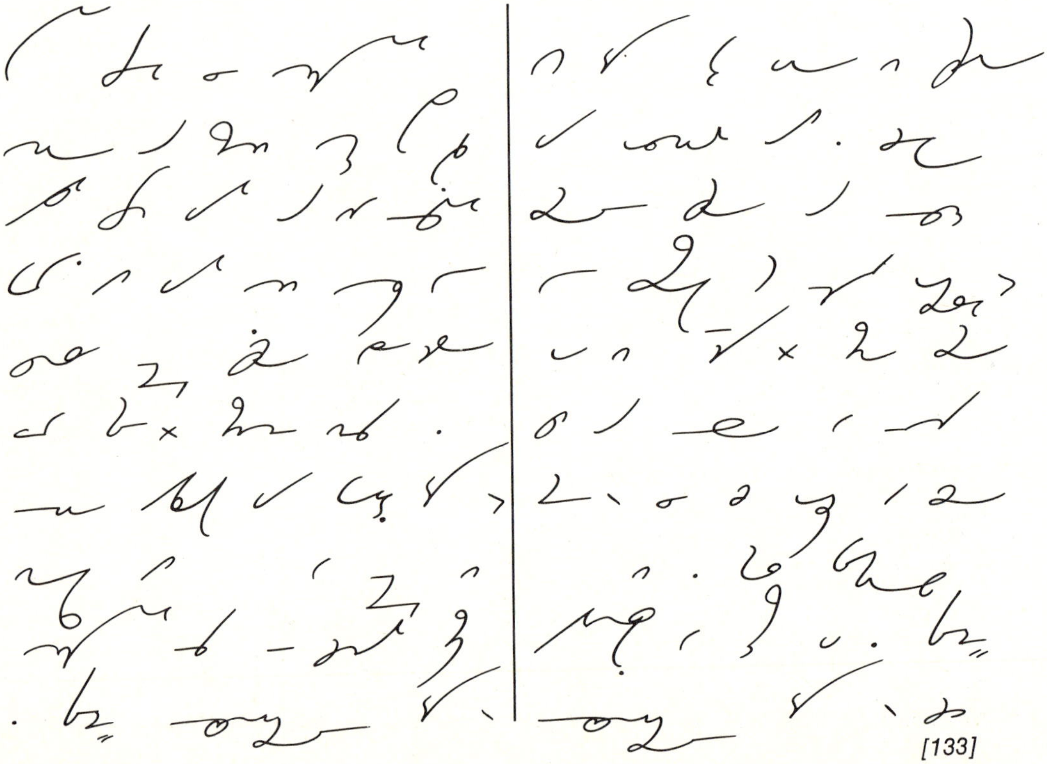

[133]

LESSON 

Lesson 47

Building Phrasing Skill

390 USEFUL BUSINESS-LETTER PHRASES

That

Several

Want

Every

1 That is, that is not, that the, that they, as that, is that, that have, that have not, that will be.

2 Several days ago, several months, several months ago, several times, several other, several others.

3 You want, if you want, we want, I wanted, who want, she wants, do you want, they want.

4 Every month, every way, every day, every other, every minute, every one of the.

391 GEOGRAPHICAL EXPRESSIONS

1 Danville, Knoxville, Jacksonville, Nashville, Brownsville, Louisville.

2 New Hampshire, Louisiana, Maryland, Michigan, Nebraska, Nevada, Massachusetts.

Building Transcription Skills

392 SIMILAR-WORDS DRILL ■ real-reel

real Genuine.

The flowers are *real.*

reel Spool.

We used a *reel*-to-*reel* recorder.

393 Business Vocabulary Builder

unique Unlike any other.

flexible Useful in a variety of ways.

optional Not compulsory.

Reading and Writing Practice

394 Phrase Letter

ex·hib·it

ap

par

intro

ap

ser

Transcribe: Model 1818

ex·pen·sive
cal·cu·la·tor

nc
;

[158]

395

choose

well-trained
hyphenated before noun

[141]

396

intro
,

conj
,

than

par

conj

flex·i·ble

par

com·pa·ny's

[138]

397

de·scribes
Transcribe:
Howard 1211

ap

1211

conj

clar·i·ty

ear·phones

re·ceived

when

1211

[154]

398

ser

conj

dis·ap·point·ing

[97]

399 Transcription Quiz For you to supply: 6 commas—2 commas parenthetical, 2 commas series, 1 comma *as* clause, 1 comma *if* clause; 2 missing words.

[154]

Developing Word-Building Power

400 WORD FAMILIES

-point

1

-ary

2

-cation

3

Des-, Dis-

4

1 Point, appoint, appointment, pointless, disappoint, disappointment, reappoint.
2 Secretary, budgetary, library, necessary, temporary, customary.
3 Education, location, communication, application, vacation, indication.
4 Designed, decide, designate, designer, disagree, disseminate.

Building Transcription Skills

401 SPELLING FAMILIES ■ words in which *y* is changed to *i* in the past tense and in the *s* form

ap·ply	**ap·plied**	**ap·plies**
re·ply	**re·plied**	**re·plies**

im·ply	im·plied	im·plies
sup·ply	sup·plied	sup·plies
com·ply	com·plied	com·plies

402 **Business Vocabulary Builder**

defer To put off; to postpone.

prior Before.

letterhead Preprinted business stationery.

Reading and Writing Practice

403

ap

Transcribe: 1502

1502

ap

Transcribe: 9 o'clock

9

ser

par

sup·plies

[110]

404

un·for·tu·nate·ly

ap

intro

nc

intro

li·brary

conj

pur·chas·ing

intro

[124]

405

Transcribe:
27th

27

ap

intro

16-page
hyphenated
before noun

16=

pri·or

if

Black's

[114]

406

if

its

if

de·ci·mal

sec·re·tary's

when

sim·ply

im·pres·sion

intro

when

ser

switch

[187]

407

fire·proof

conj

conj

93,

Transcribe: 93 percent

and o

when

[141]

408 Transcription Quiz For you to supply: 5 commas—3 commas introductory, 1 comma *as* clause, 1 comma *if* clause; 2 missing words.

[143]

LESSON 49

Developing Word-Building Power

409 WORD BEGINNINGS

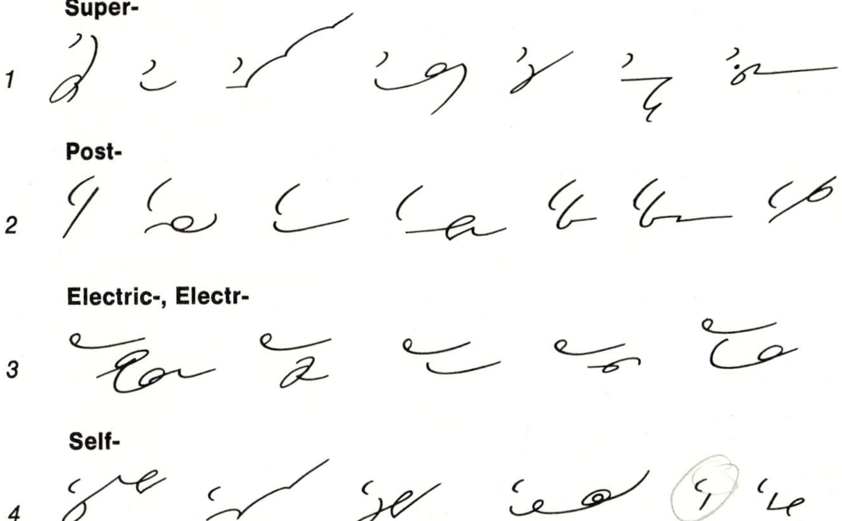

1 Supervise, superior, superintendent, superlative, supersede, superimpose, superhuman.

2 Postage, postcard, postal, postmaster, postpone, postponement, postdate.

3 Electric typewriter, electric wire, electrical, electronic, electroplate.

4 Self-addressed, self-contained, self-satisfied, self-reliant, selfish, selfishness.

Building Transcription Skills

410 COMMON PREFIXES ■ pro-

pro- in many words, *pro* means *before, forward, ahead,* or *future.*

proceed To go ahead.

procedure The process of going ahead.

program A plan for the future.

promote To move ahead.

progress To move ahead; forward movement.

411 Business Vocabulary Builder

compact Small; put together solidly.

ingenious Very clever.

clearinghouse Central agency for collecting, classifying, and distributing information.

Reading and Writing Practice

412

Su·pe·ri·or

ap

Transcribe: $200

fea·tures

intro

intro

su·per·vi·sors

per·son·nel

intro

[180]

413

sec·re·taries

if

par

when

than

piece

ser

whole

conj

intro

sam·ple

[153]

414

1776

42

Transcribe:
42 Street

nc

in·ge·nious

pro·ce·dures

ap

well-qual·i·fied
hyphenated
before noun

ser

cr

[128]

415

nc

de·scribed

Transcribe:
No. 1161

and o

self-con·tained

as

[146]

416

yes·ter·day's

if

ser

suc·cess·ful·ly

intro

nc

intro

con·se·quent·ly

conj

intro

[131]

417 Transcription Quiz For you to supply: 8 commas—4 commas apposition, 1 comma *when* clause, 2 commas parenthetical, 1 comma introductory; 1 missing word.

13

[102]

Developing Word-Building Power

418 SHORTHAND VOCABULARY BUILDER

Ēa, Ĭa

1

-tition, Etc.

2

Oi

3

Ya, Ye

4

1 Area, create, initiative, brilliant, miniature, appreciate, negotiate.

2 Condition, addition, commissioned, station, edition, quotation, permission.

3 Noise, voice, employ, invoice, appoint, disappoint, royal.

4 Yard, yarn, Yale, yellow, yield, yes, yelling.

Building Transcription Skills

419 Business Vocabulary Builder

drab State of being colorless.

clusters Small groups.

distracting Disturbing; taking attention away from.

skeptical Doubtful.

420 Office Landscaping

ser

over·grown

when

ba·si·cal·ly

intro

per·son's

drab·ness

ser

when

Many

met·al

ser

con·cept

intro

intro

crit·i·cal·ly

ser

col·or

intro

ar·eas

Sound control

well-land·scaped
hyphenated before noun

ser

conj

breaking

intro

Transcribe: 30 percent

20 30,

skeptical

par

[330] —Adapted from *Today's Secretary*

421 Secretarial Work

primarily

nc

glamorous

par

company's

intro

firsthand

nc

intro

intro

ser

crit·i·cism

Personal Conduct.

intro

par

ap·pear·ance

fac·tor

conj

[280]

LETTERS

422

re·fur·nish

intro

nonr

24

24

if

in·te·ri·or

conj

24

[109]

423

scan·ning

first-class hyphenated before noun

up to date no noun, no hyphen

intro

if

64-page hyphenated before noun

ap

intro

when

[161]

424

intro

intro

intro

par

Transcribe: 10 percent

[100]

11 Personnel

Developing Word-Building Power

425 BRIEF FORMS AND DERIVATIVES

1 Over, overcome, overcame; part, depart, parted.

2 Present, presentation, presented; probable, probably, probability.

3 Progress, progressed, progressive; publish-publication, unpublished, publishing.

4 Recognize, recognizes, recognition; question, questionable, questioned.

5 Request, requested, requesting; satisfy-satisfactory, satisfying, dissatisfied.

6 Send, sends, sender; short, shortcomings, shortly.

Building Transcription Skills

426 Business Vocabulary Builder

appealing Attractive.

analyze Consider very carefully; check completely.

complimentary Free.

eligible Qualified for.

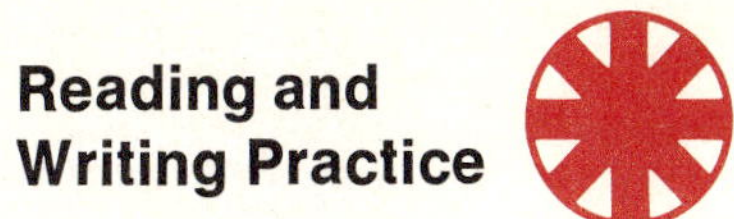

Reading and Writing Practice

427 Brief-Form Letter

[133]

cli·ents

ser

years'

conj

intro

ap·peal·ing

428

em·ploy·ees

if

ap

ap

ex·pe·ri·ence

an·a·lyze

Smith's

out·sid·er's

ser

if

reap

com·pli·men·ta·ry

par

[158]

429

ap

well-planned
hyphenated before noun

25

ap

trea·sur·er

25,

Transcribe:
25 percent

[128]

430

its

rec·om·men·da·tion

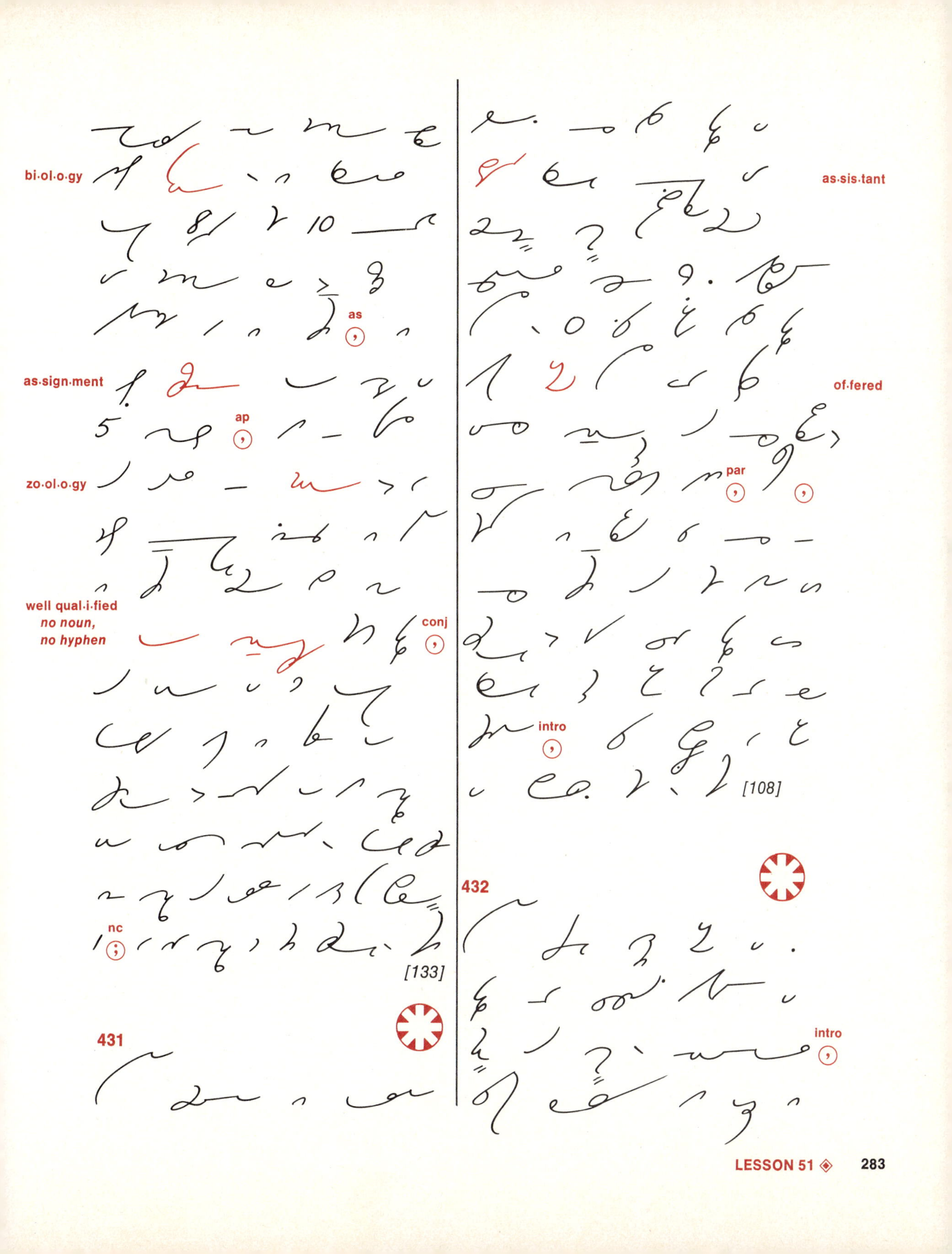

bi·ol·o·gy

as

as·sign·ment

ap

zo·ol·o·gy

well qual·i·fied
no noun,
no hyphen

conj

nc

[133]

431

as·sis·tant

of·fered

par

intro

[108]

432

intro

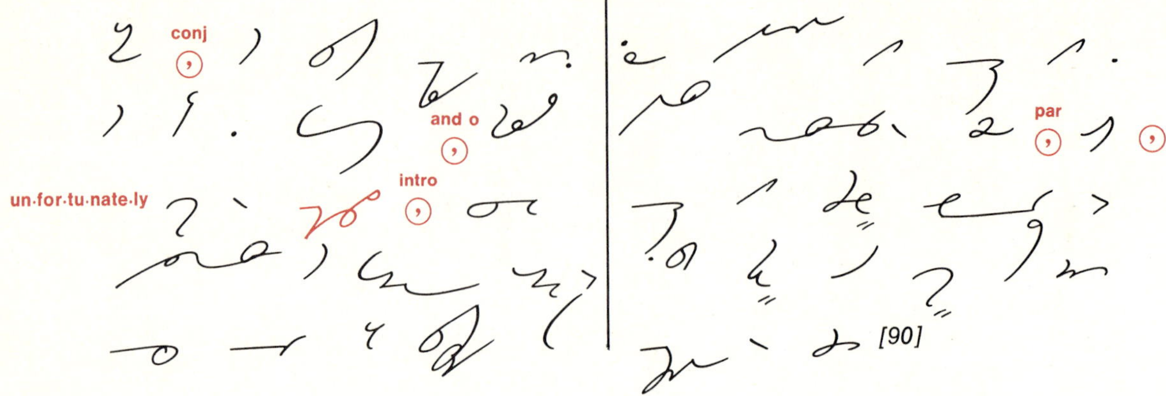

433 Transcription Quiz For you to supply: 7 commas—2 commas conjunction, 1 comma *and* omitted, 1 comma introductory, 2 commas series, 1 comma *if* clause; 2 missing words.

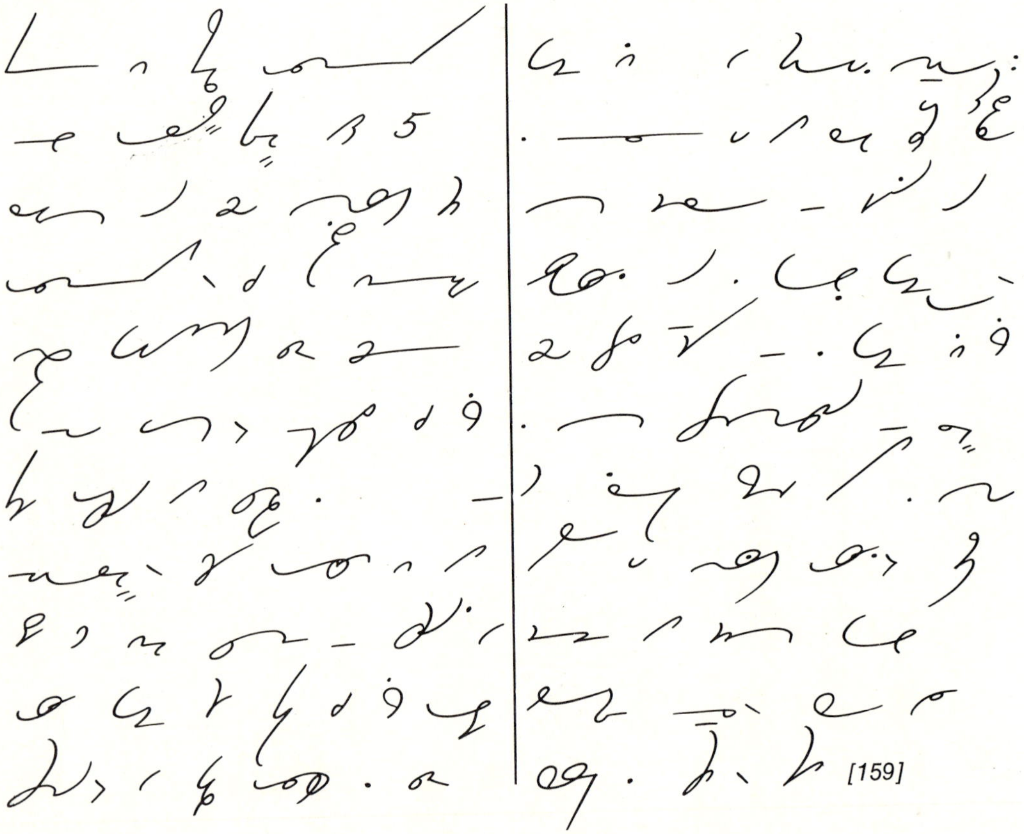

[159]

Building Phrasing Skill

434 USEFUL BUSINESS-LETTER PHRASES

Of

Us

You

Hope

1 Of the, of your, of which, of them, of that, of these, of our, of their, of this, of those.

2 For us, by us, from us, on us, with us, gave us, give us, inform us.

3 You are, you aren't, you did, you didn't, you wouldn't, you have, you haven't, you will.

4 I hope, I hope you are, I hope you will, we hope, we hope you are, we hope you will, we hope you will be, we hope you will be able.

435 GEOGRAPHICAL EXPRESSIONS

1 Detroit, New York, Syracuse, Milwaukee, San Antonio, Buffalo.

2 North Dakota, South Dakota, Oklahoma, Tennessee, Vermont, Wyoming.

Building Transcription Skills

436 SIMILAR-WORDS DRILL ■ prominent, permanent

prominent Standing out; noted.

He played a *prominent* part in the meeting.

permanent Lasting; not subject to change.

He will make his *permanent* home in New York.

437 Business Vocabulary Builder

inducted Admitted as a member.

initiative Ability to do work without direction.

confirm Verify.

Reading and Writing Practice

438 Phrase Letter

nonr

past

as

Moore's

ad·vice

intro

three-month hyphenated before noun

when

and o

de·pend·able

intro

ap

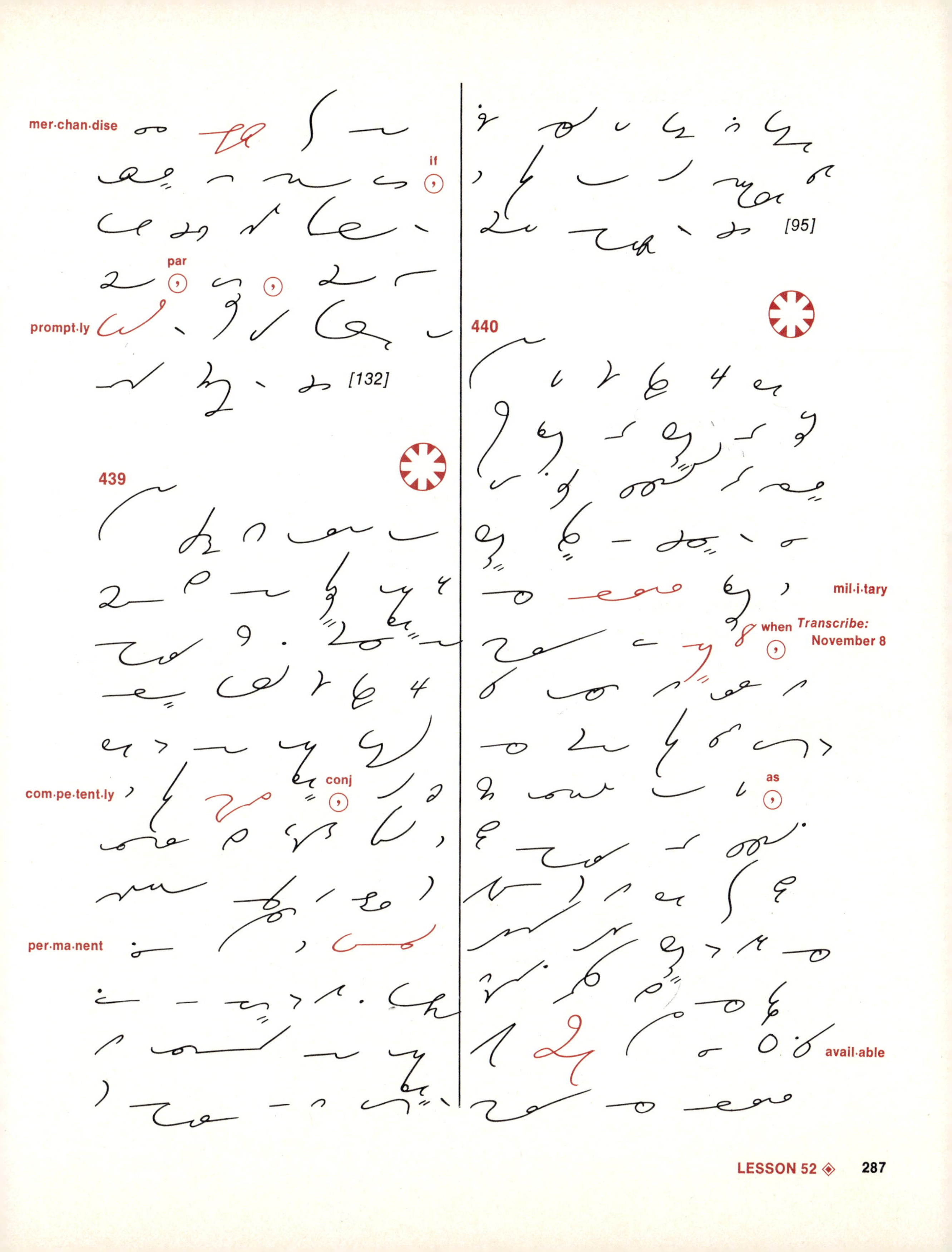

mer·chan·dise

if

par

prompt·ly

[132]

439

com·pe·tent·ly

conj

per·ma·nent

[95]

440

mil·i·tary

when

Transcribe: November 8

as

avail·able

[117]

441

intro

as

intro

nc

con·se·quent·ly

intro

up to date
no noun,
no hyphen

[107]

442

al·ready

per·ma·nent

as

conj

intro

al·ways

ini·tia·tive

prom·i·nent

if

be·lieve

[120]

443

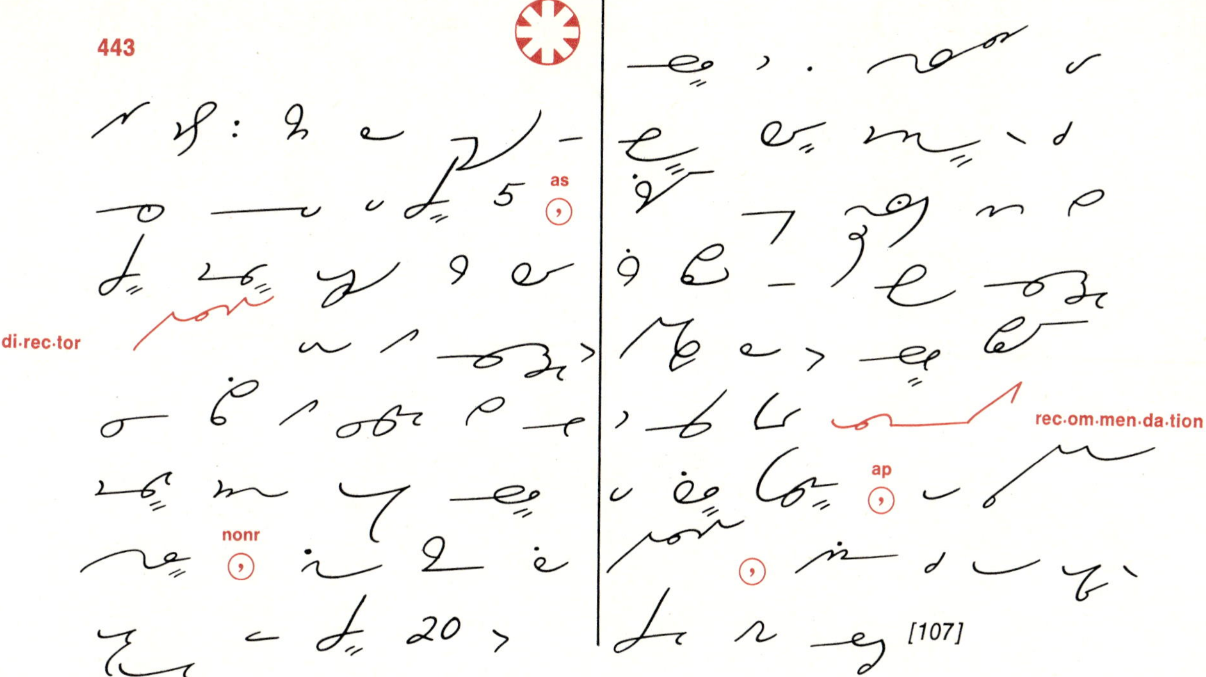

444 Transcription Quiz For you to supply: 5 commas—2 commas series, 1 comma introductory, 2 commas parenthetical; 1 missing word.

[106]

Developing Word-Building Power

445 WORD FAMILIES

-olve

1

-son

2

-ply

3

Rec-

4

1 Solve, resolve, involve, dissolve, evolve, absolve.
2 Son, person, personal, Jackson, reasonable, comparison, season.
3 Reply, supply, apply, comply, oversupply, misapply.
4 Recommend, recall, reclaim, reconsider, recollect.

Building Transcription Skills

446 COMMON PREFIXES ■ ex-

ex- in a great many words, *ex* means *from, out, out of.*

exhaust To tire out; to run out of.

exceedingly Very; beyond the measure of.

exit A way out.

expand To spread out.

expense A paying out; cost.

exterior The outside of something.

expenditure That which is paid out or used up.

447 **Business Vocabulary Builder**

monotonous Repetitive; dull.

diligent Hardworking.

pharmacists Persons who prepare and dispense medicines.

Reading and Writing Practice

448

En·ter·prises

coun·try's

as

conj

ap

phar·ma·cists

[113]

449

glam·our

if

ser

tem·po·rary

mo·not·o·nous

intro

choose

rea·son·ably

if

col·ors

[156]

450

intro

se·niors

ex·penses

ea·ger

ap

part-time
hyphenated before noun

nonr

ser

120

pleas·ant

and o

re·ply·ing

[175]

451

part time
no noun, no hyphen

nonr

part-time
hyphenated before noun

as

par

past

[103]

452

conj

if

ap

Transcribe:
2 p.m.

fur·ther

[67]

453

law·yer's

if ,

[127]

454 Transcription Quiz For you to supply: 5 commas—3 commas parenthetical, 1 comma *if* clause, 1 comma *and* omitted; 1 missing word.

[123]

LESSON 54

Developing Word-Building Power

455 WORD BEGINNINGS AND ENDINGS

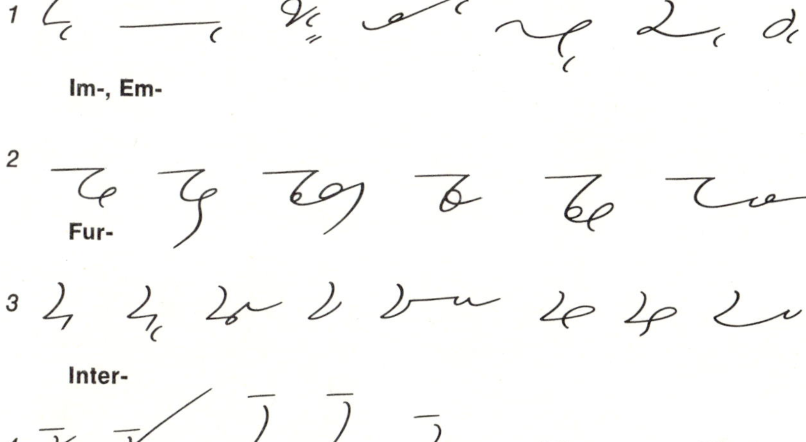

1 Openings, mornings, Hastings, readings, clippings, feelings, sayings.
2 Impress, impressive, imperative, empire, embarrass, employment.
3 Furnish, furnishings, furniture, further, furthermore, furnace, furnaces, furlough.
4 Interest, interested, interview, interviewing, interference, internal, interior.

Building Transcription Skills

456 GRAMMAR CHECKUP ■ may, can

may Implies *permission* or *possibility.*

May *I come for an interview?*

can Implies *ability* or *power.*

I can *do the work.*

457 **Business Vocabulary Builder**

impressive Forceful.

dynamic Powerful.

alleviated Relieved.

Reading and Writing Practice

458

as

as·sis·tant

Transcribe: June 20

im·pres·sive

conj

ap·ply·ing

if

[104]

459

dy·nam·ic

ap

world's

af·fil·i·ated

ser

em·braces

Ten·nes·see

30

trav·el·ing

nc

if

[167]

460

ser

as

well qual·i·fied
no noun,
no hyphen

conj

intro

[107]

461

12

ser

in·ter·views

[57]

462

sec·re·tary's

per·son·nel

ap

month's

fur·ther

if

when

ap·pre·ci·ate

[130]

463

be·gin·ning

intro

ser

intro

ser

store·rooms

intro

ser

[118]

464

per·son·nel

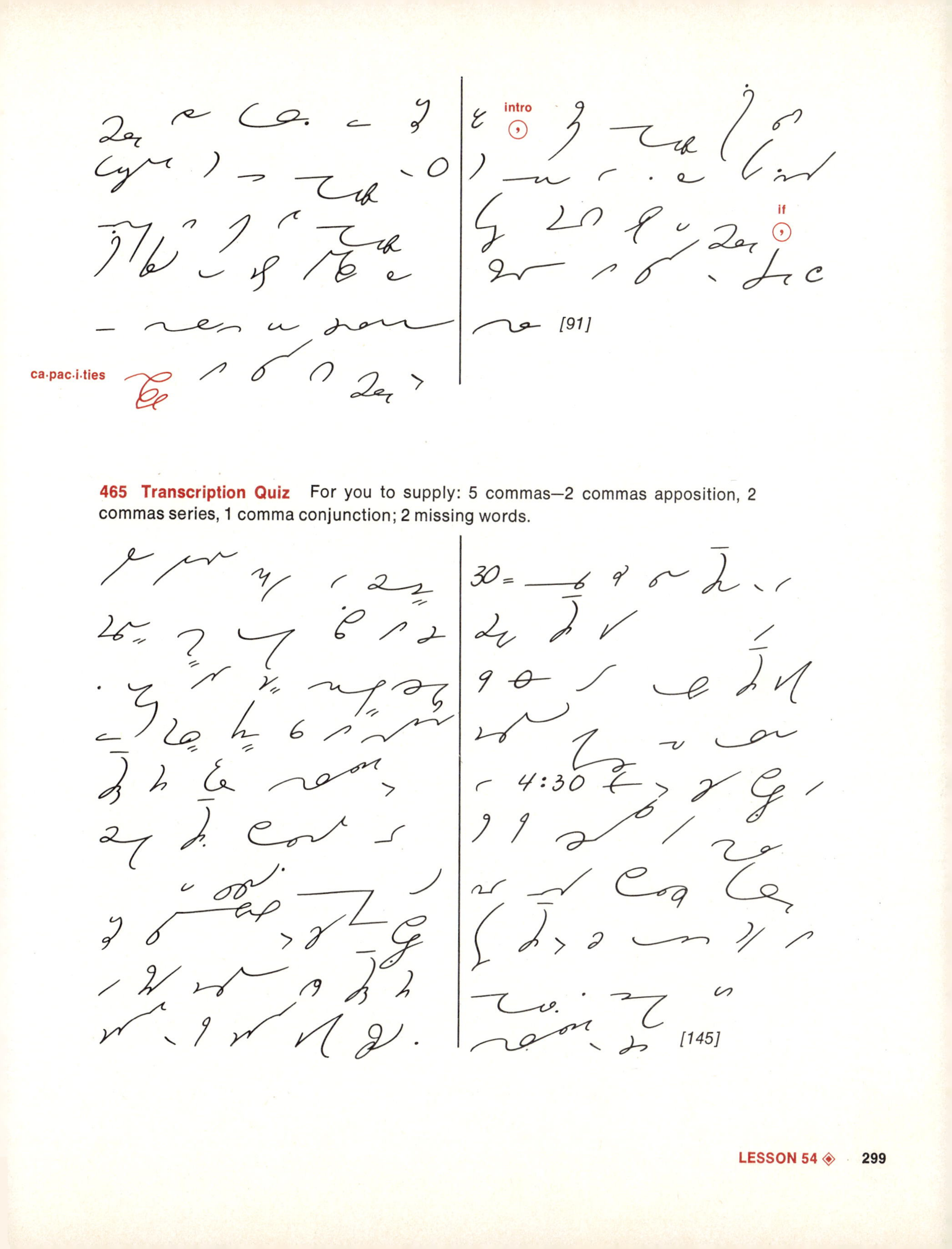

intro

if

[91]

ca·pac·i·ties

465 Transcription Quiz For you to supply: 5 commas—2 commas apposition, 2 commas series, 1 comma conjunction; 2 missing words.

30=

4:30

[145]

Developing Word-Building Power

466 SHORTHAND VOCABULARY BUILDER

-rd

1

Contractions

2

Omission of Vowel Before -tion, Etc.

3

Omission of Short U

4

1 Record, card, prepared, hardest, answered, standard, stared.

2 Haven't, don't, wouldn't, doesn't, shouldn't, couldn't, hasn't, weren't.

3 Conditional, commission, additional, station, admission, donation, omission.

4 Much, comes, summary, budget, luncheon, rushed, done.

Building Transcription Skills

467 Business Vocabulary Builder

referral Source of information.

compilation Collection; listing.

inevitably Certainly.

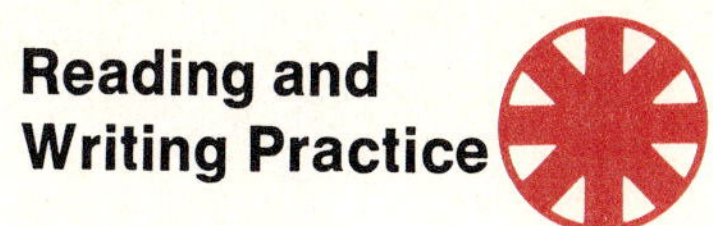

468 The Job Hunt

24-hour *hyphenated before noun*

ex·er·cise

won't

cam·paign

In launching

ca·reer

cal·en·dar

vi·tal

re·fer·ral

intro
per·ma·nent
par
than
if
nc
conj
if
match
[351]
—Adapted from *Today's Secretary*

469 Selling Yourself

com·pe·ti·tion
intro

par
intro
in·ev·i·ta·bly
346
nc
ad
ser
pre·par·ing
when
ser
com·plete·ness
conj

par

qual·i·fi·ca·tions

par

pre·vi·ous

if

You should

intro

if

sub·mit·ting

par

qual·i·fies

intro

[452]

12 Publishing

LESSON 56

Developing Word-Building Power

470 BRIEF FORMS AND DERIVATIVES

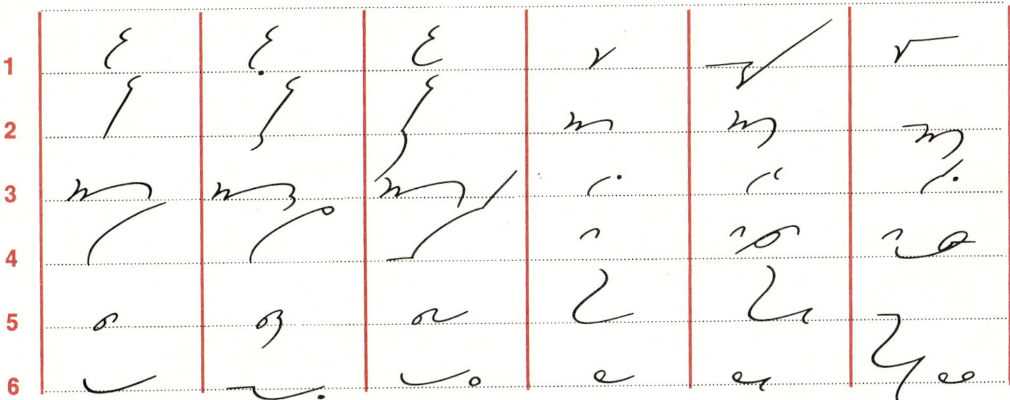

1 Speak, speaking, speaker; state, misstated, statement.

2 Subject, subjects, subjective; success, successful, unsuccessful.

3 Suggest, suggests, suggestion; thank, thanks, thanked.

4 Time, timely, untimed; under, undertake, underline.

5 Use, useful, user; value, values, invaluable.

6 Will-well, unwilling, willingly; were-year, years, yearly.

Building Transcription Skills

471 Business Vocabulary Builder

concise Brief.

electrifying Extremely exciting.

indispensable Necessary.

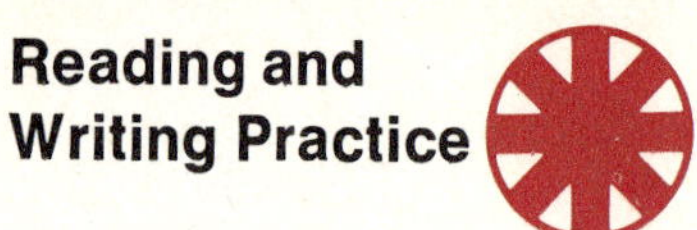

Reading and Writing Practice

472 Brief-Form Letter

To·day's

ap

rec·og·nized

conj

con·cise

and o

thor·ough·ly

if

par

[127]

473

ar·ti·cle

ap

chil·dren's

conj

ar·ea

if

Transcribe:
December 1

[141]

474

ac·cept

conj

[64]

475

gray

if

Bak·er's

ap

Over·head

nc

10= ten-day *hyphenated before noun*

if

nc

if

sim·ply

[137]

476

conj

birth·days

Christ·mas

par

25 conj

ap·proach·ing

Mys·tery

as

and o

elec·tri·fy·ing

if

if

nc

[144]

477 Transcription Quiz For you to supply: 4 commas—1 comma introductory, 1 comma conjunction, 1 comma *if* clause, 1 comma parenthetical; 2 missing words.

[121]

Lesson 57

Building Phrasing Skill

478 USEFUL BUSINESS-LETTER PHRASES

For

Upon

If

Special Phrases

1 For the, for the last, for their, for these, for whom, for his, for it, for many.

2 Upon the, upon which, upon such, upon this, upon you, upon the subject.

3 If you, if you are, if you will, if you can, if we, if we are, if my, if so, if these.

4 Your order, your orders, as soon as, as soon as possible, of course, of course it is, let us, to us.

479 GEOGRAPHICAL EXPRESSIONS

1 Framingham, Nottingham, Buckingham, Lexington, Washington, Arlington.

2 Alabama, Alaska, Arizona, Arkansas, California, Colorado.

Building Transcription Skills

480 SIMILAR-WORDS DRILL ■ addition, edition

addition Something added.

He will make a fine *addition* to our staff.

edition All copies of a publication printed at one time.

I hope you will print my article in the next *edition* of the newspaper.

481 Business Vocabulary Builder

foresee Look into the future.

integrity Complete honesty.

improper Not appropriate.

refuting Challenging; contradicting.

Reading and Writing Practice

482 Phrase Letter

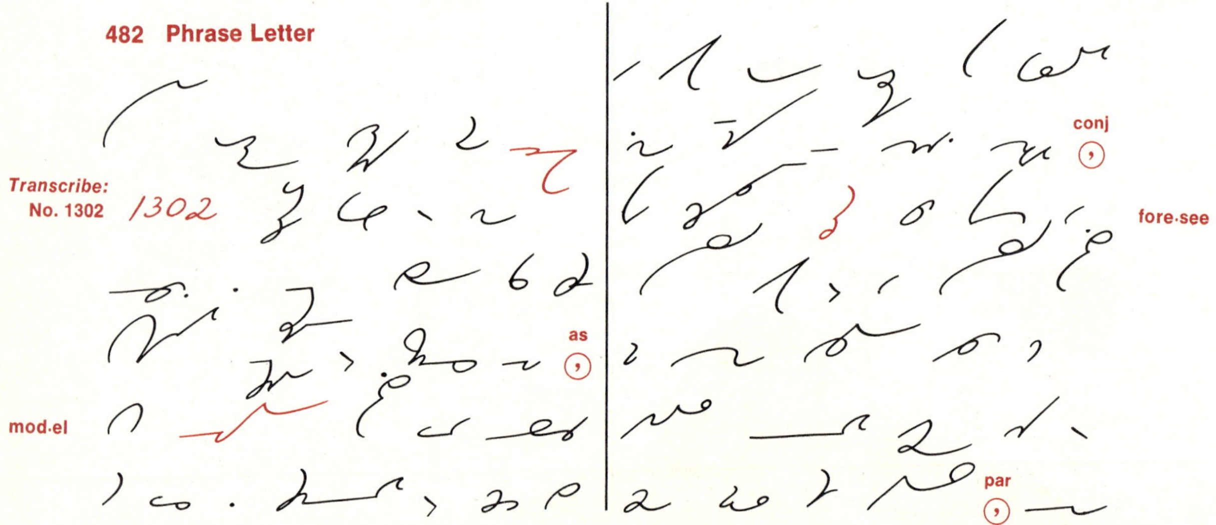

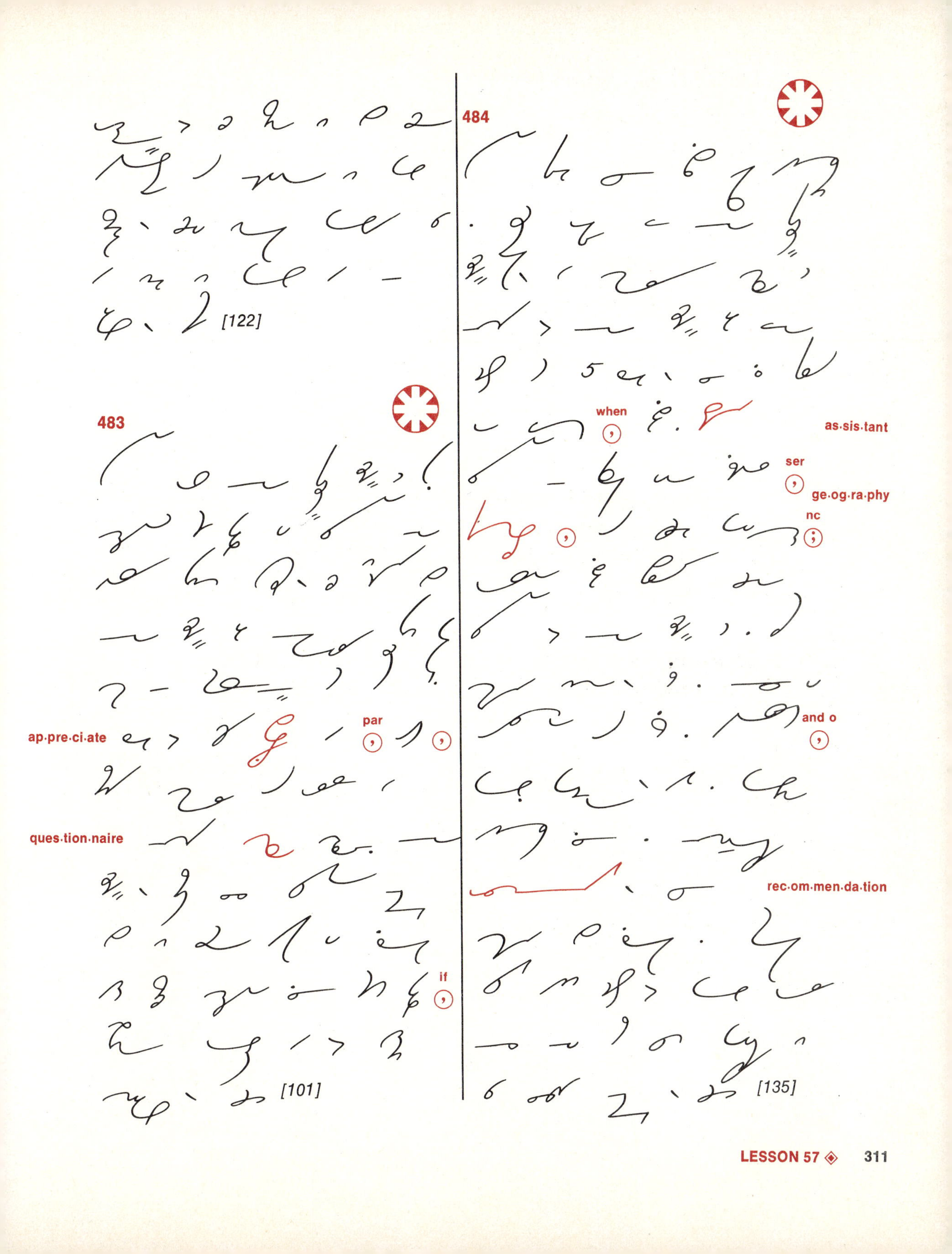

[122]

483

ap·pre·ci·ate

par

ques·tion·naire

if

[101]

484

when

as·sis·tant

ser

ge·og·ra·phy

nc

and o

rec·om·men·da·tion

[135]

485

ap

stud·ied

conj

and o

well-or·ga·nized *hyphenated before noun*

[80]

conj

lan·guage

[121]

486

child's

ser

487

conj

prof·it·ed

us·ers

well-known hyphenated before noun

suit

nc

intro

[140]

488 Transcription Quiz For you to supply: 3 commas—2 commas parenthetical, 1 comma conjunction; 2 missing words.

[118]

LESSON 58

Developing Word-Building Power

489 WORD FAMILIES

-book

1

Comm-

2

-ial

3

-ct

4

1 Book, handbook, textbook, passbook, yearbook, pocketbook, booklet.
2 Comments, committee, community, communication, commercial.
3 Editorial, material, secretarial, managerial, pictorial.
4 Inspect, defect, expect, project, respect, aspect, prospect.

Building Transcription Skills

490 SPELLING FAMILIES ■ -ance, -ence

Words Ending in -ance

guid·ance	**as·sur·ance**	**ac·cor·dance**
as·sis·tance	**ac·cep·tance**	**al·low·ance**

per·for·mance	clear·ance	sub·stance

Words Ending in -ence

con·fi·dence	ab·sence	pref·er·ence
ref·er·ence	si·lence	ev·i·dence
con·fer·ence	neg·li·gence	com·mence

491 Business Vocabulary Builder

aspects Phases; viewpoints.

defective Improperly constructed.

exhaustive Considering all possibilities.

Reading and Writing Practice

492

sec·re·tar·i·al

conj

as·sis·tance

intro

guid·ance

if

con·fer·ence

ap

[109]

493

ref·er·ence

ap

per·for·mance

as

par

if

[101]

[109]

494

495

edi·tion

dis·turbed

ap

Mod·ern

role

ser

ex·haus·tive

intro

par

par

re·me·di·al

par

[130]

496

ap

book·let's

nonr

par

ap·peal

am·bi·tious

wheth·er

if

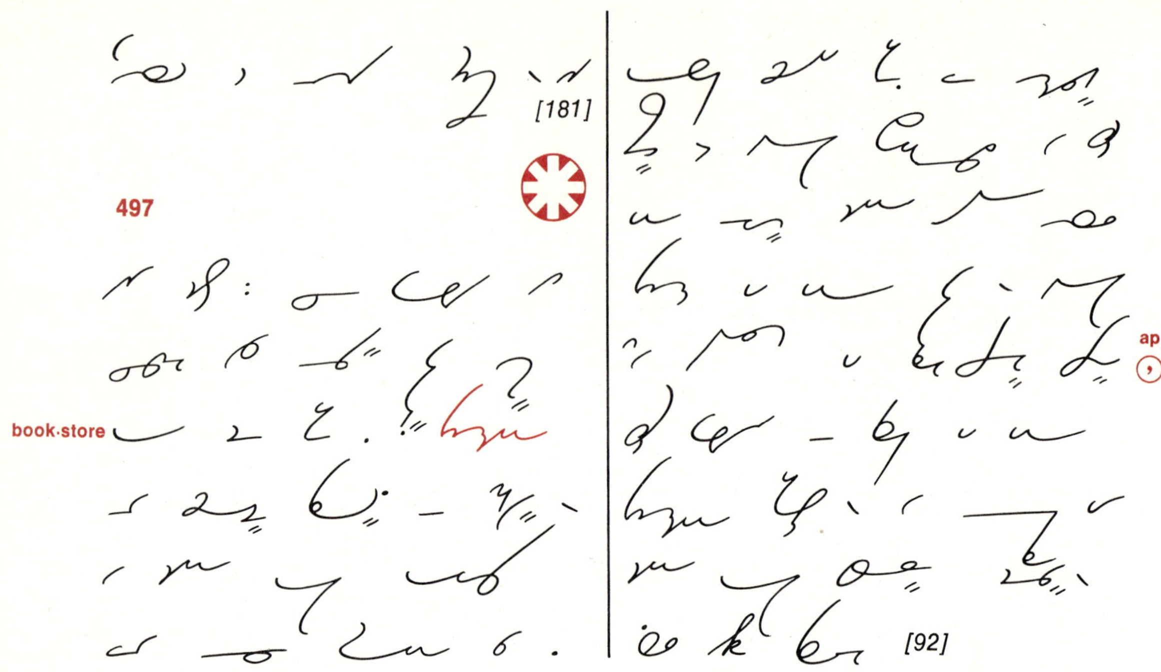

498 Transcription Quiz For you to supply: 6 commas—1 comma *as* clause, 2 commas apposition, 1 comma conjunction, 1 comma *when* clause, 1 comma *if* clause; 2 missing words.

[99]

Developing Word-Building Power

499 WORD ENDINGS

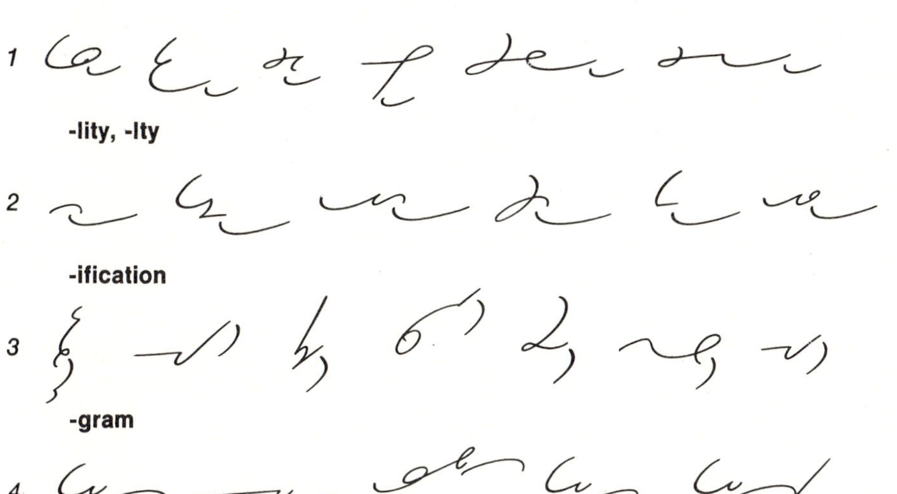

1 Priority, popularity, sincerity, majority, familiarity, similarity.

2 Quality, personality, locality, faculty, penalty, royalty.

3 Specifications, modification, justification, identification, verification, classification, notification.

4 Program, monogram, radiogram, programmer, programmed.

Building Transcription Skills

500 GRAMMAR CHECKUP ■ either, or; neither, nor

The correlative conjunctions *either-or, neither-nor* are usually used in pairs. Do not mix the members of the pairs by using *or* with *neither* or *nor* with *either.*

I must do the work either *today* or *tomorrow.*

Neither *Jane* nor *Alice is here.*

501 Business Vocabulary Builder

backlog A reserve supply.

artwork Such items as pictures, graphs, maps, etc.

formerly At a time in the past. (Do not confuse with *formally,* which means in a stately, grand, or formal manner.)

Reading and Writing Practice

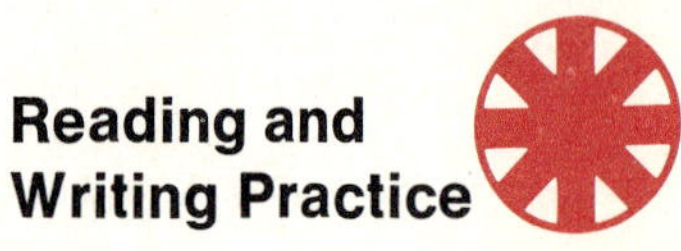

502

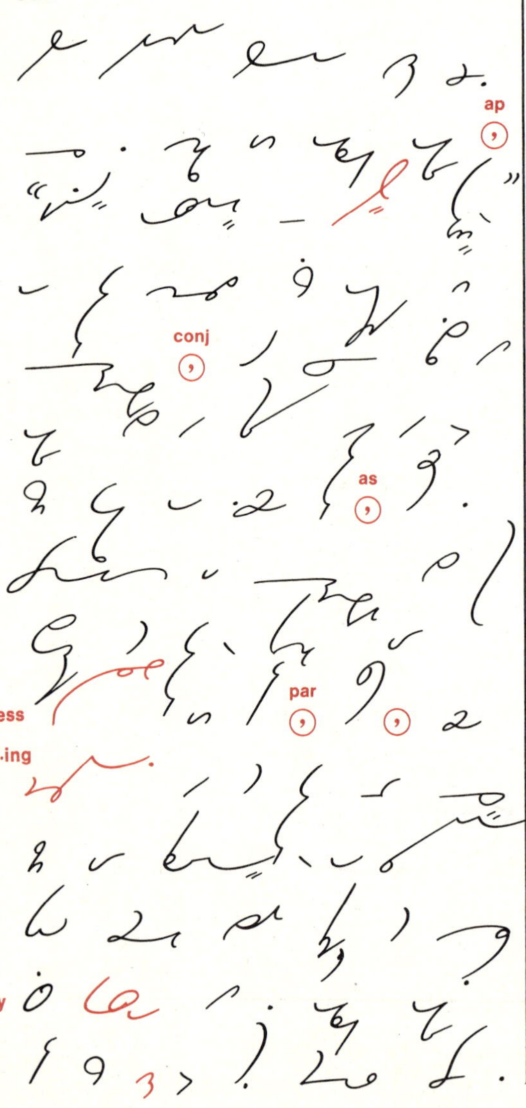

ap

To·day's

conj

as

time·li·ness

par

sched·ul·ing

pri·or·i·ty

yours

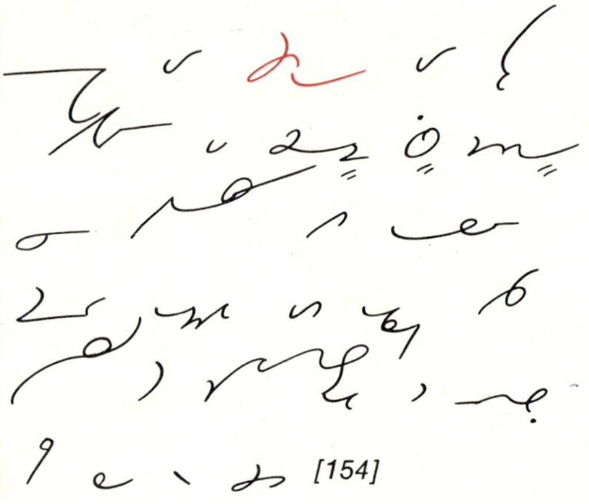

fac·ul·ty

intro

[154]

503

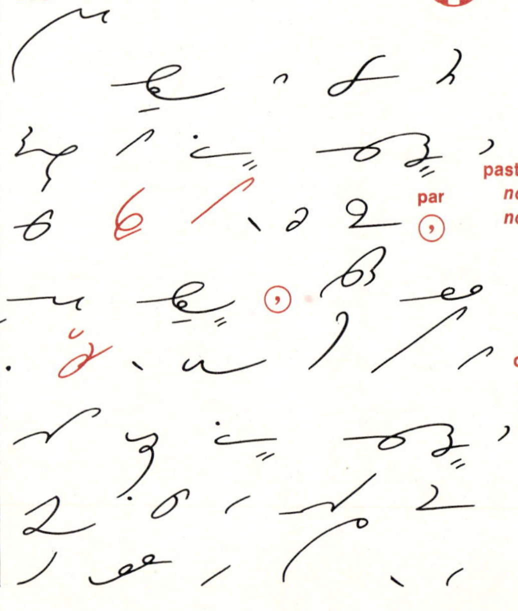

past due *no noun, no hyphen*

par

over·sight

off

nc

nc

rec·i·pes

stretch

intro

[106]

Transcribe:
$4
$7

4/

7/

4/

conj

[106]

504

Transcribe:
December 2

as

sub·scrip·tion

Transcribe:
1405
88202

1405

88202

505

sup·plies

ser

jour·nals

ac·quaint

intro

35

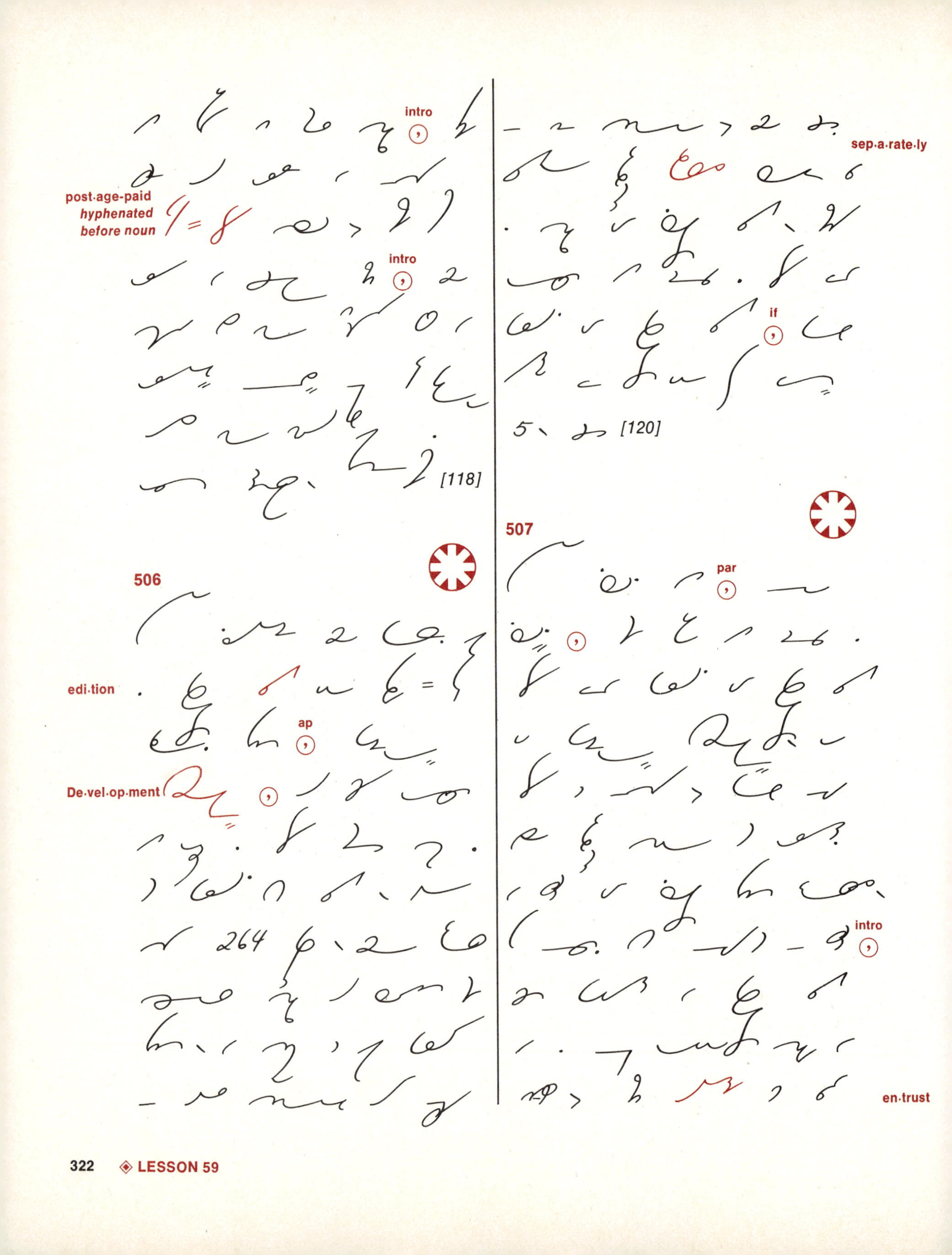

intro

post·age-paid
hyphenated before noun

intro

[118]

sep·a·rate·ly

if

5 [120]

506

edi·tion

ap

De·vel·op·ment

264

507

par

intro

en·trust

[106]

508 Transcription Quiz For you to supply: 6 commas—4 commas series, 1 comma apposition, 1 comma *if* clause; 1 missing word.

[123]

■ *In keeping with the increased pace of business, the executive finds that he no longer has time to attend to much of his own detail work. He must now depend on his secretary to take care of many important matters that he formerly handled. He wants a truly competent and responsible assistant. If you can meet these requirements, many a harried executive will be eager and ready to roll out the red carpet for you—wall to wall!*

LESSON 60

Developing Word-Building Power

509 SHORTHAND VOCABULARY BUILDER

-ng

1

-ngk

2

Ted, Etc.

3

Dem, Tem

4

1 Bring, wrong, angle, lengthy, longingly, belong.

2 Frank, inkling, drink, distinctive, succinct, functional.

3 Adapted, created, creditor, debtor, detail, deduct.

4 Damage, demand, customer, system, contemplate, medium, seldom.

Building Transcription Skills

510 Business Vocabulary Builder

inducing Persuading; convincing.

patronage The trade of customers.

grievances Complaints.

litigation Legal action.

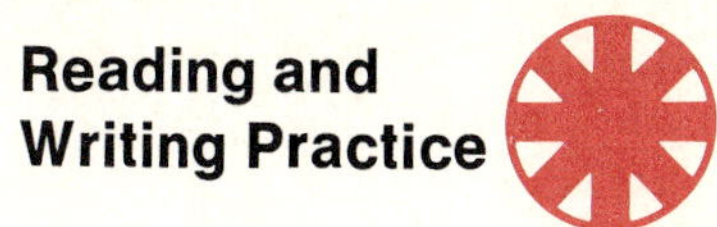

511 The Business Letter and Collections

de·lin·quent

up to date
no noun,
no hyphen

par

whole

Each company

fac·tors

conj

vari·a·tion

ser

lat·ter

ser

self-in·ter·est

col·lec·tion

if

fre·quent·ly

when

stunt

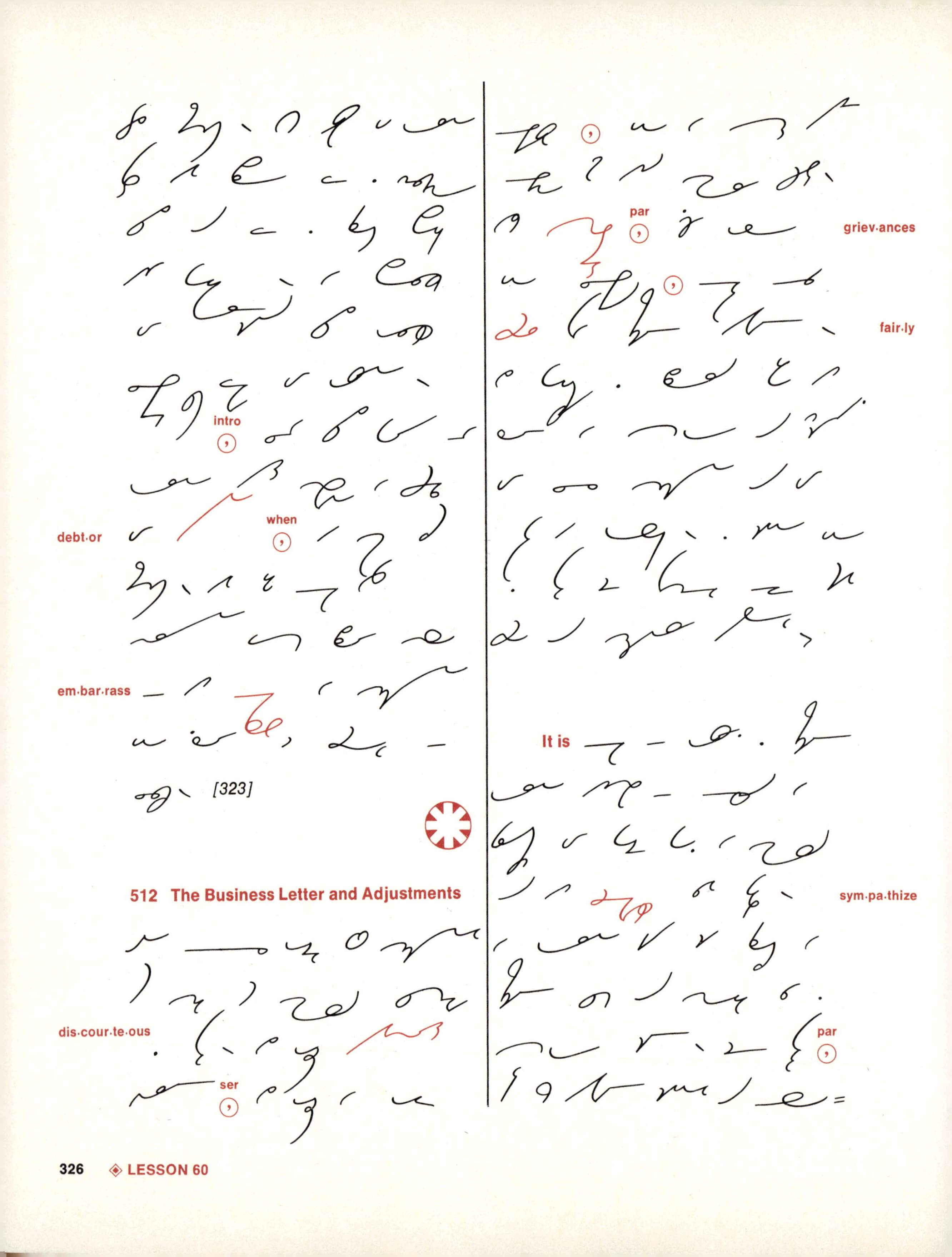

debt·or

em·bar·rass

[323]

512 The Business Letter and Adjustments

dis·cour·te·ous

griev·ances

fair·ly

It is

sym·pa·thize

prompt·ly

when

em·bar·rass·ment

if

cus·tom·er's

[233]

513 The Sales Letter

intro

[82]

up to date
no noun, no hyphen

LETTER

514

5

ap

intro

leath·er-bound
hyphenated before noun

nonr

8.50

nonr

loose-leaf
hyphenated before noun

6.60

[76]

DICTATION IN THE OFFICE

At this stage of your shorthand progress you have read and written many thousands of words. You have also taken thousands of words of dictation on familiar material as well as new material. Consequently, your shorthand skill has grown considerably—probably much more than you realize. You could now take dictation in a business office, provided the dictation was not too fast or too difficult.

Until now, your study of shorthand has been carefully controlled. The dictation has been given under ideal conditions. It has been given smoothly and evenly because your skill develops best in that way. Most of the dictation you have taken has been timed, enabling you to progress easily from one level to the next. The timing has also made measurement of your skill possible.

You will find, however, that taking dictation in an office is quite different from taking dictation in the classroom.

OFFICE-STYLE DICTATION

Your employer is not concerned with the development of your shorthand speed. He assumes that you have adequate skill the first day that you report for work. In order to keep up with the dictation, it is very important for you to develop your shorthand speed to the highest possible level.

The businessman will not always dictate smoothly and evenly. Depending on the flow of his thoughts, his dictation will be slow at times and very fast at other times. Your responsibility as a stenographer will be to keep up with the dictation regardless of the speed. It is essential that you have a reserve which will enable you to take even the fastest dictation. You will quickly become accustomed to office-style dictation if you have sufficient speed. The more speed you possess, the easier office-style dictation will be for you.

Sometimes a businessman will decide to change a sentence while he is dictating or after he has finished dictating. At other times he may ask that you take out a word, a sentence, or an entire paragraph. After the dictation has been completed, he may ask that a word or more be inserted or transposed. And the dictation will never be timed! This type of dictation is normal in every business office, and the stenographer must learn to make changes in her notes easily and quickly.

In order to help you learn to take office-style dictation, beginning with Lesson 61—and in the first lesson of each chapter thereafter—you will study some of the problems you will meet when you take dictation in a business office.

You will learn how to make short deletions during dictation and after the dictation has been completed. You will learn the easiest way to make insertions in your shorthand notes in case the dictator wants to add something after he has finished dictating a sentence. You will also learn the most efficient way to restore words, phrases, or sentences to your shorthand notes if the dictator decides to put back something he has told you to delete. You will also learn the best way to handle both short and long transpositions if the dictator decides to change the order of words, phrases, or sentences.

By following the instructions given in the lesson, you will soon be able to take and transcribe office-style dictation efficiently and accurately.

13 Real Estate

LESSON 61

Developing Word-Building Power

515 BRIEF FORMS AND DERIVATIVES

1 What, whatever; when, whenever; recognize, recognition.

2 Where, wherever, anywhere; wish, wishes, wishful.

3 Work, working, worker; world, worldly, worlds.

4 Worth, worthless, worthy; subject, subjected, subjective.

5 Short, shortly, shorten; object, objected, objective.

6 State, states; street, streets; value, valuable.

Building Transcription Skills

516 Business Vocabulary Builder

tract Area of land.

authorization Official permission.

untoward Adverse; unlucky.

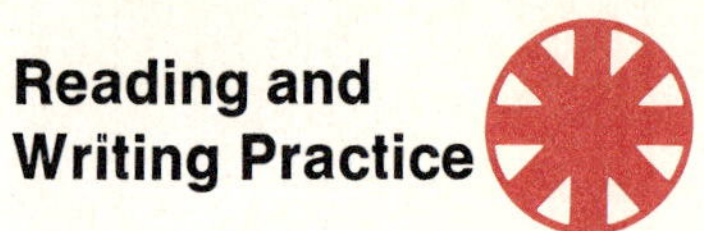

517 Brief-Form Letter

Transcribe: $24,000

intro

ac·cept

as

Chi·ca·go

ur·gent

par

ap

[120]

518

if

Transcribe: March 19 9 a.m.

ap

tract

nonr

intro

par

de·vel·op

site

when

if

[162]

519

intro

ap

con·fer·ence

par

ap

con·trary

intro

[62]

520

as

sep·a·rate

au·tho·ri·za·tion

if

15

intro

un·to·ward

if

touch

[110]

521

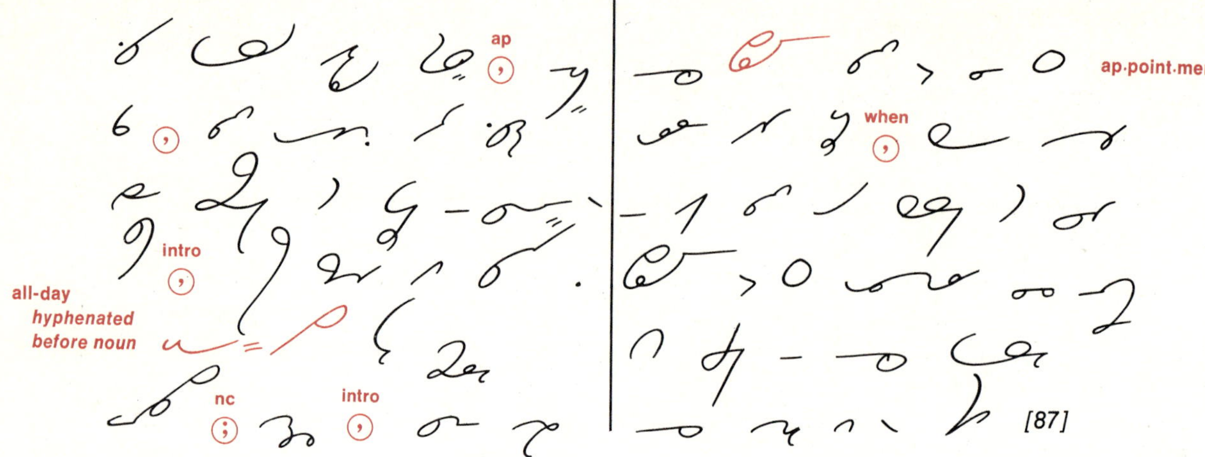

522 Transcription Quiz Up to this point, you have been told the type of punctuation that was necessary to punctuate each Transcription Quiz correctly. You have also been told how many missing words you were to supply. Beginning with this lesson, it will be necessary for you to determine without any guidance which marks of punctuation are necessary and what words are missing.

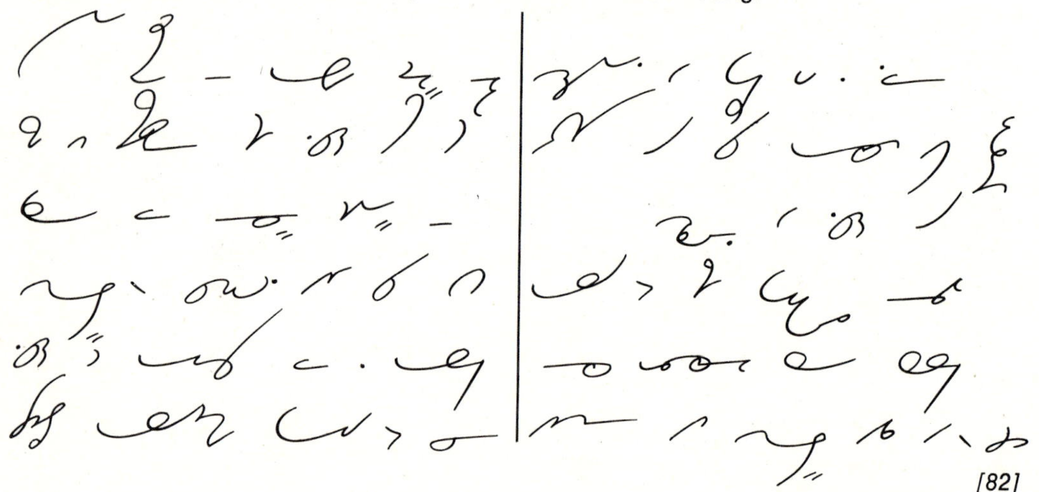

■ *The secretary with an eye to the future takes her responsibilities seriously and gives her best to every assignment.*

Short Deletions

A businessman will occasionally decide to delete—take out—a word or a phrase or even a sentence that he has dictated. For example, he may say:

> *The pamphlet describes completely the investments we suggest—take out* **completely.**

To indicate this deletion, you would simply strike a heavy downward line through the word thus:

Sometimes he may simply repeat the sentence without the word or phrase that he wishes to omit. He may say:

> *The enclosed pamphlet describes and illustrates what we have in mind—no,* **the enclosed pamphlet describes what we have in mind.**

To indicate this deletion, you would mark out in your notes not only the word *illustrates* but the word *and* as well.

If only one word or short expression is to be taken out, use a heavy downward line; if several words are to be taken out, use a wavy line. The dictator may say:

> *I feel, therefore, that I cannot accept your offer—no, scratch it out.*

In your notes you would show this deletion thus:

523 Illustration of Office-Style Dictation

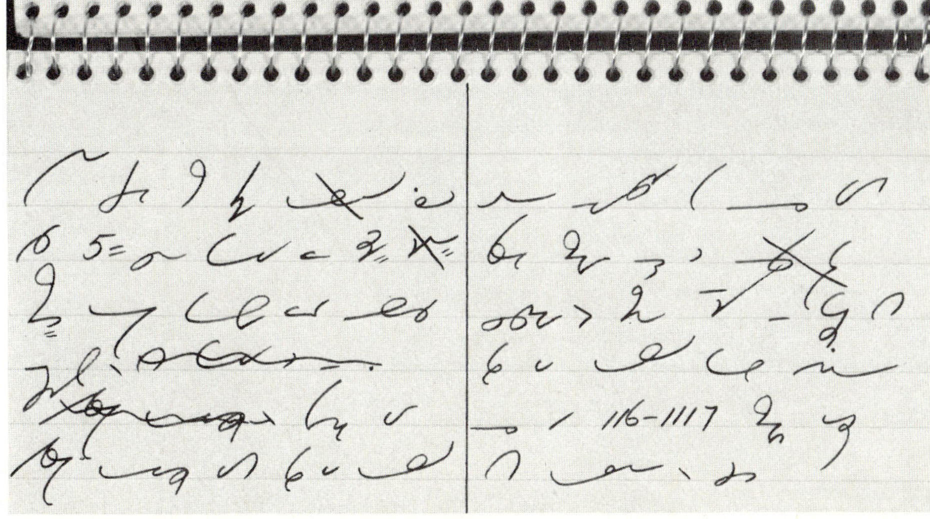

Building Phrasing Skill

524 USEFUL BUSINESS-LETTER PHRASES

Thank

Each

For

Omission of Words in Phrases

1 Thank you, thank you for, thank you for your, thank you for your order, thank you for this, to thank you for, I thank you, we thank you.

2 Each one, each month, each other, each morning, each time, each day, each night.

3 For me, for myself, for ourselves, for themselves, for yourself, for its, for the.

4 One or two, two or three, three or four, one of the, some of these, none of them, many of the.

525 GEOGRAPHICAL EXPRESSIONS

1 Philadelphia, Medford, Billings, Madison, Boise, Pierre.

2 Georgia, Montana, Connecticut, Delaware, Florida, Hawaii, California.

Building Transcription Skills

526 SIMILAR-WORDS DRILL ■ hole, whole

hole An opening.

There is a *hole* in the floor.

whole Entire.

The *whole* job is done.

527 Business Vocabulary Builder

vibrating Shaking; quivering.

thermostat Device to regulate heat.

hazardous Dangerous.

Reading and Writing Practice

528 Phrase Letter

ar·ea

par

if

bar·gain

when

wheth·er

[105]

529

past

as

whole

intro

intro

im·me·di·ate

gauge

vi·brat·ing

hole

haz·ard·ous

[114]

530

oc·cu·pan·cy

as

al·ways

nc

intro

[103]

531

trans·ferred

com·pa·ny's

conj

ap

Transcribe:
10 a.m.

[78]

532

ap

swim·ming

well-trained
hyphenated
before noun

161-1188

[101]

533

par

fore·casts

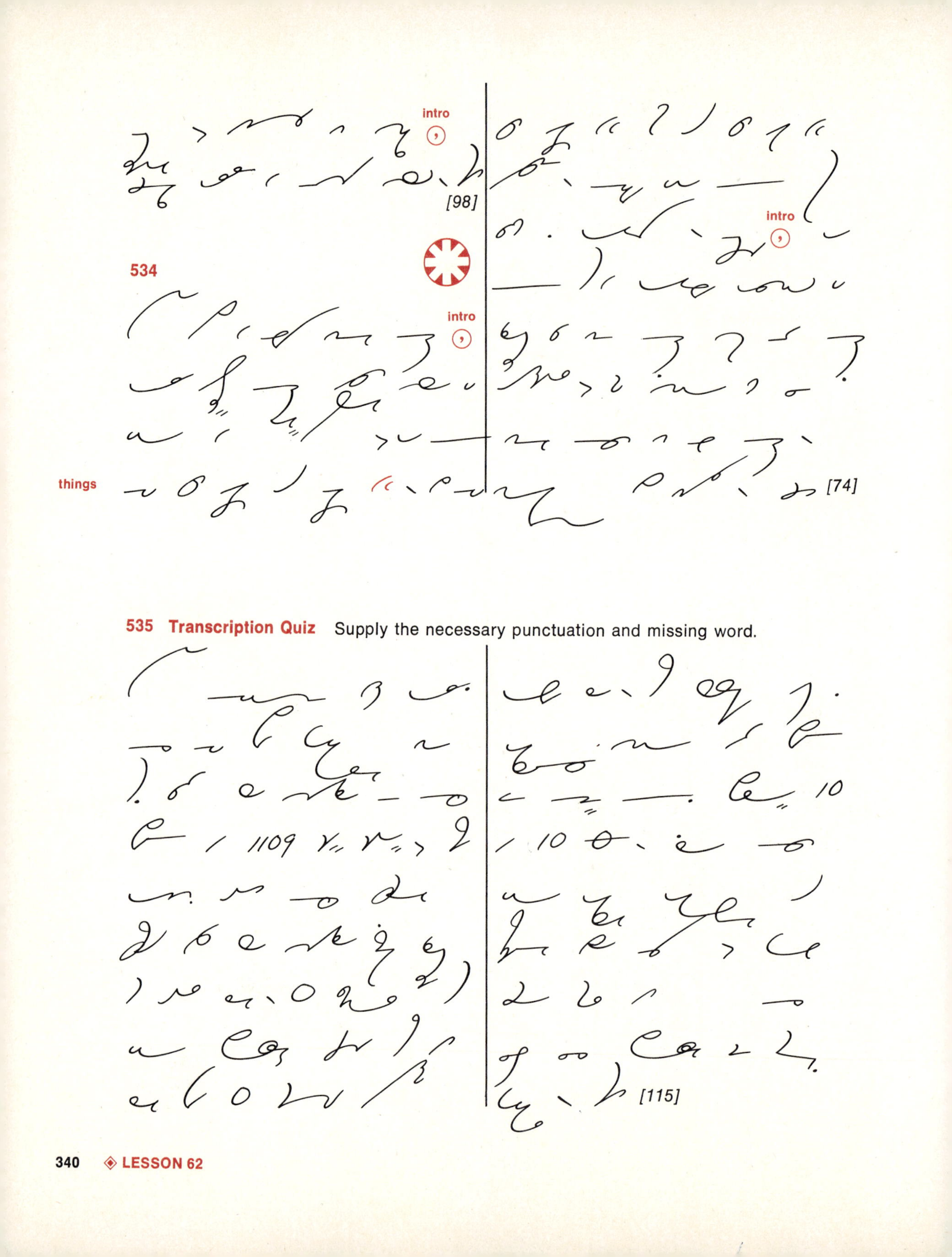

intro

[98]

intro

534

intro

things

[74]

535 Transcription Quiz

Supply the necessary punctuation and missing word.

1109

10

10

[115]

LESSON 63

Developing Word-Building Power

536 WORD FAMILIES

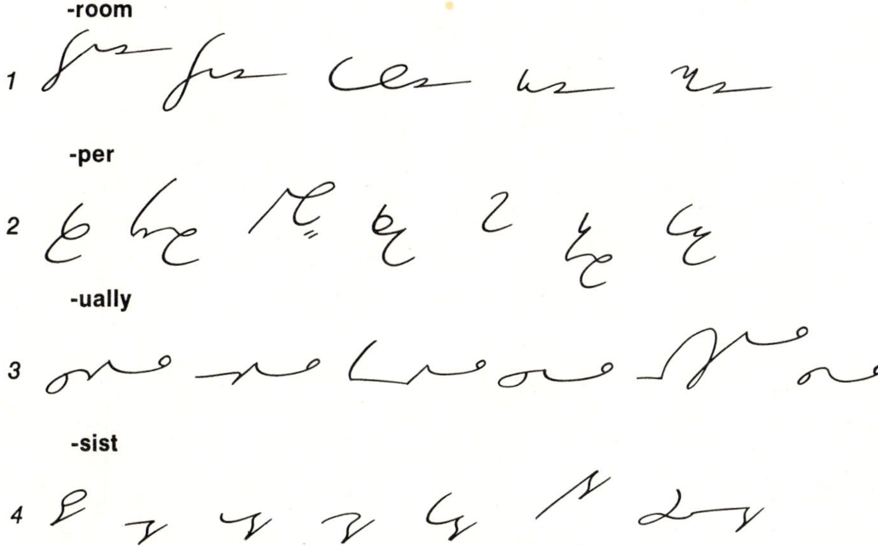

1 Bedroom, bathroom, playroom, showroom, washroom.

2 Paper, bookkeeper, Draper, sharper, upper, shopkeeper, proper.

3 Actually, mutually, punctually, annually, individually, equally.

4 Assist, insist, resist, consist, persist, desist, pharmacist.

Building Transcription Skills

537 SPELLING FAMILIES ■ ie, ei

One of the most troublesome letter combinations in the English language is the *ie, ei* pair. A few basic rules cover most of the words in which these letters appear.

1 i comes before e:

con·ve·nient	**niece**	**friend**
piece	**chief**	**be·lieve**

2 **except**

(a) **after c:**

re·ceive **re·ceit** **de·ceit**

(b) **when the combination has the sound of a:**

eight **heir** **neigh·bor**

But, unfortunately, there are some exceptions:

ei·ther **ef·fi·cient** **lei·sure**

Watch for the *ie, ei* combinations in the Reading and Writing Practice.

538 Business Vocabulary Builder

appropriate (*adjective*) Satisfactory.

punctually Exactly on time.

pros and cons Reasons for and against.

Reading and Writing Practice

539

ap·pre·ci·ate

if

de·scrip·tive

[78]

540

ap

book·keep·er

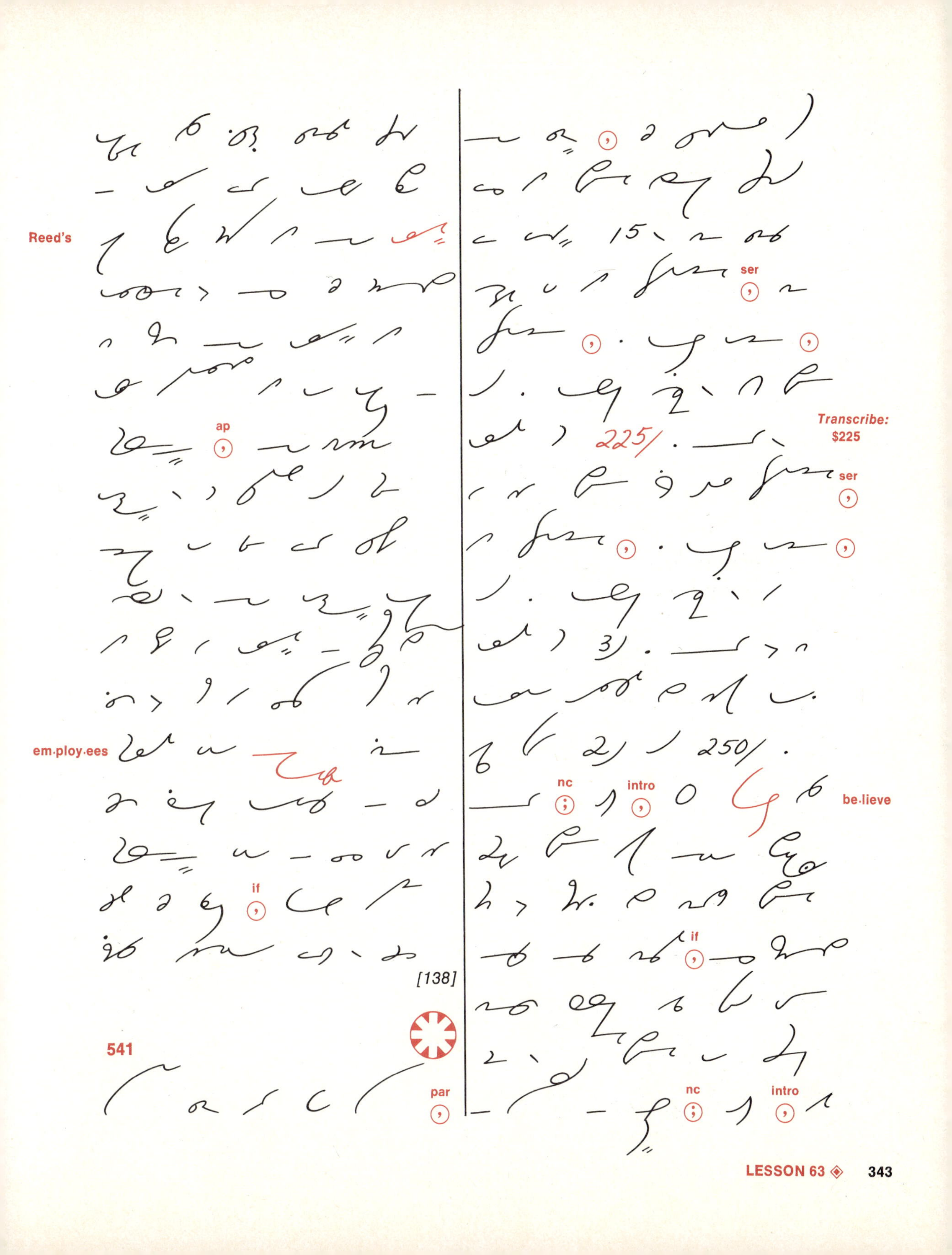

Reed's

ap

em·ploy·ees

if

[138]

541

par

ser

ser

Transcribe: $225

nc

intro

be·lieve

if

nc

intro

un·like·ly

[157]

ap

[121]

542

as

piece

intro

pros

cons

45

5

6

40

if

punc·tu·al·ly

10

543

ap

16

10

intro

es·sen·tial

[70]

544

oc·cu·pan·cy

20

when

gra·cious

acres

35

ser

5

intro

rec·re·ation·al

679-8900

[113]

545 **Transcription Quiz** Supply the necessary punctuation and the missing word.

[130]

Placing Short Letters by Judgment

When you become a stenographer, you will, of course, be expected to take dictation and transcribe it accurately and rapidly. You will be expected to spell all words correctly and to supply proper punctuation.

You will, in addition, be expected to place each letter attractively on the letterhead so that the appearance of the letter will make a good impression on the person to whom it is addressed.

Experienced stenographers acquire the knack of placing letters by judgment; they do not use a placement scale. They glance at their notes and decide that the left-hand margin should be "about here" and the right-hand margin "about there"—and produce letters that are pleasing to the eye.

Most of the average businessman's dictation consists of short letters—letters of approximately 100 words. The suggestions given below will help you acquire the knack of placing short letters by judgment.

On page 347 you will find Letter No. 17 of *Gregg Shorthand for Colleges, Volume Two*—a short letter—as it was written in shorthand by an experienced stenographer and the transcript she produced. Notice that the shorthand for this letter required a little more than half a column in her notebook.

Make a shorthand copy of Letter No. 17 and determine how much space this short letter requires in your shorthand notebook. If your notes are small, they may require less space than the notes on page 347; if they are large, they may require more space.

Whenever your notes for a dictated letter require approximately the same space in your notebook that they require for Letter No. 17, here is what you should do to place the letter attractively on the letterhead, assuming that your machine has elite—small—type:

1. Set your margin stops about two inches at the left and two inches at the right.
2. Insert your paper or stationery pack and type the date two lines below the last line of the letterhead.
3. Start the inside address about 4 inches from the top of the paper. (About 3½ inches from the top if your machine has pica—large—type.)
4. Then transcribe the body of the letter.

If you follow these suggestions for placing a short letter of approximately 100 words, you will always produce letters that will make a good first impression on the reader.

Connecticut State College

EASTFORD, CONNECTICUT 06242

July 1, 197-

Miss Janet Weber
753 Main Avenue
New Haven, Connecticut 06513

Dear Miss Weber:

We think you have made a wise choice in deciding to further your education by attending college. More jobs will be open to you when you graduate, and you will be able to earn a higher salary.

After reviewing your high school records, Miss Weber, we find that you are eligible to apply for several scholarships here at Connecticut State College. Enclosed are the application forms for these scholarships. We are also sending you our general catalog.

Very sincerely yours,

Joseph R. Davis

Joseph R. Davis
Registrar

JRD:DS

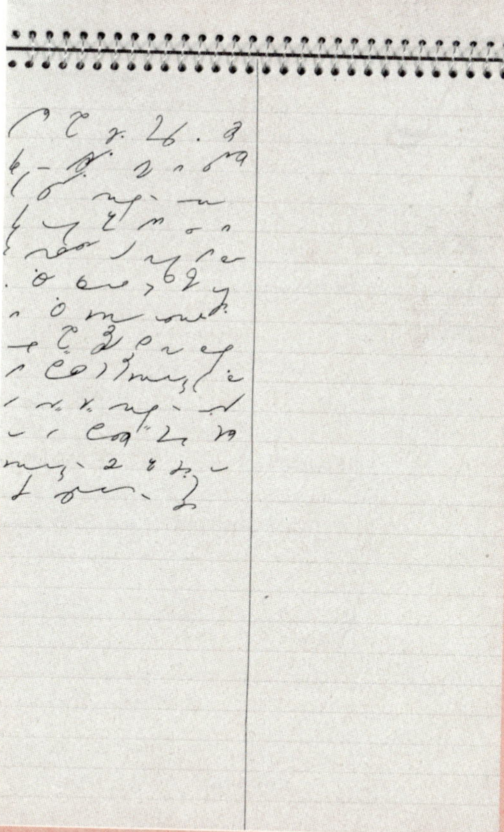

Developing Word-Building Power

546 WORD ENDINGS

-ingly

-ily

-ment

-burg

1 Exceedingly, unhesitatingly, appealingly, entertainingly, overwhelmingly, willingly.

2 Family, easily, readily, temporarily, steadily, heavily, heartily.

3 Development, elementary, basement, assessments, temperament, moment.

4 Pittsburgh, Plattsburg, Petersburg, Gettysburg, Greensburg, Williamsburg, Newburgh.

Building Transcription Skills

547 COMMON PREFIXES ■ im-

im- not

immobile Not movable; fixed.

impassable Not passable; inaccessible.

impossible Not possible; not capable of occurring.

impollite Not polite; rude.

immature Not mature; undeveloped.

548 Business Vocabularly Builder

realty Real estate; property.

converted changed over; remade.

mart Store; market.

unhesitatingly Promptly.

Reading and Writing Practice

549

Re·al·ty

nonr

col·leagues

ser

if

conj

ar·eas

[97]

550

ap

rec·om·mend

if

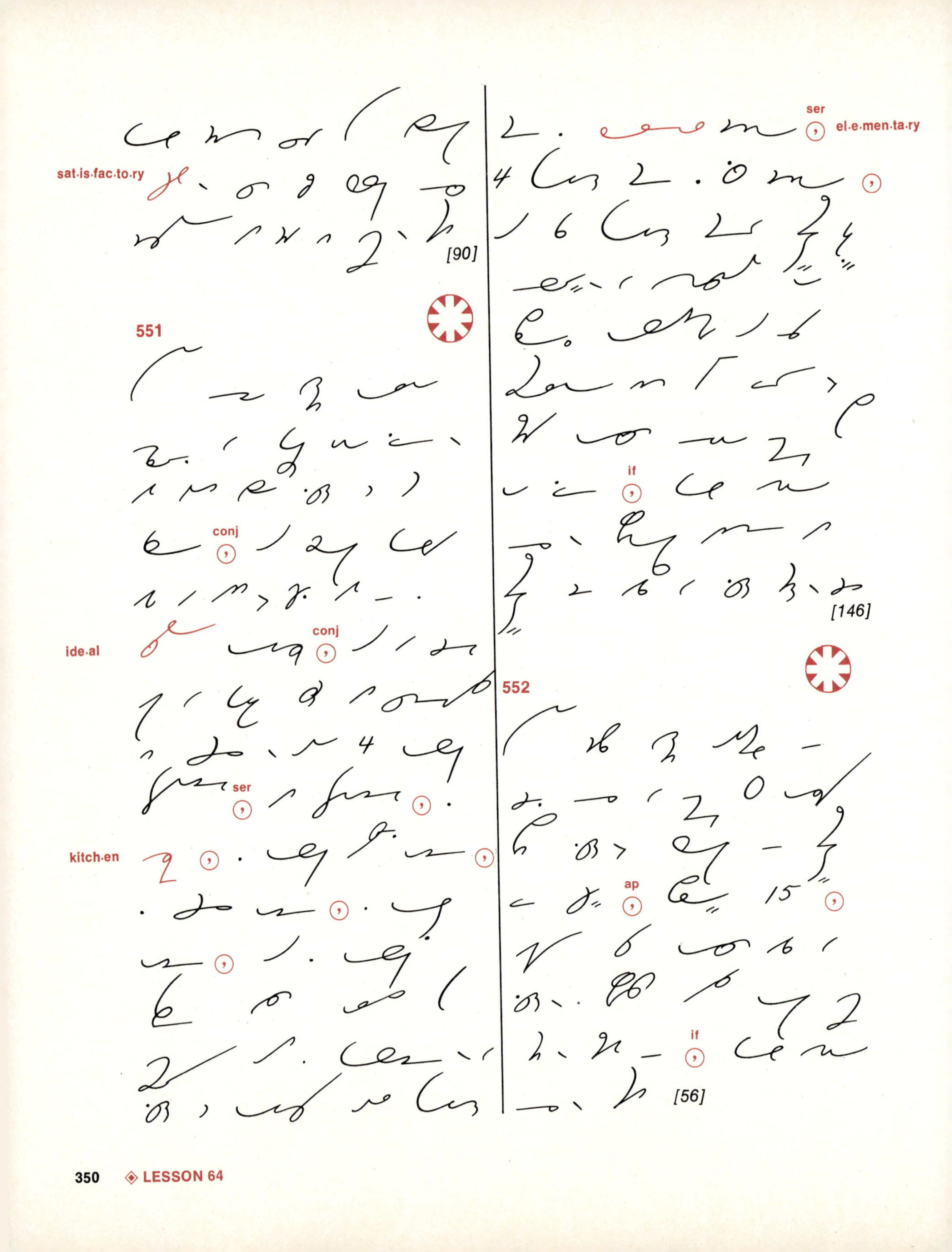

sat·is·fac·to·ry

[90]

551

conj

ide·al

conj

ser

kitch·en

ser

el·e·men·ta·ry

if

[146]

552

ap

if

[56]

553

five-room *hyphenated before noun*

fam·i·ly's

ap

when

al·ready

conj

oc·cu·pan·cy

par

[113]

554

Transcribe: 85 percent

intro

intro

ten·ant

month's

par

ser

year-round 24-hour *hyphenated before noun*

if

ser

[145]

555

when

man's

trans·ferred

if

[84]

556 Transcription Quiz Supply the necessary punctuation and the missing words.

[118]

LESSON 65

Developing Word-Building Power

557 SHORTHAND VOCABULARY BUILDER

Ī

1

Ow

2

Ēa, Ĭa

3

Tern, Term, Etc.

4

1 Simplify, familiarize, provide, buyer, decide, price.

2 House, around, ground, surround, allow, town.

3 Area, create, negotiate, appreciated, brilliant, initiate.

4 Pattern, turn, attorney, term, determine, terminal.

Building Transcription Skills

558 Business Vocabulary Builder

familiarize To aquaint.

reputable Of good reputation; respected.

negotiations Business transactions.

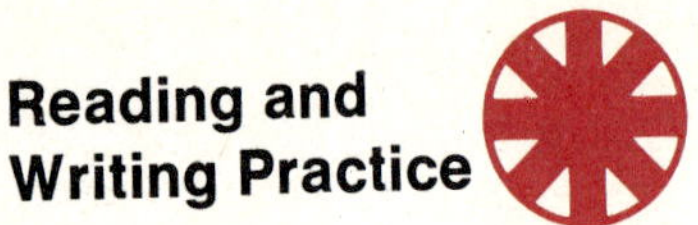

Reading and Writing Practice

559 Buying a Home

fa·mil·iar·ize

par

conj

rep·u·ta·ble

intro

ap

mul·ti·ple

Some dealers

conj

tour

Before you

intro

ex·act·ly

ser

bath·rooms

too

when

am·ple

when

intro

plan·ning

[385]

560 Selling a Home

It is

kitch·en

conj

intro

enough

intro

intro

ne·go·ti·a·tions

You can

intro

com·pa·ra·ble

com·pet·i·tive

par

intro

top-notch *hyphenated before noun*

and o

ser

ga·rage

If you have

if

conj

if

intro

le·gal

at·tor·ney

if

buy·er

[331]

LETTER

561

Lei·sure

nonr

30

ser

sev·er·ing

intro

[142]

14 Retailing

LESSON 66

Developing Word-Building Power

562 BRIEF FORMS AND DERIVATIVES

1 Acknowledge, acknowledged, acknowledgment; recognize, recognition, recognized.
2 Advantage, advantages, advantageous; newspaper, newspaperman, newspapermen.
3 Advertise, advertised, advertisement; responsible, responsibility, responsibilities.
4 After, afternoon, afterward; experience, experienced, inexperienced.
5 Business, businessman; important-importance, unimportant; ordinary, ordinarily.
6 Character, characters, characterize; probable, probably, improbable.

Building Transcription Skills

563 Business Vocabulary Builder

deteriorate To waste away.

deprive To keep from the enjoyment of something; deny.

recipient One who receives.

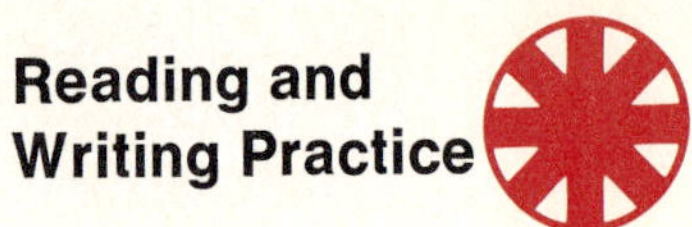

Reading and Writing Practice

564 Brief-Form Letter

suit·cases

nc ;

when ,

good-look·ing *hyphenated before noun*

when ,

qual·i·ty

intro ,

[130]

565

intro ,

er·ror

[87]

566

par

intro

intro

when

[90]

567

Pol·ly's

intro

par

its

ac·cept

ap

nonr

and o

de·te·ri·o·ra·tion

if

in·te·ri·or

ex·te·ri·or

conj

col·or·ful

prod·ucts

[157]

568

ser

pa·tience

intro

par

par

intro

de·prive

for·ev·er

[124]

569 **Transcription Quiz** Supply the necessary punctuation and the missing word.

[180]

Short Insertions and Changes

Occasionally a businessman may change his mind about a word or phrase after he has completed a sentence. He may say:

I am enclosing 11 copies of the form—change **11 to 15.**

You would indicate this change in your notes thus:

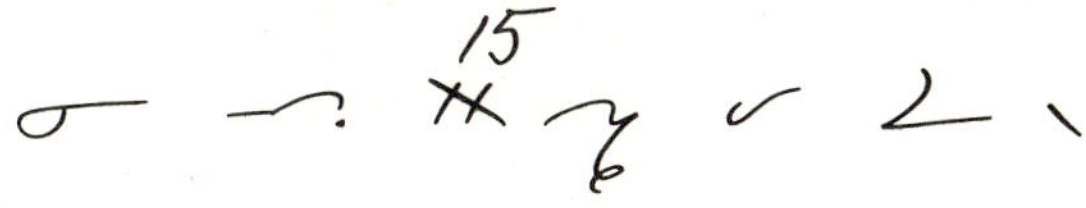

Sometimes the businessman may wish to insert a word or a phrase in a sentence he has dictated. He may say:

I am enclosing 15 copies of the form—make that **15 copies of the latest form.**

You must be on the alert so that you can quickly find the point at which the addition is to be made. When you find the point, insert the word or phrase with a carat, just as you would in longhand, thus:

570 Illustration of Office-Style Dictation

Building Phrasing Skill

571 USEFUL BUSINESS-LETTER PHRASES

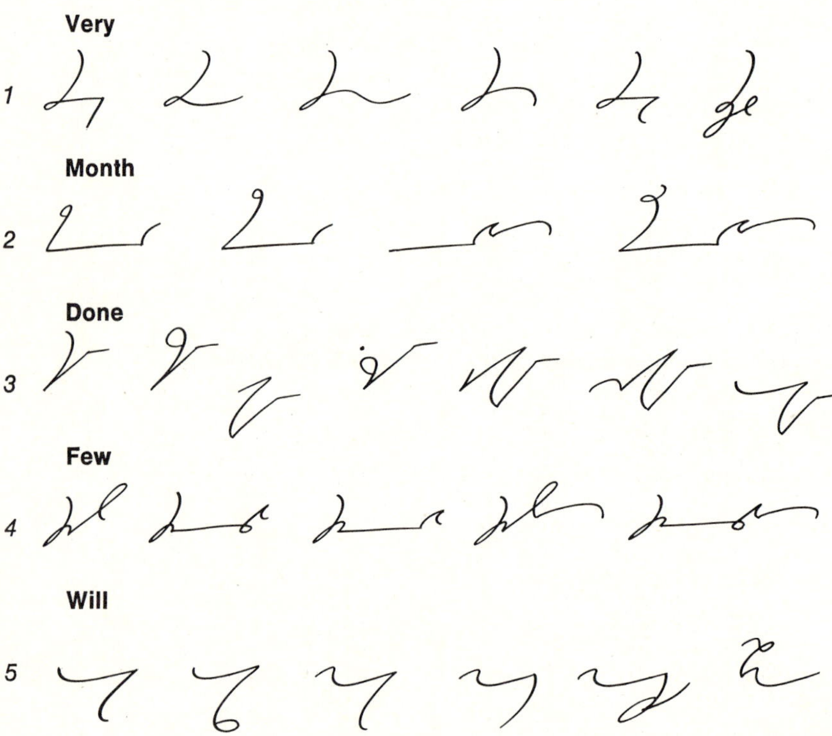

1 Very much, very well, very glad, very good, very important, very satisfactory.

2 Each month, every month, months ago, several months ago.

3 Have done, I have done, to be done, has done, should be done, could be done, will be done.

4 Few days, few minutes, few months, few days ago, few minutes ago.

5 Will be, will be able, you will be, you will have, you will find, we hope you will.

572 GEOGRAPHICAL EXPRESSIONS

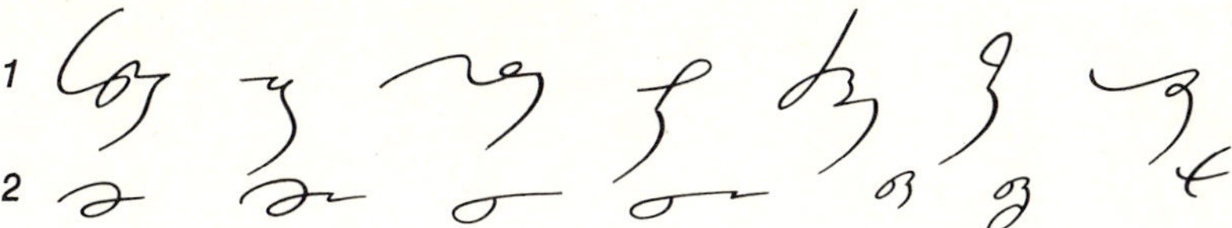

1 Brownsville, Knoxville, Greenville, Nashville, Jacksonville, Ashville, Louisville.

2 Canada, Canadian, America, American, United States, United States of America, Puerto Rico.

Building Transcription Skills

573 SIMILAR-WORDS DRILL ■ purpose, propose

purpose *(noun)* An intention.

Our *purpose* is to create goodwill.

propose *(verb)* To offer for consideration.

Here is the plan that we *propose.*

574 Business Vocabulary Builder

portable Easily movable.

alternative Different route or method.

in vogue In fashion; popular.

Reading and Writing Practice

575 Phrase Letter

crowd·ed

if

when

rolls

wheels

intro

week's

intro

ser

fau·cet

[142]

576

intro

par

ev·ery·body's

intro

if

cer·tain·ly

if

cr

par

[173]

577

brows·ing

nc ;

when ,

and o ,

well-trained hyphenated before noun

[62]

578

intro ,

raise

ser ,

over·head ,

ab·sorb

par ,

,

15

cus·tom-made hyphenated before noun

15,

if ,

billed

15 [143]

579

par

rec·om·mend

ap

dem·on·stra·tor

sug·gest·ed

ap

Transcribe:
9 a.m.
5 p.m.

ap

[111]

580 Transcription Quiz Supply the necessary punctuation and the missing words.

[145]

Developing Word-Building Power

581 WORD FAMILIES

-or

1

-ert

2

Adv-

3

Thing

4

1 Floor, store, bookstore, more, nor, original.
2 Expert, alert, insert, exert, concert, assert, dessert.
3 Advance, adventure, advise, adverse, advancement, advocate.
4 Thing, something, anything, nothing, everything, plaything.

Building Transcription Skills

582 COMMON PREFIXES ■ en-

en- in, into

enact To make into law.

enroll To register in.

enter To go in.

entrance A way in.

583 Business Vocabulary Builder

precision Exactness.

functional Workable; useful.

browse Look around leisurely.

Reading and Writing Practice

584

fash·ions

ap

ser

one-half

and o

well-trained hyphenated before noun

[93]

585

as

men's

intro

wom·en

la·dies'

ap

ser

pre·ci·sion

and o

ad·ven·ture

[127]

586

if

par

Frank·lin's

75

func·tion·al

nc

beau·ti·ful·ly

[142]

587

Nash's

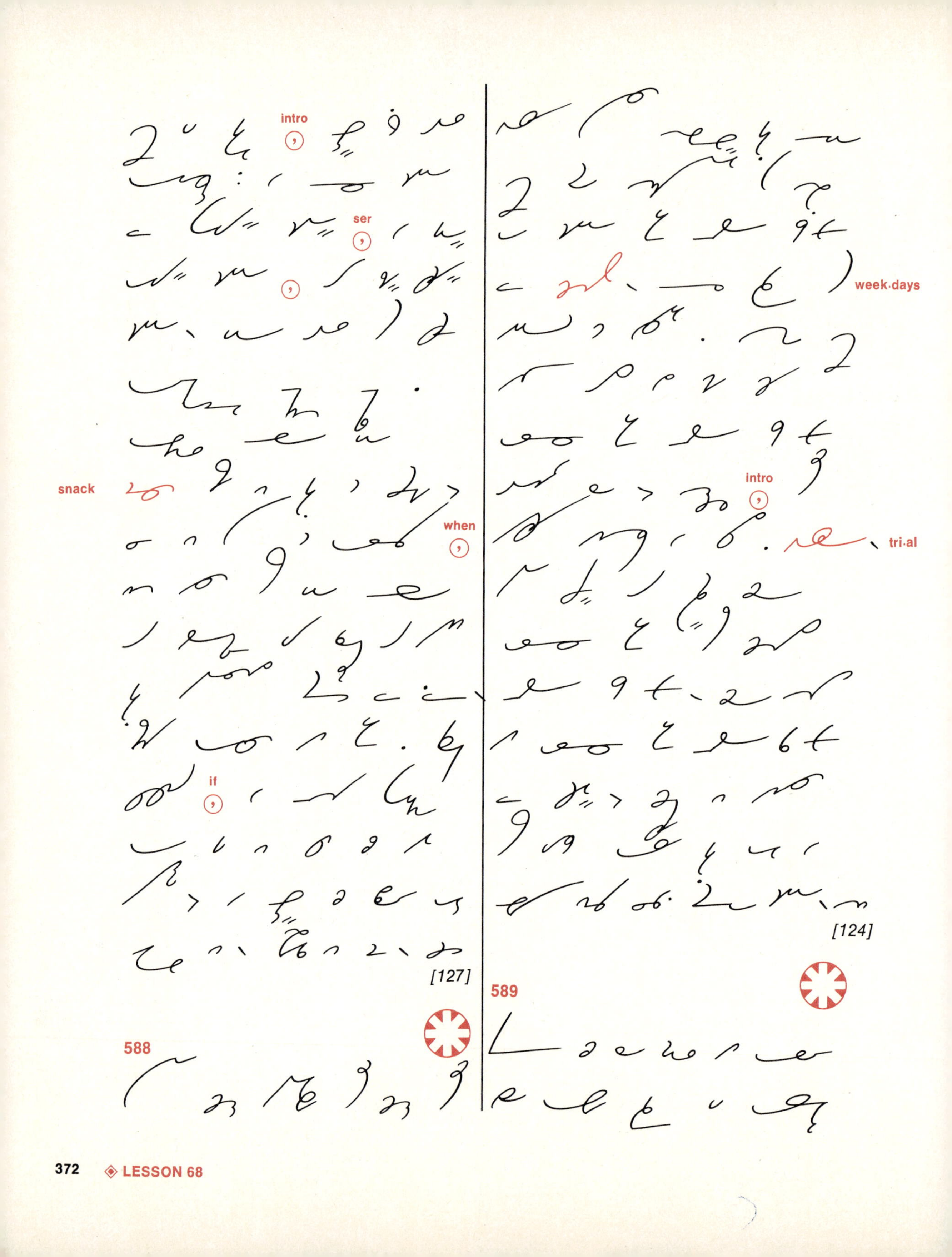

intro

ser

snack

when

if

[127]

588

week·days

intro

tri·al

[124]

589

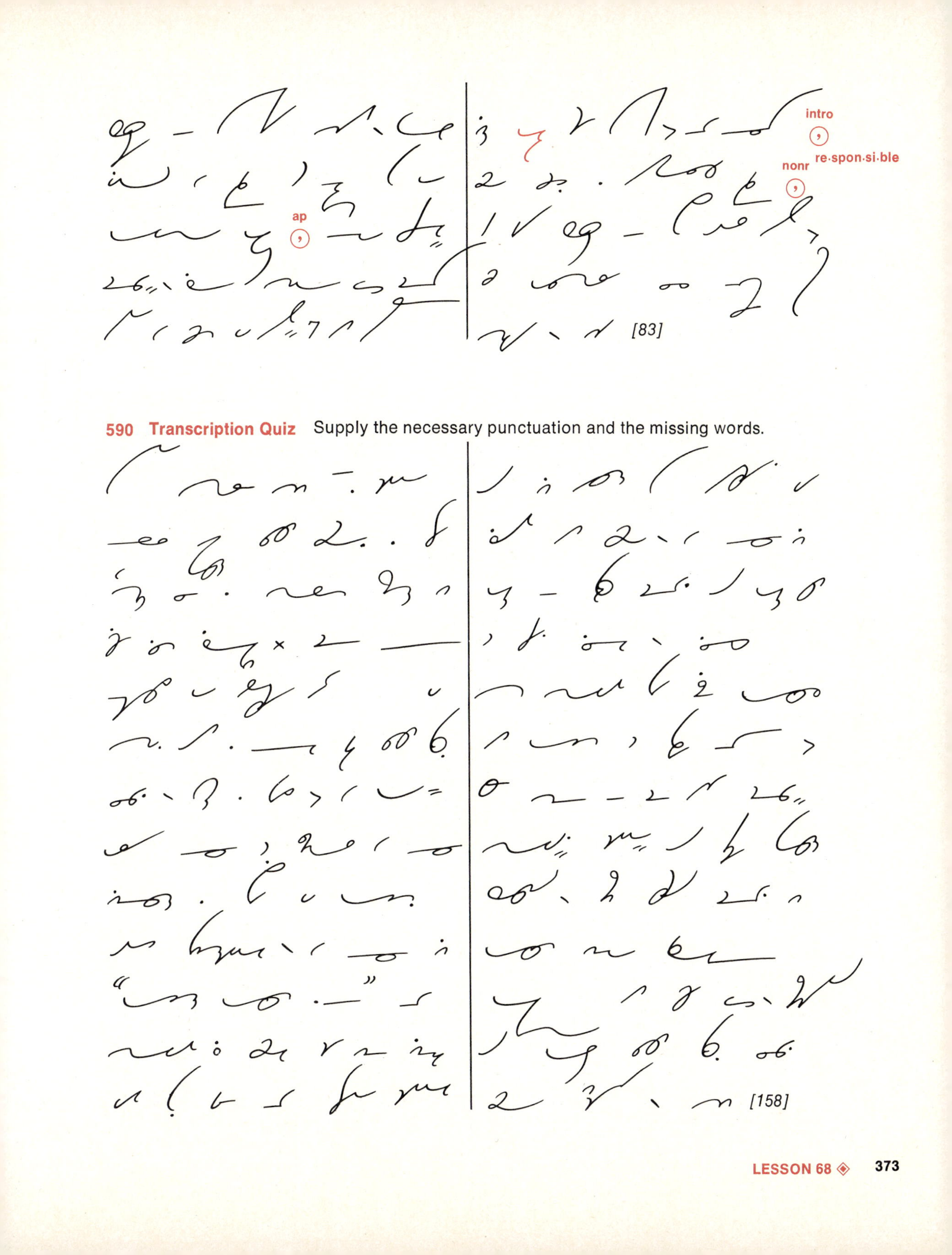

intro

nonr

re·spon·si·ble

ap

[83]

590 Transcription Quiz Supply the necessary punctuation and the missing words.

[158]

Developing Word-Building Power

591 WORD BEGINNINGS AND ENDINGS

Mis-

1

-gram

2

Ex-

3

-ington

4

1 Mistake, misplace, misprint, misrepresent, misinterpret, misunderstood.

2 Telegram, diagram, cablegram, radiogram, monogram.

3 Express, expect, exactly, extend, example, examine, extra.

4 Wilmington, Lexington, Washington, Huntington, Burlington.

Building Transcription Skills

592 GRAMMAR CHECKUP ■ possessive with gerund

A gerund is a verbal noun ending in *ing.*

Verb	*Gerund*
work	working
need	needing
take	taking

Be sure to use the possessive case for nouns and pronouns that precede gerunds.

Joan's working *caused her family no problem.*

Our commission depends on our *(not* us) finishing *on time.*

◈ Note: Be especially careful when transcribing the pronoun *your* before a gerund. Stenographers often transcribe the brief form *you-your* as *you.*

I would appreciate your *(not* you) checking *into this matter.*

593 Business Vocabulary Builder

partial Part; incomplete.

illegally Unlawfully; outside the law.

suites Sets of furniture.

Reading and Writing Practice

594

suites

par

intro

[122]

595

par

conj

at·mo·sphere

par

rea·sons

per·ma·nent

past

nonr

when

par

[157]

596

intro

your

[109]

597

Cos·met·ics

ap

ser

ap

ser

nonr

well-known
hyphenated before noun

nc

intro

conj

20-min·ute
hyphenated before noun

par

[130]

598

piece

nc

when

scratches

intro

de·vel·ops

Transcribe: 10 a.m.

nc

[137]

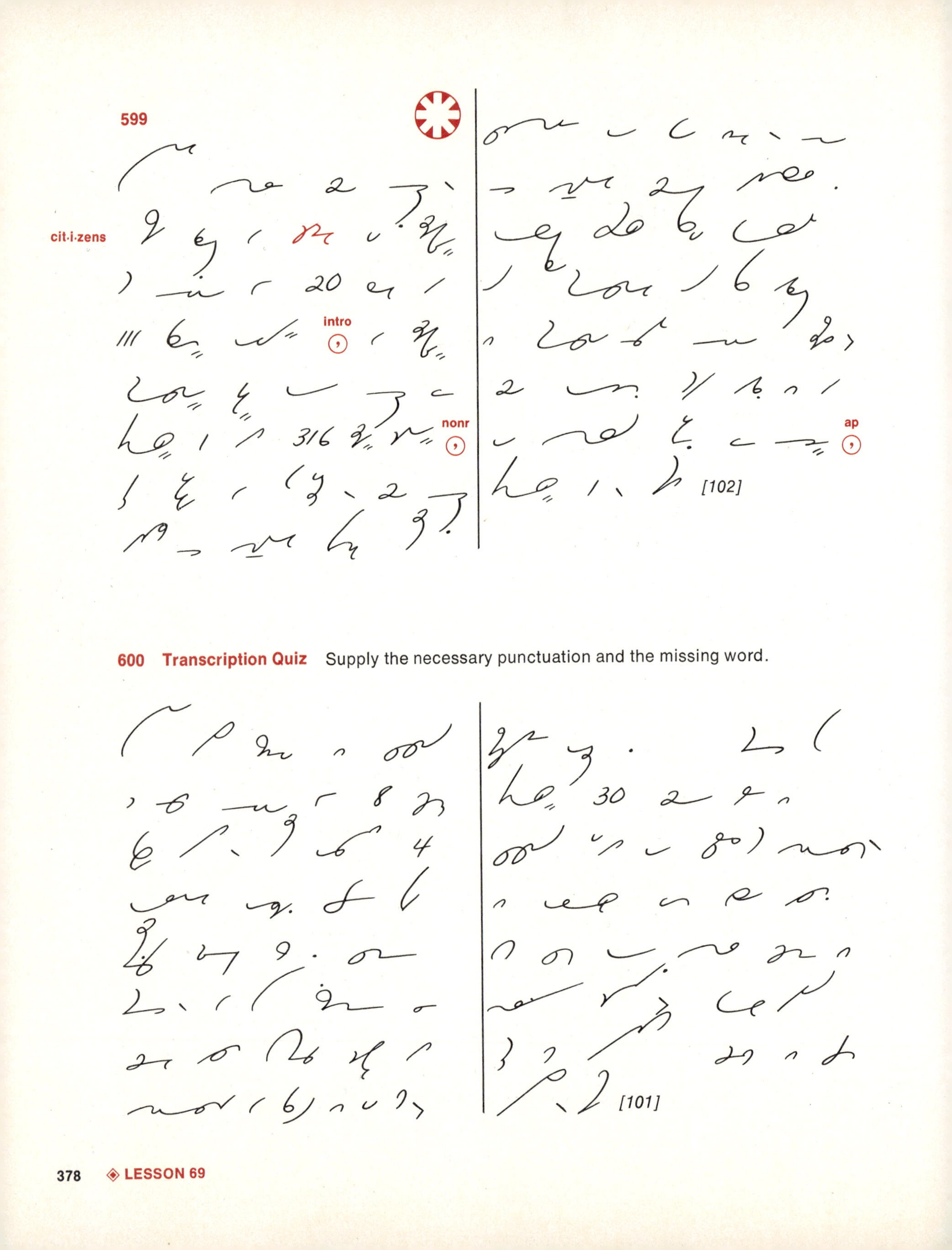

599

cit·i·zens

intro

nonr

ap

[102]

600 **Transcription Quiz** Supply the necessary punctuation and the missing word.

[101]

Developing Word-Building Power

601 SHORTHAND VOCABULARY BUILDER

Compounds

Dev, Etc.

Nd, Nt

Ow

1 However, within, worthwhile, notwithstanding, someone, somewhere, everybody.

2 Development, devoted, device, different, differences, definite, defray.

3 Industry, indicate, independent, center, central, continent.

4 Counter, discount, allowed, surrounded, recounted, countless.

Building Transcription Skills

602 Business Vocabulary Builder

innovations New developments; new inventions.

frugality Thriftiness.

phenomenal Remarkable.

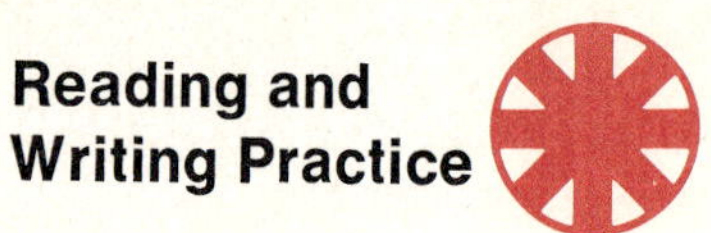

Reading and Writing Practice

603 Changes in Retailing

Amer·i·ca's

ap

sym·bol

conj

nonr

full-line *hyphenated before noun*

spe·cial·ty

par

sub·urbs

fam·i·lies

when

intro

pla·zas

par

This change

par

nonr

de·pen·dent

al·lowed

oc·cur·ring

con·ges·tion

intro

24= 24-hour *hyphenated before noun*

ser

intro

conj

ap

[297]

604 The Discount Store

intro

than

lie

per·son·nel

nc

intro

in·te·ri·or

par

fru·gal·i·ty

The sales

check-out *hyphenated before noun*

conj

intro

conj

quan·ti·ties

phe·nom·e·nal

conj

[264]

LETTERS

605

when

break·age

[83]

606

choose

ser

when

ser

[130]

607

Transcribe: No. 1181

intro

whole·sal·ers

nonr

416

[102]

608

nc

ser

Yon·kers

if

[84]

15 Transportation

Developing Word-Building Power

609 BRIEF-FORMS AND DERIVATIVES

1 Circular, circulars; govern, government; railroad, railroads.
2 Company, companies, accompanies, accompanied; never, nevertheless.
3 Correspond-correspondent, corresponded, correspondingly; worth, worthless, worthy.
4 Enclose, enclosing, enclosure, enclosed; opportunity, opportunities.
5 Envelope, envelopes; ordinary, extraordinary; work, workable.
6 Ever-every, everyone, everywhere, everybody; purpose, purposely.

Building Transcription Skills

610 Business Vocabulary Builder

counselors Guidance personnel.

destination The ending place of a journey.

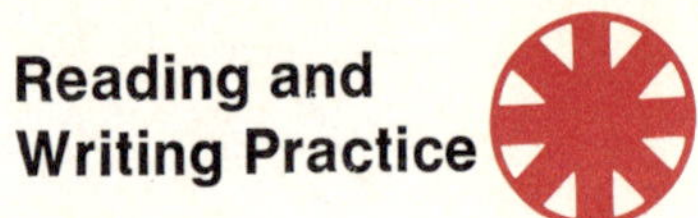

611 Brief-Form Letter

intro ,

de·picts

if ,

[114]

612

well-known hyphenated before noun

coun·sel·ors

ac·com·mo·da·tions

ea·ger

intro ,

[123]

613

when

weighs

any·where

conj

ev·ery·where

intro

shelved

week·end

if

nc

then

par

[120]

614

ap

21

en·trance

re·mod·el·ing

ser

es·ca·la·tor

conj

tem·po·rar·i·ly

[105]

615

itin·er·ar·ies

intro
intro
intro
conj
intro
re·ceipt
if
[130]
owe

616 Transcription Quiz Supply the necessary punctuation and the missing word.

[100]

Restorations

There will be times when your employer will dictate the word or phrase and then change it. Upon reflection, however, he will decide that the original word or phrase was better. He might say:

The work he did was satisfactory—no **passable;** *oh, perhaps* **satisfactory** *is better.*

The best way to handle this situation is to write the restored word or phrase as though it were a completely new form. You write the word *satisfactory;* then strike it out and substitute *passable;* finally, strike out *passable* and rewrite *satisfactory.* Your shorthand notes would look like this:

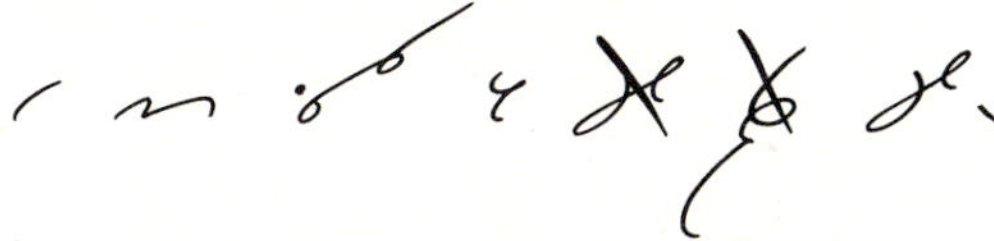

Do not try to indicate that the original outline for *satisfactory* is to be restored. This attempt may make your notes difficult to read, with the result that you may not be able to transcribe them correctly.

617 Illustration of Office-Style Dictation

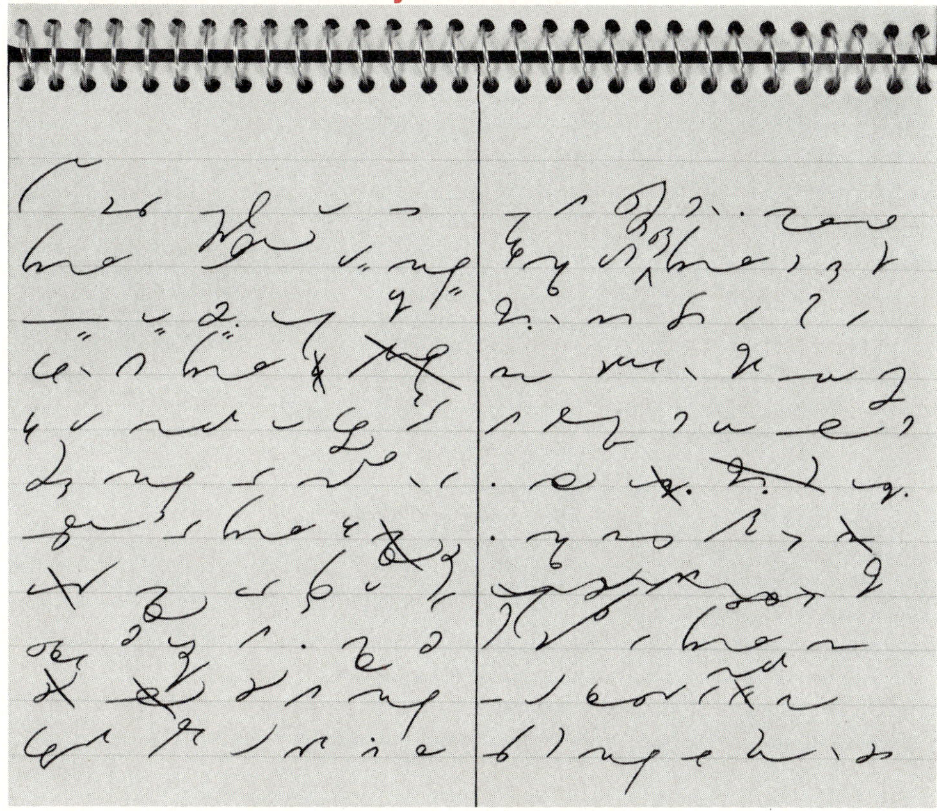

Building Phrasing Skill

618 USEFUL BUSINESS-LETTER PHRASES

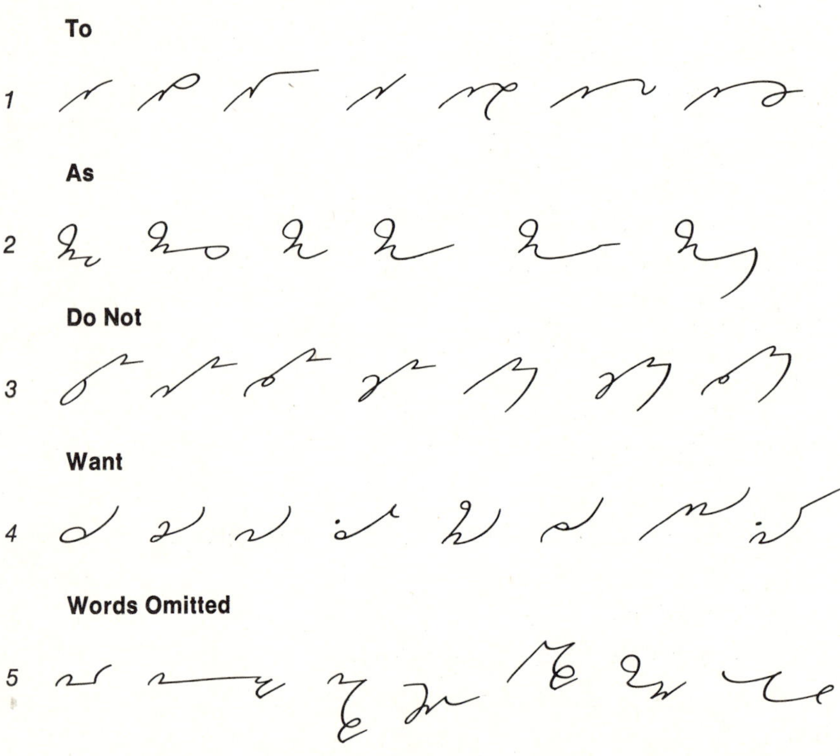

1 To the, to that, to them, to it, to keep, to go, to gain.

2 As you know, as you may, as you are, as you will, as you will not, as you will have.

3 I do not, you do not, they do not, we do not, do not have, we do not have, they do not have.

4 I want, we want, you want, he wants, if you want, they want, do you want, who wanted.

5 One of the, one of the most, one of the best, in the future, during the past, as a result, will you please.

619 GEOGRAPHICAL EXPRESSIONS

1 Chicago, New York, Pittsburgh, Parkersburg, Greensburg, Harrisburg, Plattsburg.
2 Illinois, Iowa, Kansas, Kentucky, Texas, Utah, Idaho, Montana.

Building Transcription Skills

620 SIMILAR-WORDS DRILL ■ affect, effect

affect To influence; to change.

The transaction will *affect* our financial picture.

effect *(noun)* Outcome; result.

What *effect* will the discussion have on the audience?

effect *(verb)* To accomplish; to bring about.

We want to *effect* a settlement of your account.

621 Business Vocabulary Builder

working capital Cash available for general business expenses.

acute Critical.

revitalize Bring new spirit or life to.

Reading and Writing Practice

622 Phrase Letter

as

cap.i.tal

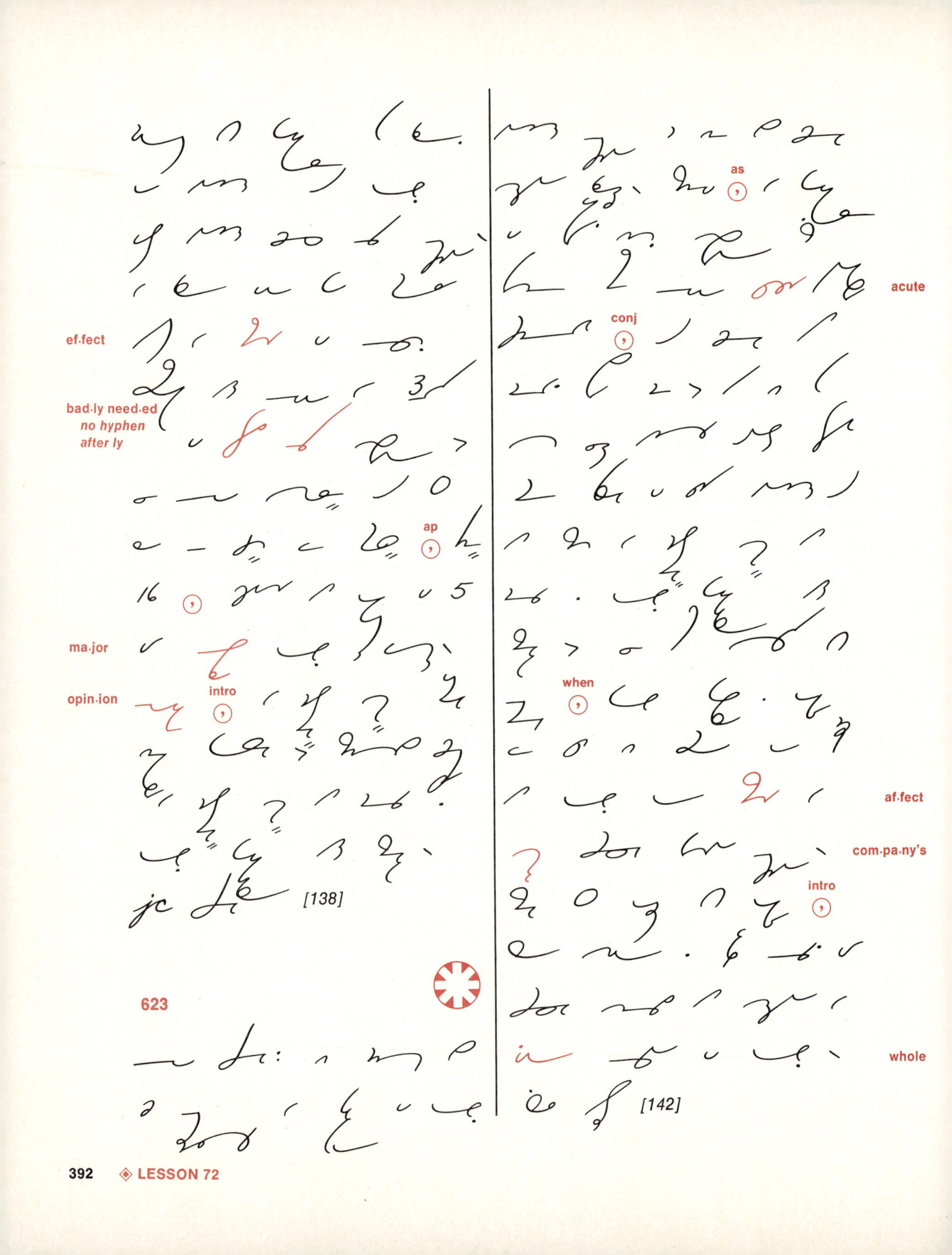

ef·fect

bad·ly need·ed
no hyphen after ly

ap

ma·jor

opin·ion

intro

[138]

623

as

acute

conj

when

af·fect

com·pa·ny's

intro

whole

[142]

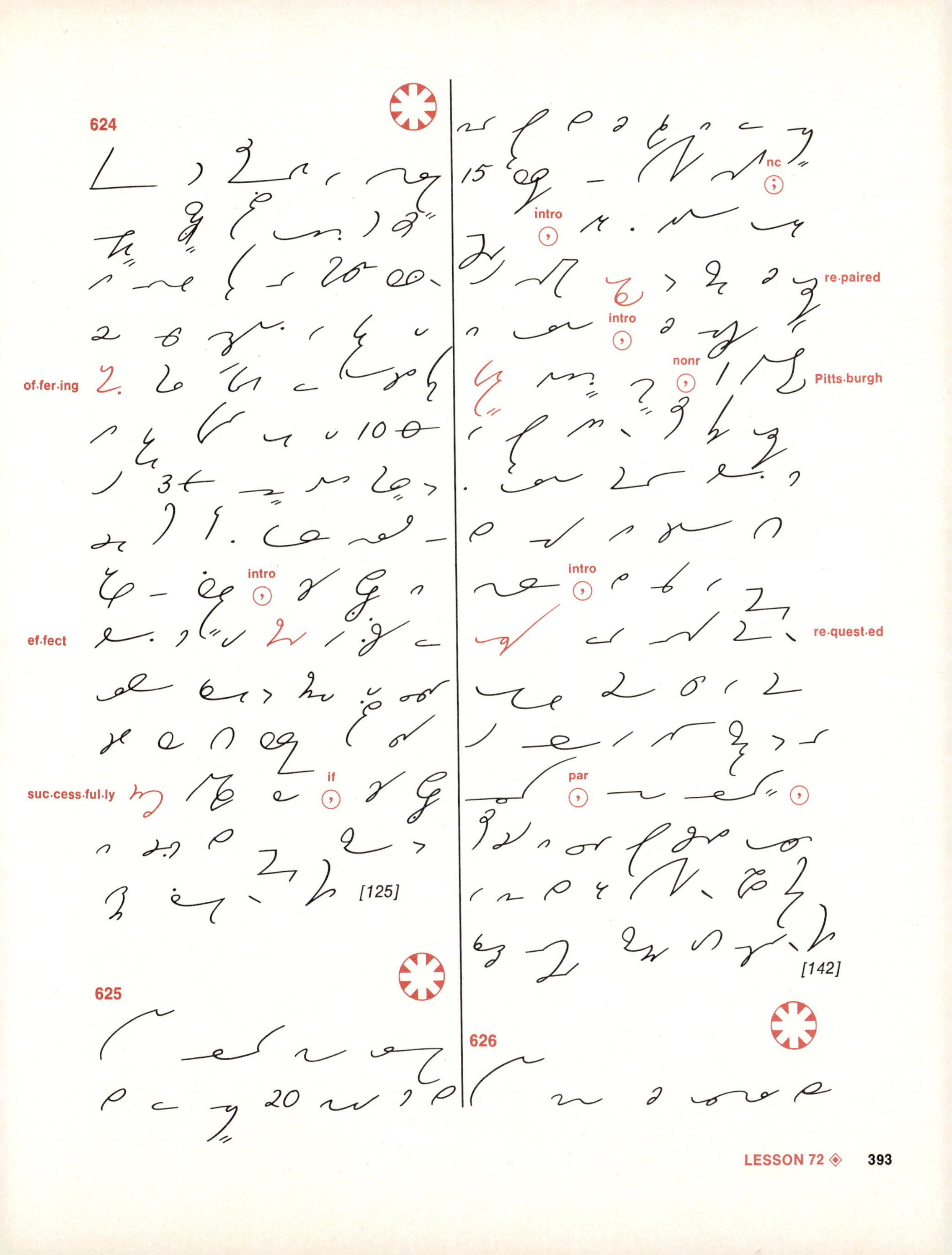

624

of·fer·ing

ef·fect

suc·cess·ful·ly

intro

intro

if

[125]

625

nc

intro

re·paired

intro

nonr

Pitts·burgh

intro

re·quest·ed

par

[142]

626

conj

at·tempt·ing

lit·tle-used *hyphenated before noun*

fre·quent·ly used *no hyphen after ly*

as

ef·fect

intro

com·plete·ly

conj

strain

[138]

627 Transcription Quiz Supply the necessary punctuation and the missing words.

[122]

Developing Word-Building Power

628 WORD FAMILIES

Ins-

-tention

-holder

-sult

1 Instant, install, instruct, institute, instigate, instrument.
2 Attention, intention, detention, contention, pretention, inattention, retention.
3 Holder, stockholder, shareholder, leaseholder, householder.
4 Result, consult, insult, resulted, consulted, insulted.

Building Transcription Skills

629 SPELLING FAMILIES ■ des-, dis-

Words beginning *des* and *dis* are often pronounced alike in such words as *describe* and *disturb.* Study the words in the following list so that you will know how to spell them correctly.

Words Beginning with Des-

de·spite	**de·scribe**	**de·stroy**
de·sire	**de·sign**	**de·spair**

Words Beginning with Dis-

dis·turb	**dis·cern**	**dis·agree·ment**
dis·ap·point	**dis·agree**	**dis·burse**

630 Business Vocabulary Builder

debris (pronounced *de·brē*) Remains of something broken or destroyed; rubble.

agenda A list of things to be done.

proxy Written authorization to act for another.

Reading and Writing Practice

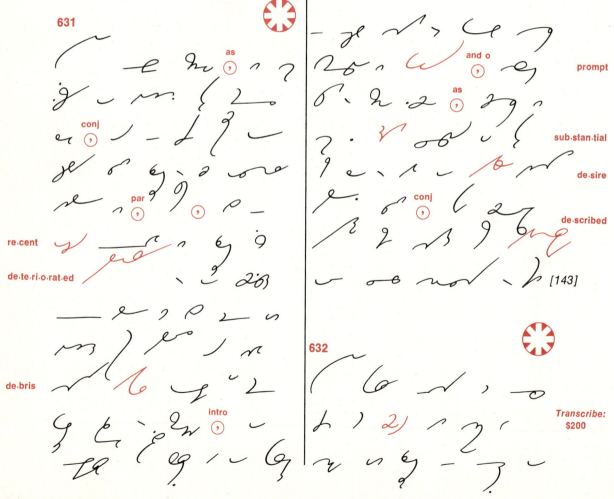

631

as

conj

par

re·cent

de·te·ri·o·rat·ed

de·bris

intro

and o

prompt

as

sub·stan·tial

de·sire

conj

de·scribed

[143]

632

Transcribe: $200

ap 18

when

Com·pa·ny's

intro

[126]

ap 15

10 2011

Transcribe:
10 a.m.
Room 2011

three-year
hyphenated before noun

freight

if

proxy

[117]

633

634

50

buy·ing

intro

cap·i·tal

[83]

635

spec·i·fied

as

as

top-notch *hyphenated before noun*

nonr

cities

if

well-trained *hyphenated before noun*

if

if

Transcribe: Extension 1161

[210]

636 Transcription Quiz Supply the necessary punctuation and the missing word.

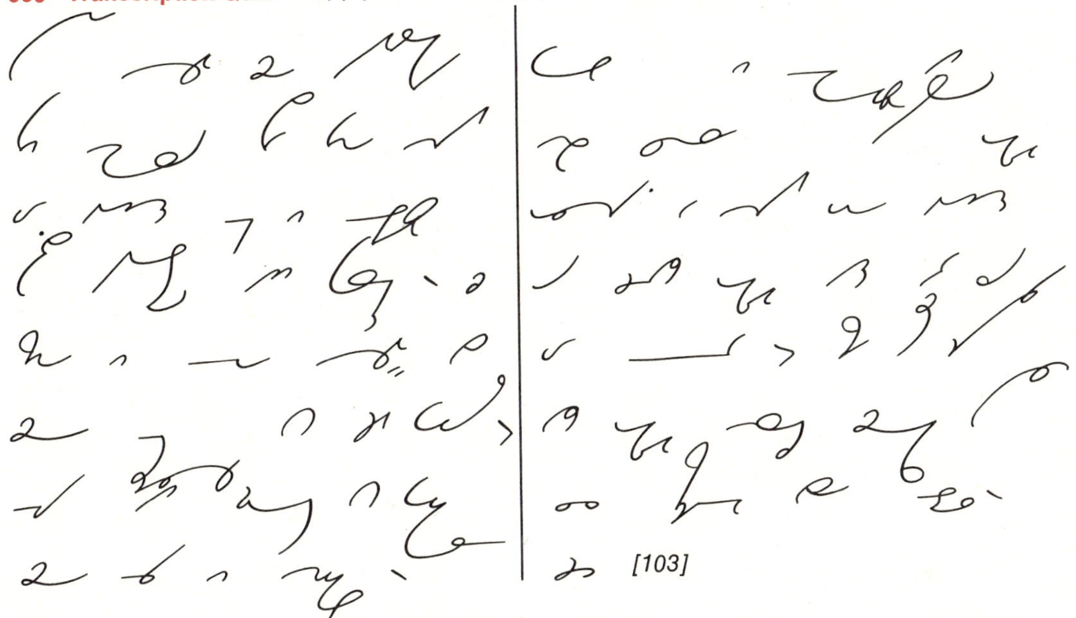

[103]

■ *Morale in the individual is his zest for living and working—or lack of it. The person with high morale believes in himself, in his future, and in others. He thinks his work is worth doing and that he is doing a good job at it. High morale helps him to take minor irritations in stride, to work under pressure when necessary without blowing up, to get along with people who want to take more than they give. High morale makes a person unbeatable.*—Laird and Laird

LESSON 74

Developing Word-Building Power

637 WORD BEGINNINGS AND ENDINGS

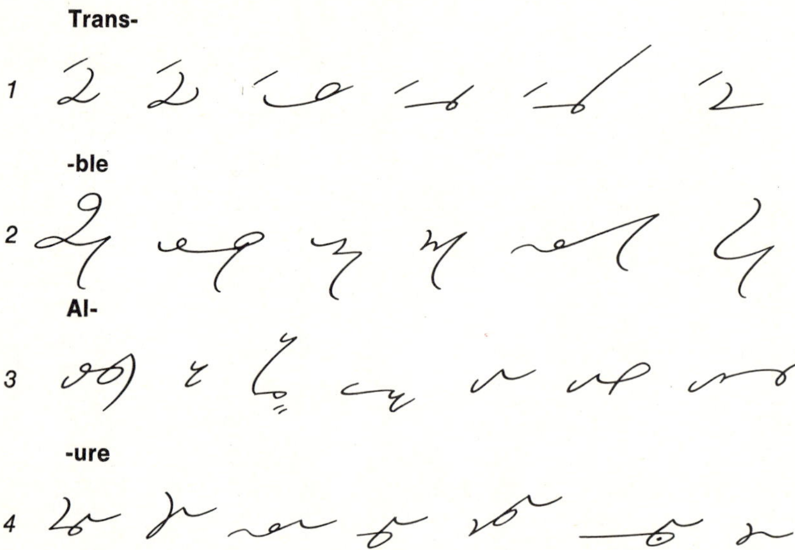

1 Transfer, transferred, translate, transmit, transmitted, transform.
2 Available, reliable, reasonable, suitable, creditable, valuable.
3 Alternative, also, Albany, almost, alter, alteration, altogether.
4 Furniture, feature, creature, nature, stature, miniature, secure.

Building Transcription Skills

638 GRAMMAR CHECKUP ■ pronoun after than or as

You can determine which pronoun to use after *than* or *as* by mentally adding the words that make a complete clause.

I want to go with you rather than him. *(rather than go with him)*

Jane can type the paper as well as I. *(can type the paper)*

No one knows better than I *that you are dependable. (better than I know that you are dependable)*

639

Business Vocabulary Builder

fragile Easily broken.

meticulous Extremely careful.

effects *(noun)* Movable property.

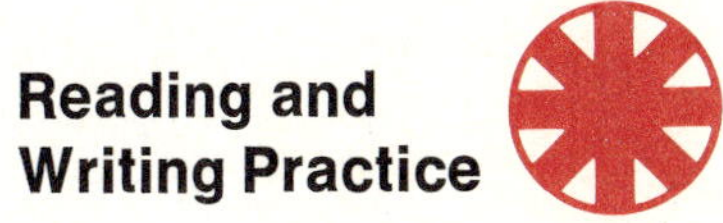

Reading and Writing Practice

640

yours par

oc·ca·sion·al·ly

ex·pen·sive as par

em·ploy·ee

when

ser cloth·ing

[211]

641

as

fac·tor

par

intro

ap

trans·ferred

[145]

ap·pre·ci·ate

642

intro

day's

if

if

idle

112-1122

rea·son·able

nc ;

[180]

well-trained *hyphenated before noun*

[134]

643

intro ,

pre·par·ing

644

lives

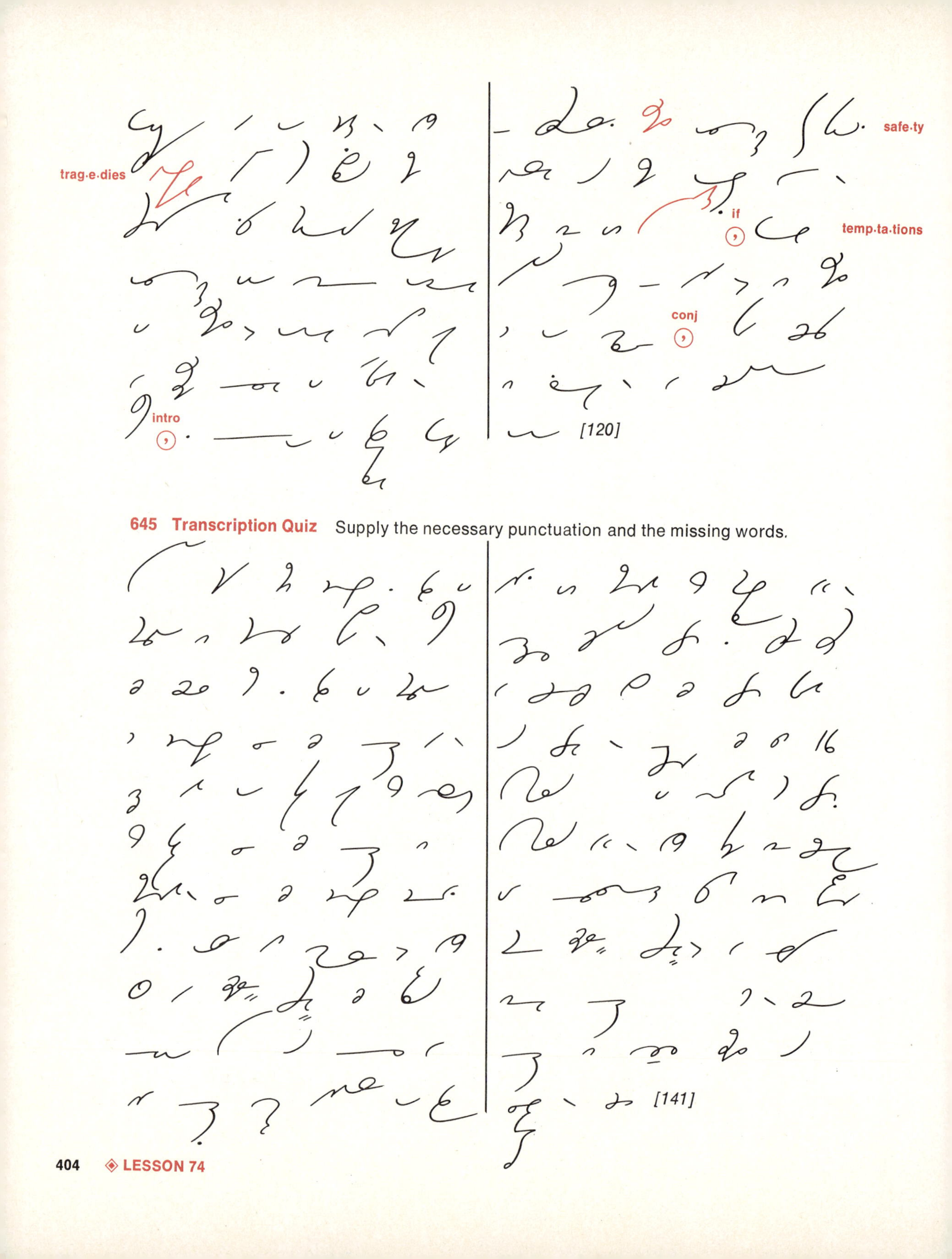

trag·e·dies

intro

safe·ty

if

temp·ta·tions

conj

[120]

645 Transcription Quiz Supply the necessary punctuation and the missing words.

[141]

LESSON 75

Developing Word-Building Power

646 SHORTHAND VOCABULARY BUILDER

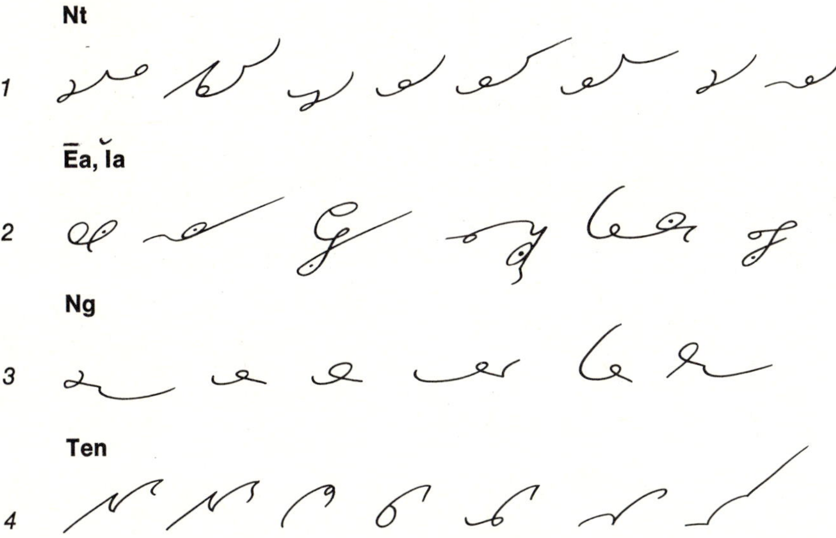

1 Century, dependent, recent, rent, rented, rental, sent, current.

2 Areas, created, appreciated, negotiations, brilliance, initiate.

3 Single, ring, rang, length, bring, tangle.

4 Distance, distances, tennis, attention, retention, continue, intended.

Building Transcription Skills

647 Business Vocabulary Builder

traumatic Shattering; staggering.

alleviate Lessen; relieve.

alter Change. (Do not confuse with *altar* which is a place of worship.)

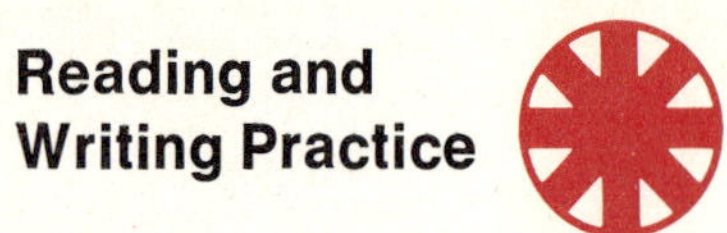

Reading and Writing Practice

648 Revolution in Transportation

intro

dra·mat·ic

horse-drawn *hyphenated before noun*

par

Amer·i·ca's

nonr

role

intro

par

intro

de·vel·op·ments

high-speed *hyphenated before noun*

par

ar·eas

The development

intro

Kit·ty Hawk

ser

par

intro

al·ready

un·for·tu·nate

conj

intro

ef·fect

pol·lu·tion

con·ges·tion

The first

ap

Man

par

[483]

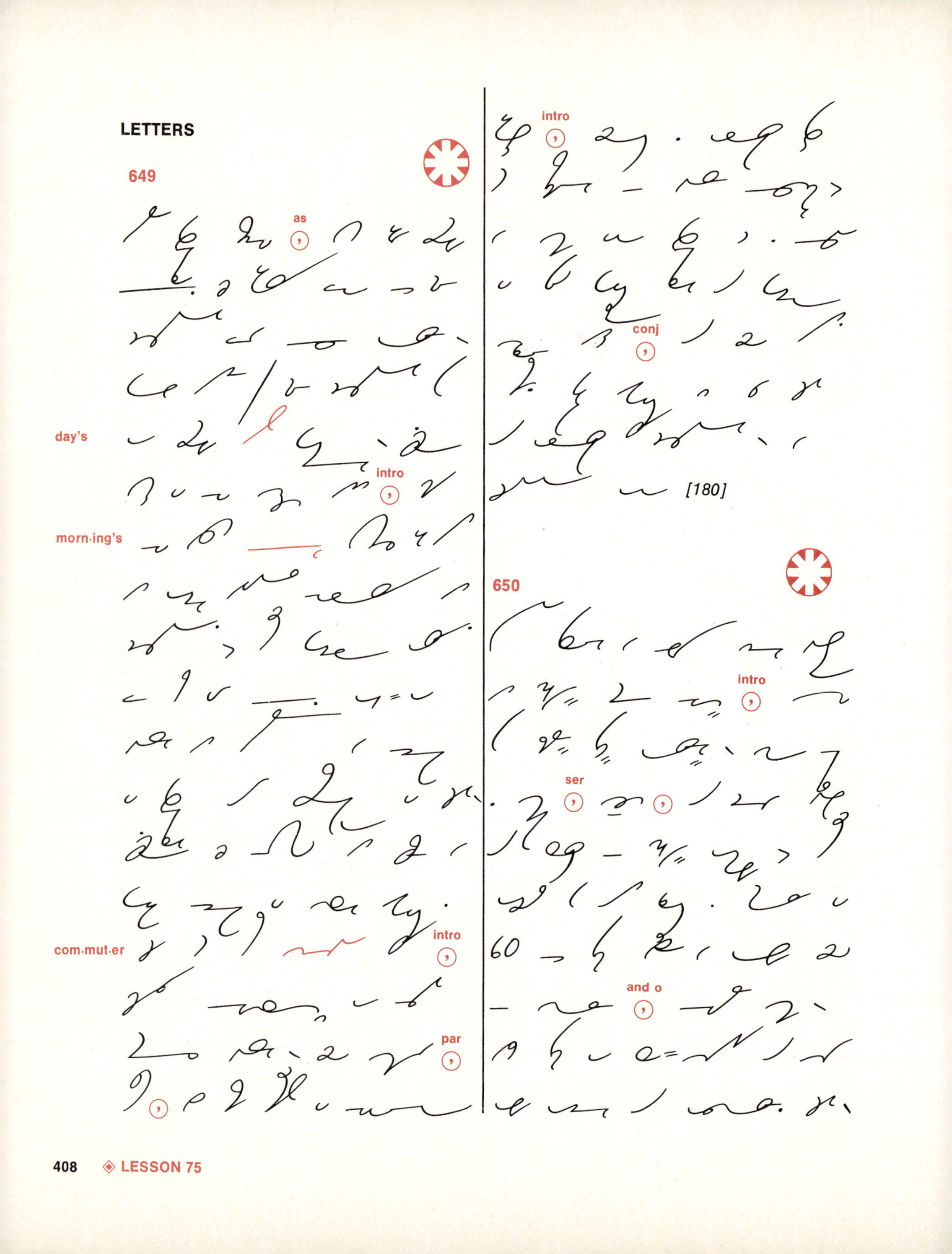

LETTERS

649

as

day's

intro

morn·ing's

com·mut·er

intro

par

intro

conj

[180]

650

intro

ser

and o

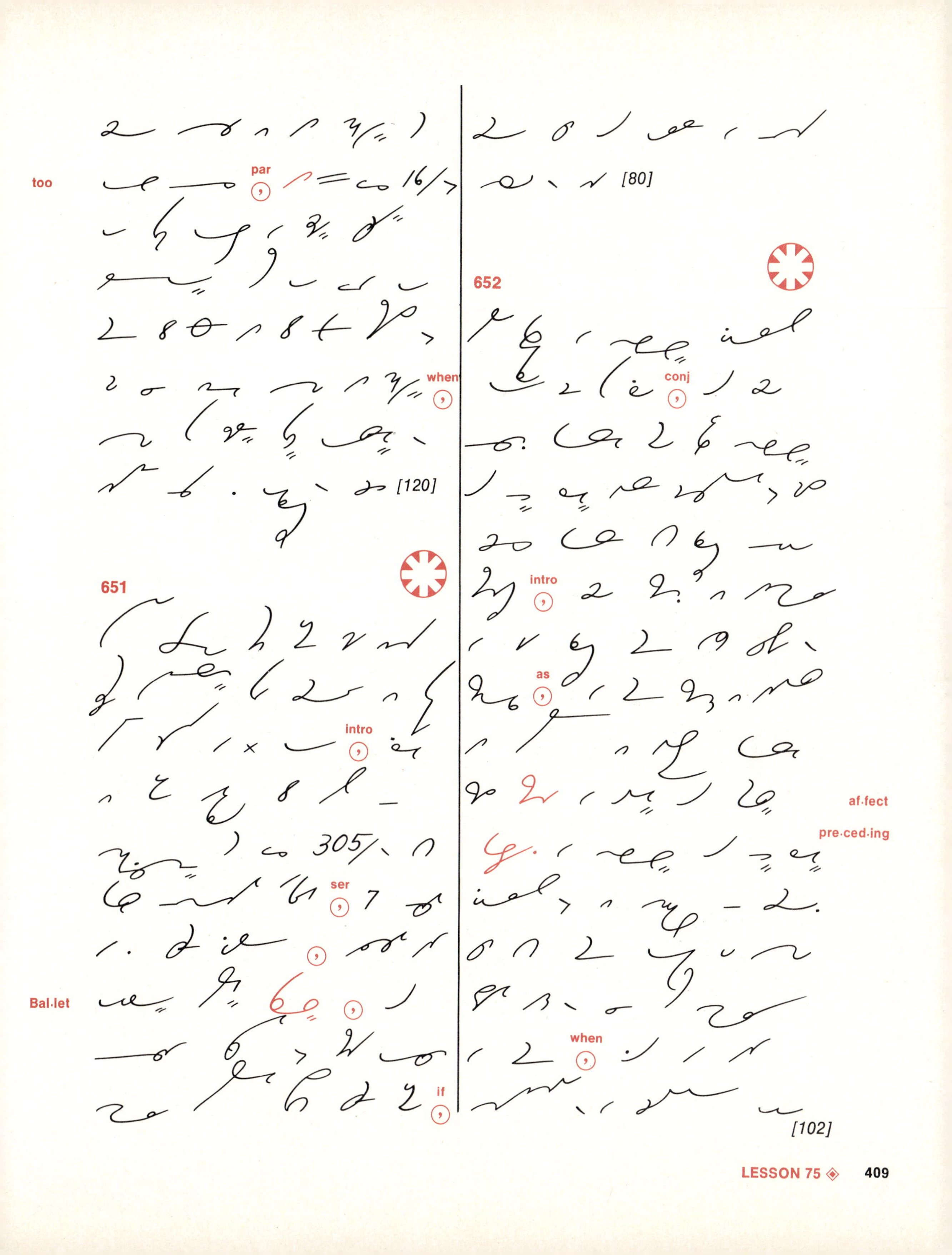

too

par

16/

when

[120]

651

intro

305/

ser

Bal·let

if

[80]

652

conj

intro

as

af·fect

pre·ced·ing

when

[102]

16 Travel

LESSON 76

Developing Word-Building Power

653 BRIEF FORMS AND DERIVATIVES

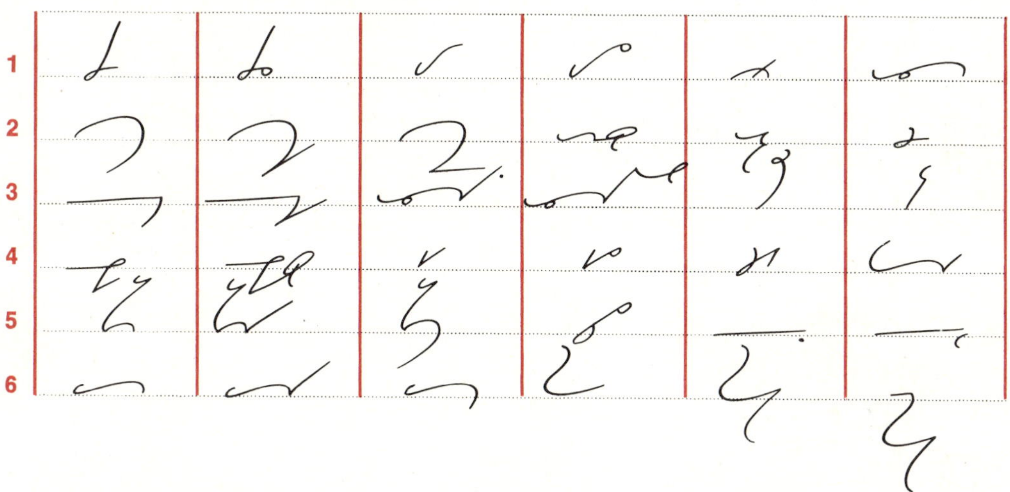

1 General, generally; ordinary, ordinarily; quantity, regular.
2 Govern, governed, government; recognize, responsible, send.
3 Manufacture, manufactured; regarding, regardless; several, such.
4 Merchant, merchandise; short, shortly; situation, progressed.
5 Object, objected; objective, idea, morning, mornings.
6 Organize, organized, organization; value, valuable, invaluable.

Building Transcription Skills

654 Business Vocabulary Builder

scenic Beautiful.

itineraries Detailed plans for trips.

wistfully Longingly; wishfully.

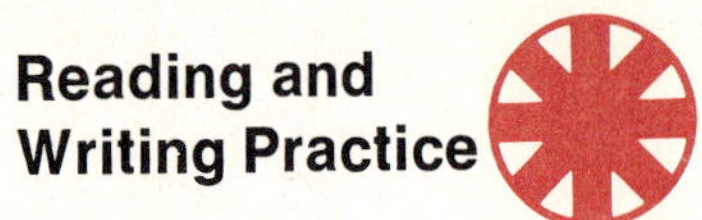

655 Brief-Form Letter

routes

nc

sce·nic

if

at·ten·dants

[130]

656

ap

Transcribe: 8 a.m.

intro

available

conj

if

[107]

657

ser

itin·er·aries

par

for·ward

[141]

658

if

ad·ver·tise·ments

conj

par

ad·ven·ture

re·al·i·ty

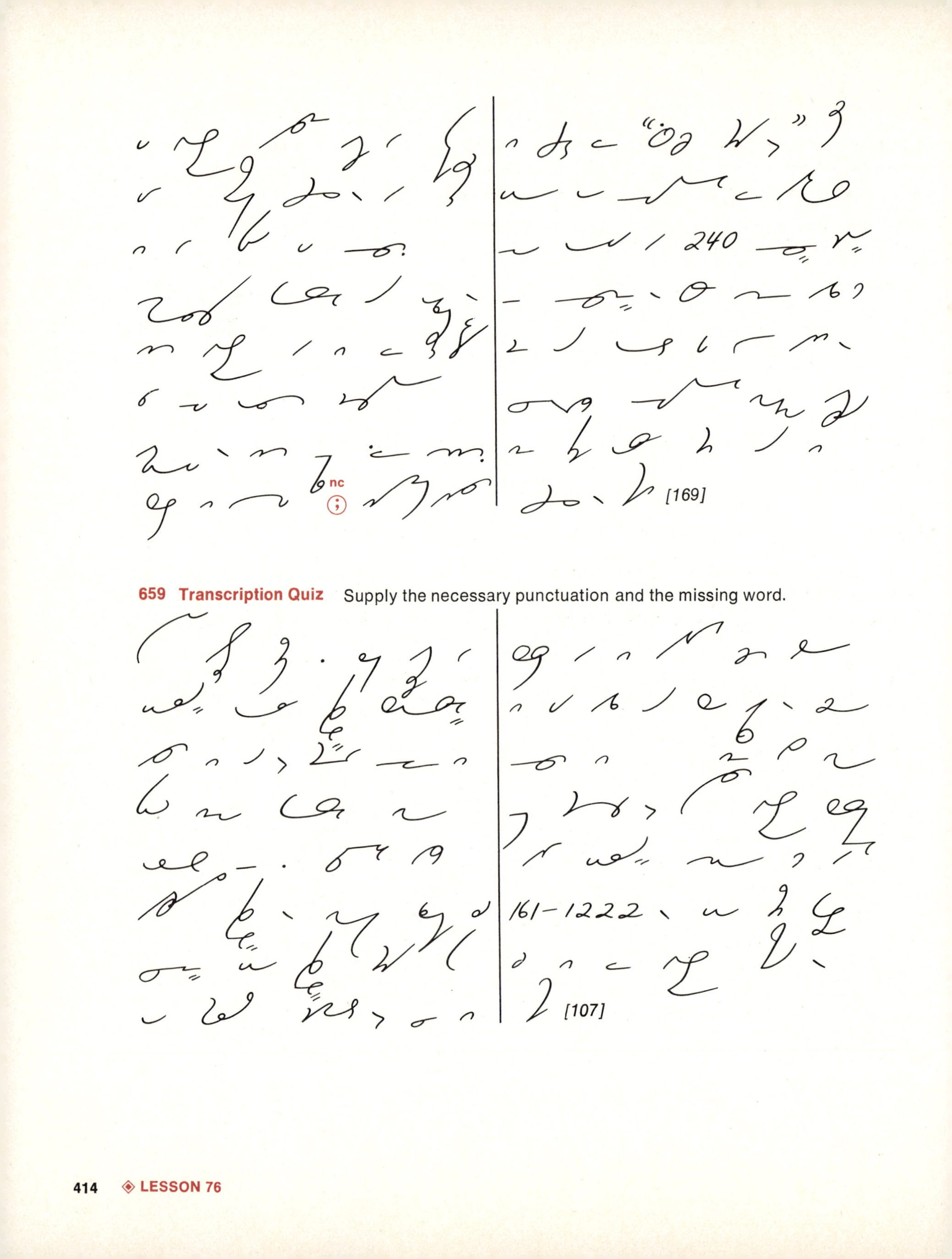

240

[169]

659 Transcription Quiz Supply the necessary punctuation and the missing word.

161-1222

[107]

Short Transpositions

A businessman may decide to transpose a word or phrase for emphasis or some other reason. The simplest way to indicate the transposition of a word or phrase is to use the printer's sign for transposition. The businessman might say:

> *We are conducting a campaign for our cars in both weekly and monthly magazines—make that* **monthly and weekly magazines.**

In your notes you would indicate the transposition thus:

You should then be careful, when you transcribe, to type the word *and* after the word *monthly.*

660 Illustration of Office-Style Dictation

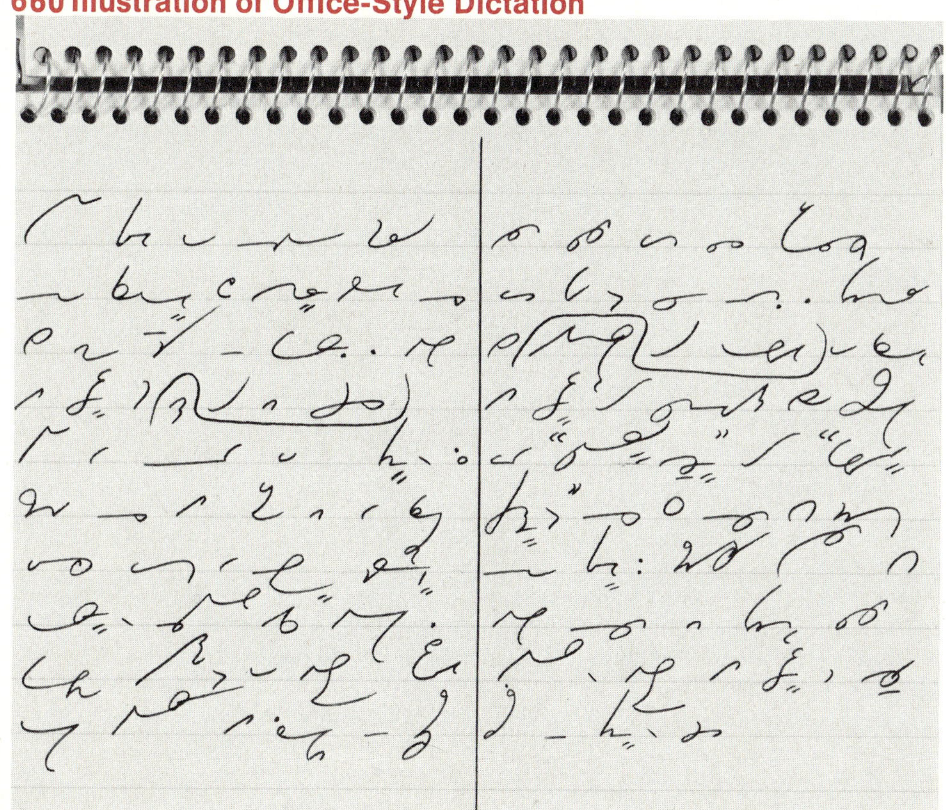

Building Phrasing Skill

661 USEFUL BUSINESS-LETTER PHRASES

Let Us

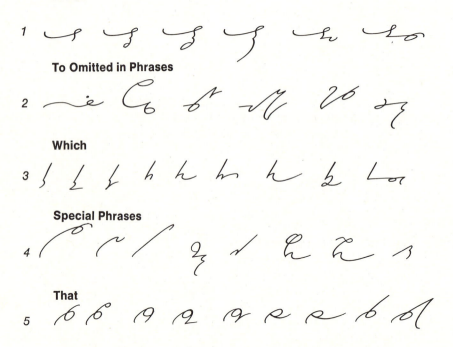

1

To Omitted in Phrases

2

Which

3

Special Phrases

4

That

5

1 Let us, let us see, let us say, let us have, let us know, let us make.

2 Glad to hear, able to say, in addition to the, in order to obtain, up to date, seems to be.

3 Which is, which is not, which is the, which you, which you are, which you can, which you will, which we are, which means.

4 To make, to know, to do, as soon as possible, your order, I hope you are, we hope you will, to us.

5 That the, that they, that is, that is not, that is the, that are, that will, that would, that would be.

662 GEOGRAPHICAL EXPRESSIONS

1 England, France, Germany, Spain, Norway, Denmark, Sweden.
2 United States, America, Pacific, Europe, Asia, Africa.

Building Transcription Skills

663 SIMILAR-WORDS DRILL ■ fair, fare

fair Just; clear weather.

We want to be *fair.*
The weather is usually *fair.*

fare The price of transportation.

Did you pay your plane *fare?*

664 Business Vocabulary Builder

innovations New developments.

congenial Friendly; easy to know.

departure Act of leaving.

lodging Living accommodations.

Reading and Writing Practice

665 Phrase Letter

trav·el

par

rea·son

intro

par

when

prompt

ser

intro

[117]

666

conj

guides

intro

con·ge·nial

conj

lodg·ing

ap

par

de·scribes

[144]

667

un·hur·ried

ap

cruises

ap

enjoyable

[150]

668

conj

month's

ser

par

fair

if

Scandinavia

fare

[151]

669

all-ex·pense hyphenated before noun

Cin·cin·nati

Transcribe: 8 a.m. May 6

ap

nonr

and o

de·li·cious

Lou·is·ville's

if

[120]

670 **Transcription Quiz** Supply the necessary punctuation and the missing words.

[137]

LESSON 78

Developing Word-Building Power

671 WORD FAMILIES

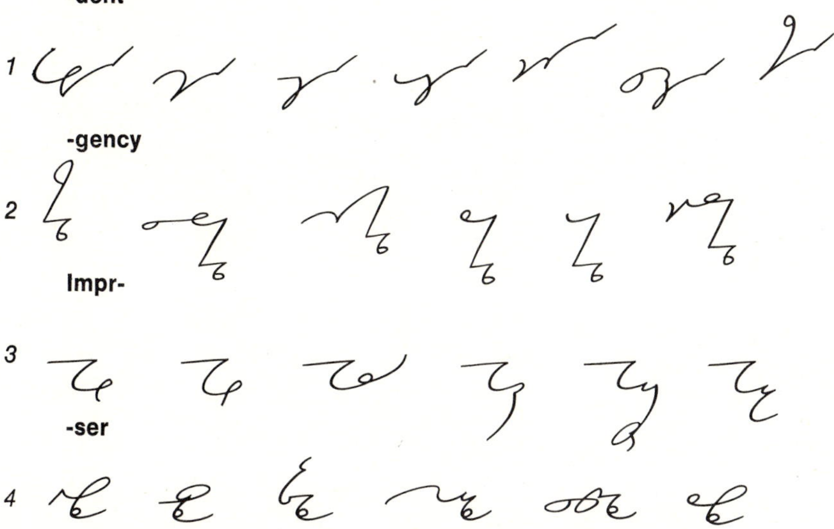

1 President, confident, incident, resident, student, accident, evident.
2 Agency, emergency, contingency, urgency, regency, stringency.
3 Impress, impression, imprint, improve, improvise, improper.
4 Tracer, nicer, sponsor, grocer, announcer, eraser.

Building Transcription Skills

672 SPELLING FAMILIES ■ -cial, -tial

Be careful when you transcribe words ending in the sound of *shul.* Sometimes it is spelled *cial;* at other times, *tial.*

Words Ending in -cial

spe·cial	**ben·e·fi·cial**	**ar·ti·fi·cial**
so·cial	**fi·nan·cial**	**su·per·fi·cial**

Words Ending in -tial

es·sen·tial	**po·ten·tial**	**res·i·den·tial**
ini·tial	**con·fi·den·tial**	**par·tial**

673 Business Vocabulary Builder

traverse To travel across or through.

thesis Written account of a research project.

reimburses Pays back.

Reading and Writing Practice

674

con·fer·ence

ap

ac·cept

conj

emer·gen·cy

intro

com·pa·ny's

if

ap

Com·mer·cial

conj

con·fi·dent

[131]

675

intro

ca·noe·ing

tra·verse

nonr

ser

if

equip·ment

[125]

676

nc

thor·ough·ly

par

nonr

broth·er's

ini·tial

first

conj

and o

en·joy·able

[140]

677

spon·sor

intro

Eu·ro·pe·an

ben·e·fi·cial

conj

re·im·burses

cul·tured

and o

if

es·sen·tial

par

[201]

678

10

ac·cept

211 21

if

nonr

Hol·i·day

5

[96]

679

shut·tle

intro

intro

[103]

680 Transcription Quiz Supply the necessary punctuation and the missing word.

[116]

Developing Word-Building Power

681 WORD BEGINNINGS AND ENDINGS

Turn, Etc.

Inter-

Ther-

-lity

1 Eastern, western, southern, turn, terminal, attorney, determine.
2 Interest, international, interview, interpret, interval, interrupt, interfered.
3 Other, together, altogether, either, neither, bothered, rather, gather.
4 Facility, responsibility, advisability, quality, reliability, personalities.

Building Transcription Skills

682 COMMON PREFIXES ■ inter-

inter- between

international Between nations.

intermediate In between; coming between two points.

interim The time between one event and another.

interval A space between two objects; a space of time between events.

intercede To come between.

intermission The period between the acts of a performance.

683 **Business Vocabulary Builder**

abroad Overseas.

wholesale Price charged to retailers for subsequent sale to public.

amended Changed.

Reading and Writing Practice

684

three-week hyphenated before noun

as

Ot·ta·wa ser

in·ter·me·di·ate

par

[110]

685

ser Can·a·da's

sep·a·rate·ly

ser

intro

par

en·joy·able

and o

[120]

686

Ho·ri·zons

ap

ar·ti·cle

nonr

abroad

intro

whole·sale

intro

re·cent·ly

conj

bur·dens

intro

[187]

687

ap

Transcribe: Flight 211

con·ve·nient

if

[104]

688 Transcription Quiz Supply the necessary punctuation and the missing word.

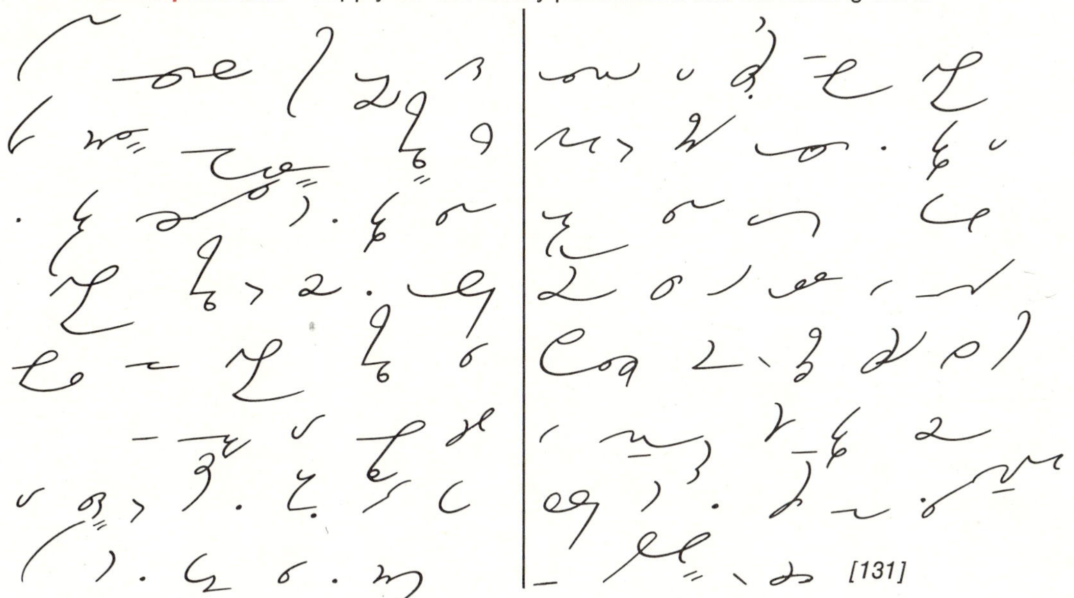

[131]

■ *An attractive, neatly typed letter signifies more than a responsible secretary; it becomes a sample of the taste and character of the company. No letter that a secretary mails out should ever be less than perfect.*

Long Transpositions

Occasionally your employer will decide that an entire sentence or even a paragraph would be more effective if it were transposed to another part of the letter. When this happens, the simplest way to show the long transposition is to encircle the material to be transposed and indicate the new position by an arrow.

689 Illustration of Office-Style Dictation

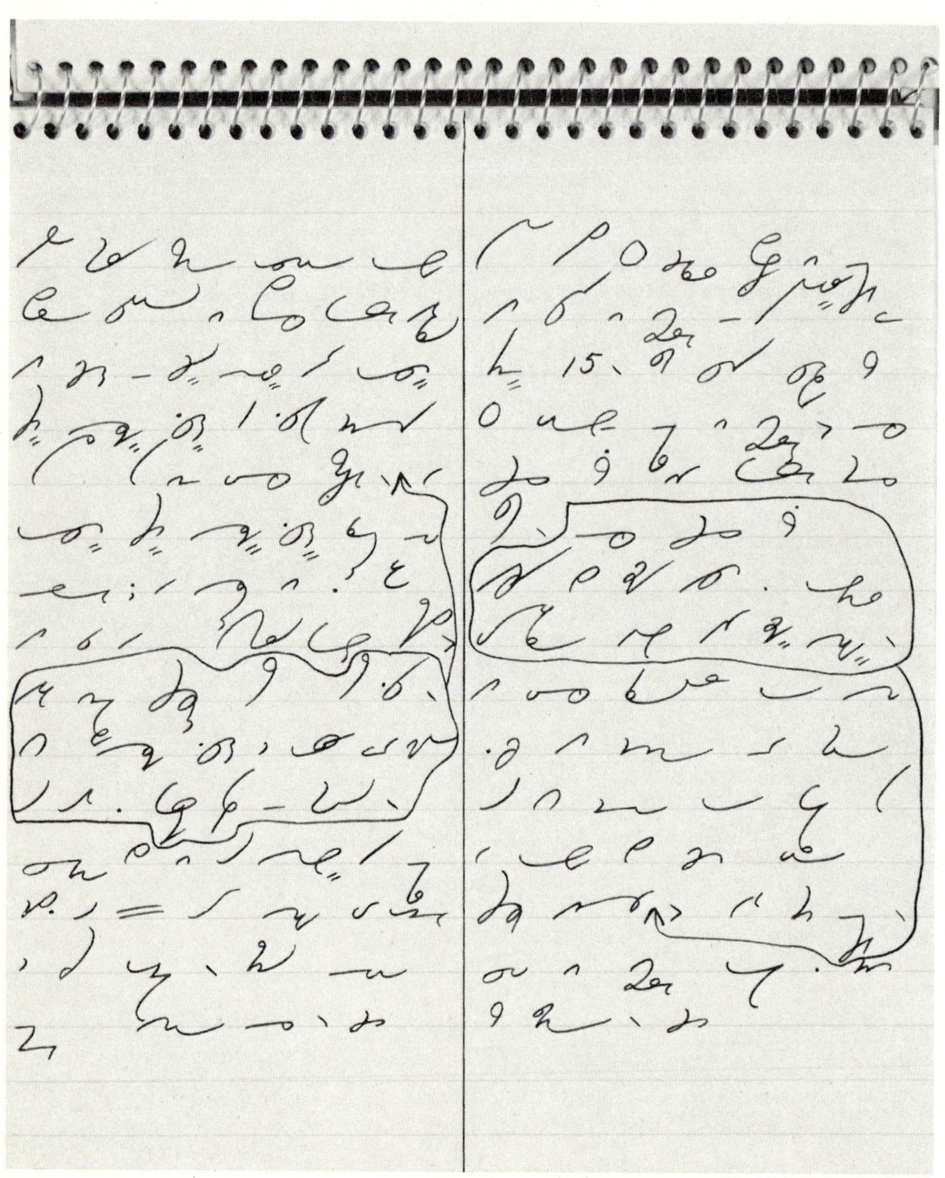

Developing Word-Building Power

690 SHORTHAND VOCABULARY BUILDER

Ten, Den, Etc.

1

Abbreviation -quire

2

Mem, Men

3

Ū

4

1 Assistance, written, maintain, fortunately, intend, guidance.
2 Inquire, acquire, acquired, require, requirement, esquire.
3 Memory, memorable, remember, mention, recommendation.
4 Excuse, reputable, human, document, humor, unique.

Building Transcription Skills

691 Business Vocabulary Builder

consul Official representative of one country residing in another.

passport Official paper granted by one's own government authorizing international travel.

carriers Transportation companies.

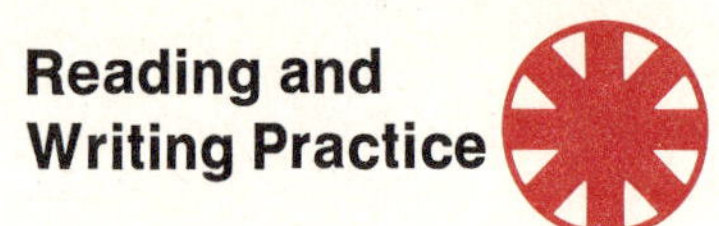

692 Travel Know-How

conj

ex·cep·tion

for·tu·nate·ly

intro

intro

car·ri·ers

phase

wear

It is

conj

ser

cus·toms

con·sul·ar

blurred

for·eign

nc

if

Always

length

vi·sas

conj

up to date
no noun,
no hyphen

first-class
hyphenated
before noun

intro

bur·den

intro

ser

med·i·cines

Don't

if

me·men·to

spe·cial·ties

conj

Don't

nc

stren·u·ous

conj

hu·mor

best-made *hyphenated before noun*

guid·ance

when

as·sis·tance

par

nonr

ser

if

ad·vice

[666]

LETTERS

693

when

Transcribe: Flight 115

nc

en·trees

menus

hon·ored

del·i·ca·cies

intro

and o

intro

115

[122]

694

Di·rec·to·ry

450

ser

intro

intro

let·ter·head

if

(600) 211-5556

and o

24

intro

[153]

APPENDIX

RECALL DRILLS

Joined Word Endings

1 -ment

2 -tion

3 -tial

4 -ly

5 -ily

6 -ful

7 -sume, -sumption

8 -ble

9 -ther

10 -ual

11 -ure

12 -self, -selves

13 -ort

14 -tain

15 -cient, -ciency

Disjoined Word Endings

16 -hood

17 -ward

18 -ship

19 -cal, -cle

20 -ulate, -ulation

21 -ingly

22 -ings

23 -gram

24 -ification

25 -lity

26 -lty

27 -rity

Joined Word Beginnings

28 Per-, Pur-

29 Em-

30 Im-

31 In-

32 En-

33 Un-

34 Re-

35 Be-

36 De-, Di-

37 Dis-, Des-

38 Mis-

39 Ex-

40 Com-

41 Con-

42 Sub-

43 Al-

44 For-, Fore-

45 Fur-

46 Tern-, Etc.

47 Ul-

DISJOINED WORD BEGINNINGS

48 Post-

49 Inter-, Etc.

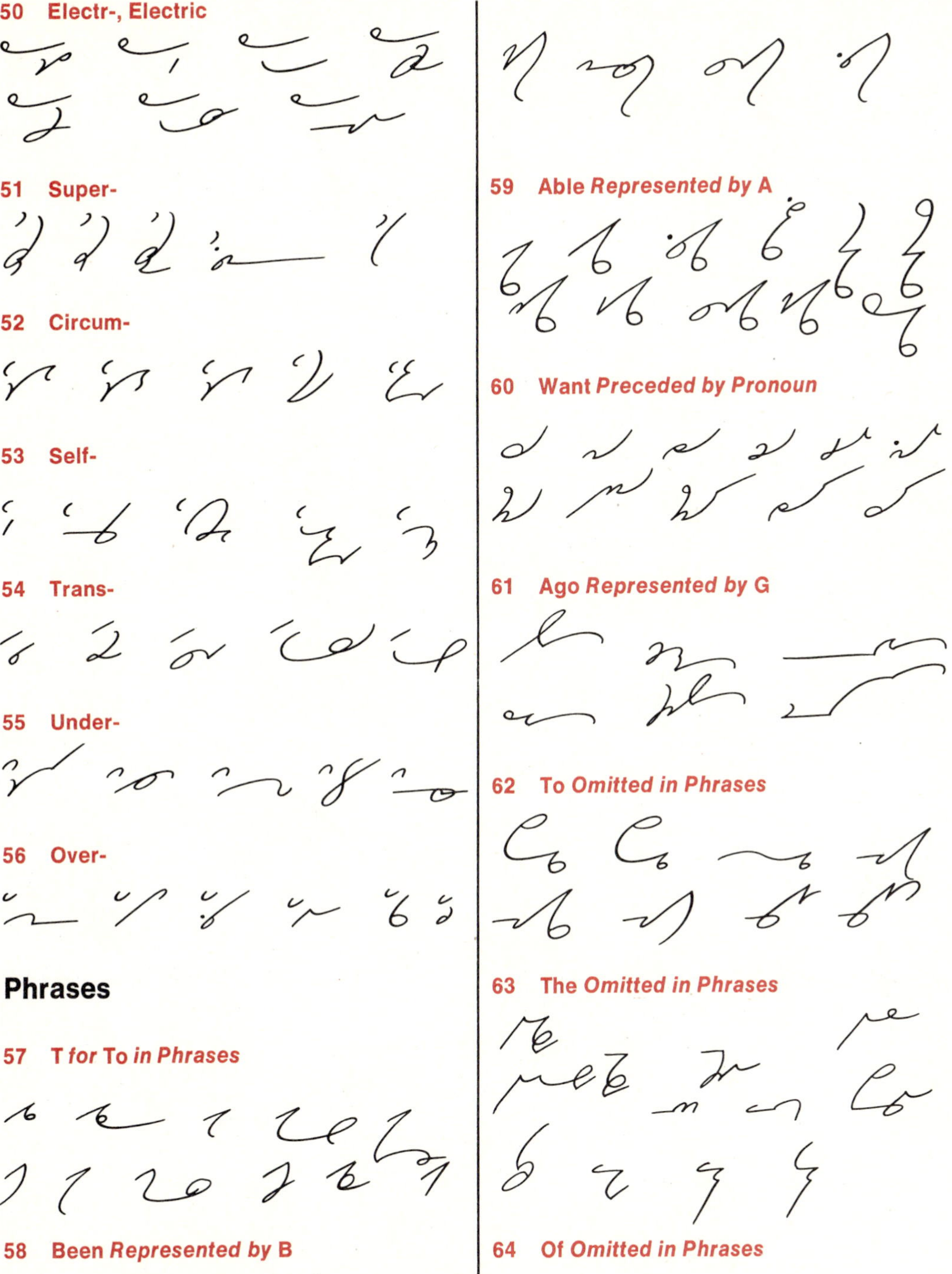
50 Electr-, Electric

51 Super-

52 Circum-

53 Self-

54 Trans-

55 Under-

56 Over-

Phrases

57 T *for* To *in Phrases*

58 Been *Represented by* B

59 Able *Represented by* A

60 Want *Preceded by Pronoun*

61 Ago *Represented by* G

62 To *Omitted in Phrases*

63 The *Omitted in Phrases*

64 Of *Omitted in Phrases*

65 A Omitted in Phrases

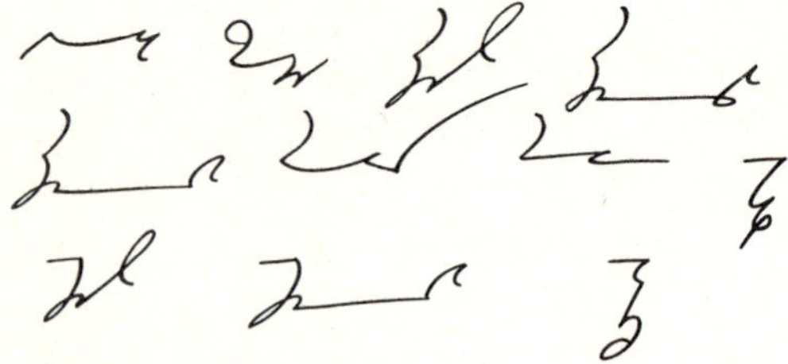

66 *Intersected Phrases*

67 *Special Phrases*

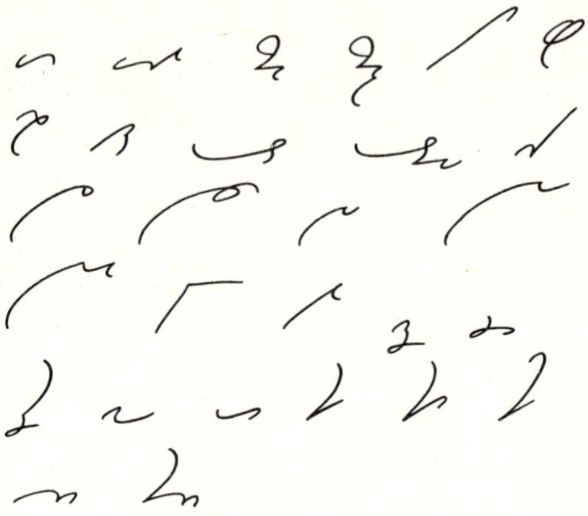

ADDRESSES FOR TRANSCRIPTION

(The numbers of the following names and addresses correspond to the numbers of the supplementary letters in the *Instructor's Handbook for Gregg Shorthand for Colleges, Diamond Jubilee Series, Volume Two, Second Edition.)*

Chapter 1

1 Miss Jane Johnson, State Realty Company, 1201 Avenue B, Elkhart, IN 46514

2 Mr. D. C. Royal, National Products Company, 206 Wilson Road, Harrison, NY 10528

3 The Honorable John Kelley, Mayor of Springfield, Springfield, TX 75214

4 Mr. George Rusk, 1801 First Street, Westport, CT 06880

5 Mr. Keith Jackson, 814 Sixth Avenue, Dover, DE 19901

Chapter 2

6 Mr. Edward C. Hunter, 128 Madison Avenue, Tacoma, WA 98411

7 Mr. A. B. Weaver, 215 Beacon Street, Boston, MA 02143

8 Mr. H. M. Jamison, Manager, Governor Smith Hotel, 201 Elm Street, Dallas, TX 75201

9 Mr. Willard Preston, 18 Green Road, White Plains, NY 10601

10 The National Service Station, 1300 Crestwood, Denver CO 80222

Chapter 3

11 Mr. K. N. Brown, 41 South Street, Rockville, NH 03301

12 Mr. Carl Jackson, 160 Franklin Avenue, St. Louis, MO 66111

13 Mr. J. T. Newton, Director, Birmingham Regional Air Terminal, Birmingham, AL 36302

14 Mr. S. T. Houston, Manager, Customer Relations, Western Airlines, 156 Fifth Avenue, Los Angeles, CA 90015

15 Wilson Aircraft Corporation, Wilson Building, Kennedy Boulevard, Jersey City, NJ 07304

Chapter 4

16 Mr. A. R. James, Vice President, Springfield National Bank, 300 Third Avenue, Springfield, OH 45512

17 Mr. Ray Snider, Virginia National Bank, 165 Lee Avenue, Falls Church, VA 22040

18 Mr. C. C. Toby, First National Bank, 151 Grand Avenue, Detroit, MI 48207

19 Mr. T. E. Hunt, Personnel Director, Chemical Bank of California, 121 Bay Street, San Francisco, CA 94120

20 The First National Bank, Main Plaza, Providence, RI 02901

Chapter 5

21 Mr. George M. Smith, Central Commercial College, Little Rock, AR 72203

22 Mr. Kenneth Baxter, Universal Computer Company, 510 Del Rey Street, Los Angeles, CA 90025

23 Mr. Albert R. Green, Coastal Electronics, 18 Eastern Parkway, Portland, OR 97250

24 Mr. Donald Harding, President, Colorado Data Processing Systems, 415 Trent Street, Pueblo, CO 81009

25 The Goldburg Company, 15 Park Place, Minneapolis, MN 55433

Chapter 6

26 Dr. Charles Evans, School of Education, Eastern State University, Newark, NJ 07118

27 Professor Gerald Burns, The Art Institute of Georgia, 15 West Street, Atlanta, GA 34615

28 Dr. J. C. Andrews, Dean, Graduate School, Western University, Helena, MT 59601

29 Mr. Charles M. Farmington, Southern Michigan Distributors, 14 Dade Boulevard, Miami, FL 33125

30 Mr. A. C. Smith, Personnel Manager, Technical Service Company, One Main Street, Montpelier, VT 05602

Chapter 7

31 Mr. L. H. Scott, The Hotel Association of Chicago, 15 Wabash Street, Chicago, IL 60655

32 Mr. James Kent, 1617 Jefferson Street, Cullman, AL 35055

33 Mrs. J. R. Fraser, 18 Lake Drive, Seattle, WA 98112

34 Mr. H. H. James, 1301 Glendale Avenue, Los Angeles, CA 90015

35 The General National Bank, One Main Place, Dallas, TX 75208

Chapter 8

36 Mr. Thomas Short, Vice President, World Insurance Company, Chicago, IL 60670

37 Mr. Joseph Harding, National Insurance Company, 30 Madison Avenue, New York, NY 10037

38 Mr. L. A. Kennedy, Mercantile Life Insurance Company, Durham, NC 27701

39 Mr. William Bauer, Reliable Insurance Company, 16 East 51 Street, New York, NY 10022

40 Mrs. Lucille Bennette, 81020 Lindhurst Drive, Los Angeles CA 90056

Chapter 9

41 Mr. Alvin C. White, General Clothing Manufacturing Company, 141 Commerce Street, Memphis, TN 38128

Chapter 9 (Continued)

42 Mr. J. C. Black, Central Manufacturing Company, 42 Park Avenue, Detroit, MI 48226

43 Mr. Horace Wilson, President, Wilson Company, 30 Franklin Square, Philadelphia, PA 19144

44 Mr. Arthur C. King, Wilson Manufacturing Company, One Madison Avenue, New York, NY 10017

45 Mrs. James Jones, 1611 Hancock, Vernon, TX 78701

Chapter 10

46 Johnson Business Systems, 30 Madison Avenue, New York, NY 10017

47 Mr. D. K. Davis, Simplex Company, 14 Parker Drive, Bloomsburg, PA 17815

48 Mr. David Anderson, Ajax Business Machines Company, 56 Harris Road, Reading, PA 19607

49 Mr. Phillip Wagner, Central Supply Company, 1516 First Avenue, Lexington, NC 27292

50 Mr. Henry Carson, 141 Second Street, New Haven, CT 06512

Chapter 11

51 Mr. P. C. Pierce, Pierce Supply Company, 416 Railroad Avenue, Milton, DE 19968

52 Miss Delphine Day, 33 Main Street, Elizabeth, NJ 07215

53 Mr. A. L. Shaw, Personnel Director, The Foley Company, 55 State Street, Chicago, IL 60655

54 Dr. Jeffrey Washing, Director, Placement Center, State College, 48 Mill Road, Houston, TX 77017

55 Mrs. Janet Mason, 130 South Boulevard, Des Moines, IA 50315

Chapter 12

56 Mr. Tim South, 18 East Broadway, Brooklyn, NY 11224

57 Mr. V. V. Green, 171 Jackson Street, Florence, AL 35904

58 Mr. Arnold Wolff, Manager, The Modern Book Company, Long Beach, CA 90801

59 Mr. Edward Crawley, 166 Garden Road, Missoula, MT 59801

60 The Basic Book Company, 16 Butler Road, Glendale, CA 91209

Chapter 13

61a Mr. G. R. Powell, 1301 Hancock Street, Cincinnati, OH 45217

61b Mr. Everett Weaver, 1816 Bensonhurst Drive, Cleveland, OH 44131

62a Mr. Paul Smith, 61 Eastern Parkway, Oak Grove, WI 53925

62b Mr. J. C. Morgan, 1209 Spaulding, Madison WI 53716

Chapter 13 (Continued)

63a Mr. Z. A. Brown, 611 Field Point Drive, Belleville, NJ 08502
63b Mr. Max Ryder, Ryder Realty, 18 Southpark Drive, Vicksburg, MS 39180
64a Mr. F. A. Strong, 14 Weber Road, Ogden, UT 84401
64b Mr. James R. West, 416 Adams Street, Charleston, SC 29404
65a Leisure Village Corporation, Smoke Rise, NJ 07070
65b Mr. Horace Jennings, 17 South First Street, Yonkers, NY 10704

Chapter 14

66a Mrs. Ethel Rogers, Retail Business Association, Milford, CT 06460
66b Mr. Benjamin Hill, Coordinator, Department of Distributive Education, Milford High School, Milford, CT 06051
67a Mr. Kenneth Casey, Casey Manufacturing Company, 16 Randolph Street, Peoria, IL 61604
67b Mr. Kenneth Casey, Casey Manufacturing Company, 16 Randolph Street, Peoria, IL 61604
68a Mr. J. P. Jones, 1611 Hancock Avenue, Kermit, TX 79732
68b Mr. J. P. Jones, 1611 Hancock Avenue, Kermit, TX 97932
69a Mr. T. C. Shaver, Nation Plumbing Company, 61 Eighth Avenue, Flint, MI 48706
69b Mr. B. T. Day, 1842 Jones Street, Flint, MI 48707
70a Mr. Boyd Hanstins, 1130 Oak Lawn, Dallas, TX 75210
70b Gersons China Shop, Central Plaza, Worcester, MA 01610

Chapter 15

71a Miss Catherine Evans, Page Elementary School, 141 Spellman Drive, Fayetteville, AR 72701
71b Mr. Jerome Green, The Railroad Institute, 316 Park Avenue, New York, NY 10017
72a Mr. Quincy Fisher, 18 Red Bluff Road, Parkersburg, PA 15104
72b Mr. Carlos Burns, Suburban Bus Company, 191 Stephen Street, Pittsburgh, PA 15205
73a Mr. Barry O'Connell, Central Railroad Corporation, 18 Wabash Street, Chicago, IL 60655
73b Mr. Barry O'Connell, Central Railroad Corporation, 18 Wabash Street, Chicago, IL 60655
74a Mr. Gary Wilson, Reliable Delivery Service, 1077 Main Street, Denver, CO 80215
74b Mr. B. W. Williams, President, Quick Print Company, 1801 South Street, Denver, CO 80223
75a The Central Railroad, 181 Benson Street, Chicago, IL 60671
75b Mr. James Kent, 130 State Street, Chicago, IL 60680

76a Mr. B. B. Carson, Public Relations Department, National Oil Corporation, Houston, TX 77004

76b Mr. Jason Worth, 1801 Canal Street, New Orleans, LA 70125

77a Mr. Rodger Taylor, World Tours, 18 East 36 Street, New York, NY 10016

77b Miss Janice Tucker, School of Education, Hartford College, Hartford, CT 06108

78a Mr. Fred Brown, 40 Court Street, Stamford, CT 06901

78b Mr. Fred Brown, 40 Court Street, Stamford, CT 06901

79a Mr. William R. Tibbs, Personnel Director, International Travel, Inc., 1401 Elm Street, Dallas, TX 75201

79b Mr. Robert McNair, 1408 Vine Street, Mobile, AL 36605

80a The Johnson Travel Agency, 1800 Madison Avenue, New York, NY 10016

80b Mr. Art Smith, 14 Almeda Road, Almeda, GA 31401

INDEX OF BUILDING TRANSCRIPTION SKILLS

The number next to each entry refers to the page in the text in which the entry appears.

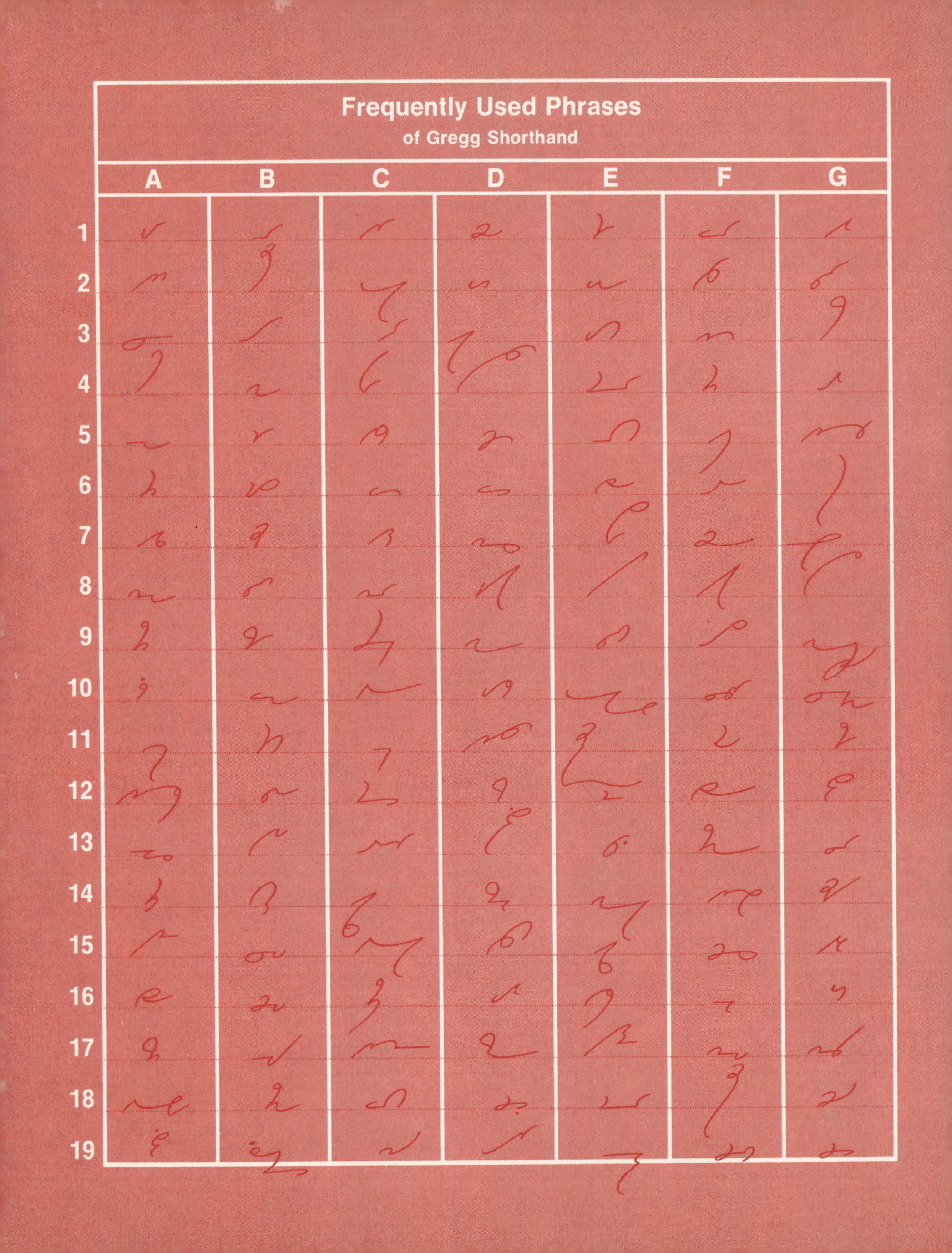

Frequently Used Phrases
of Gregg Shorthand

	A	B	C	D	E	F	G
1							
2							
3							
4							
5							
6							
7							
8							
9							
10							
11							
12							
13							
14							
15							
16							
17							
18							
19							